W9-CPC-161

Front Cover:

Front cover photo: Highway 281 south of Devils Lake, North Dakota. Photographer John Vachon, Photographic Archives, University of Louisville, Standard Oil Collection.

Back Cover:

Back cover photo: A farm truck on a county road near Carrington, North Dakota. Ca 1940. Photographer John Vachon, Photographic Archives, University of Louisville, Standard Oil Collection.

TABLE OF CONTENTS

List of Illustrations II

List of Tables..III

Acknowledgements IV

About the Authors V

Preface VI

Introduction..1

Chapter I
The Canadian Experience: A Daylight Blizzard 16

Chapter II
The American Experience:
A Night of Terror For North Dakotans...45

Chapter III
The Storm In Minnesota...171

Chapter IV
The Great Lakes Region and Northeastern United States:
The Deadly Blizzard Subsides;
Record Breaking Cold Temperatures...253

Chapter V
Aftermath and Conclusions...262

Notes...289

Works Cited..298

General Index...302

I

LIST OF ILLUSTRATIONS

Figure 1. The Track of the Storm...2

Figure 2. Weather Map for March 14, 1941 6

Figure 3. Weather Map for March 15, 1941 7

Figure 4. Weather Map for March 16, 1941 8

Figure 5. Weather Map for March 17, 1941 9

Figure 6. Yukon Territory 17

Figure 7. A Map of Canada...19

Figure 8. Alberta...21

Figure 9. General Location of Deaths in Saskatchewan..........................25

Figure 10. General Location of Deaths in Manitoba.................................34

Figure 11. A Map of Cities and Towns of North Dakota...........................47

Figure 12. General Location of Deaths in North Dakota.........................154

Figure 13. A Map of Cities and Towns of Minnesota 174

Figure 14. District No. 32 Basketball Tournament Ad............................179

Figure 15. General Location of Deaths in Minnesota 252

LIST OF TABLES

Table 1.   Wind Velocities of the March 15, 1941
Blizzard at Hector Airport..139

Table 2.   Official Wind Velocity Classifications 273

III

ACKNOWLEDGMENTS

The writers are indebted to Professor D. Jerome Tweton for his ideas on organization and structure, as well as his encouragement in pursuing this topic. Special thanks are also in order to Professors William Gard and Douglas C. Munski for their constructive criticism and comments that helped to clarify the subject.

Thanks are also due to the staff of the Chester Fritz Library at the University of North Dakota, especially the services of the interlibrary loan division. We want to thank Betty Gard and Sandy Beidler for their kindness and assistance. Also, we are grateful to Phyllis Erickson who did our illustrations and to Jerry Olson for his photographic skills. The Elwyn B. Robinson Special Collection allowed us to use material from their archives.

The authors wish to thank all those who have shared their experiences of the 1941 storm with us. Likewise, to those who wrote us letters concerning the blizzard. We are grateful to Vic and Rose Potulny of Fordville for sharing their copy of the March 18, 1941, issue of the Grand Forks Herald. Also, Betty Kunkle of Cogswell for giving one of the authors the March 18, 1941 issue of the Fargo Forum.

We wish to thank the Grand Forks Herald and the The Forum for allowing us to reproduce the front pages of their newspapers and some of the works of their photographers. Also the Stephen Messenger for their permission to use one of their advertisements for an illustration.

Regional newspapers have provided much of our information and we are grateful to each and every one of them. Their coverage of the storm in the aftermath has added much to the heritage of the region. Credit belongs to the editors and their reporters.

We wish to thank Bev Rosencrans for typing our manuscript.

For all those who offered their insights and encouragements, we are grateful.

THE AUTHORS

The authors grew up on farms close to the Red River Valley in North Dakota. Every generation remembers one or two winter storms. For the writers it is the three day blizzard of March, 1966. We still talk about the huge snow drifts from the storm. We can recall how much school we missed that winter because the roads were blocked with snow, and what great snow forts we built.

Larry Eugene Skroch was born at Oakes, North Dakota. In 1975 he graduated from Sargent Central High School in Forman, North Dakota. He then served three years in the United States Army. He received his A.S. degree in Pre Law from North Dakota State School in 1982. He then attended the University of North Dakota receiving a B.A. degree in Social Science and a M.A. degree in history in 1988. For his master's thesis he wrote, "A History of Sargent County's School District Reorganization Since 1947." While attending school he continued to work in construction and served in the North Dakota National Guard until 1991. After graduating in 1988 he has worked for Burlington Northern Railroad as a brakeman and conductor.

Douglas Ramsey attended the University of North Dakota, receiving both his B.A. and M.A. in history from them. For his master's thesis he wrote, "A History of the Northern Dakota Railway Company." Since his graduation in 1987 he has continued to farm and work as a civil engineering technician.

Preface

The power of imagination and curiosity started this project. The seed was planted by stories Douglas Ramsey heard from his parents and others who remembered the storm.

Here's a story about the 1941 blizzard that Laurence Ramsey told his son, Douglas Ramsey:

> I remember it was a nice day because there was water on the ground by the barn. I was milking the cows with my father when the storm hit suddenly. I told my dad it was storming really bad outside, but he wouldn't believe it. After finishing the milking we looked outside and everything was white. We decided to try to make it back to the house. My father put our kerosene lamp in a pail so it wouldn't blow out and we started out holding hands. We came across the clothesline and followed it towards the house. I remember seeing just a little flame. We headed toward it and made it back safely to our house.[1]

The following account is from Mrs. Laurence Ramsey:

> I lived on a farm several miles west of Crystal, North Dakota, in March 1941. On Saturday morning I went skating with my other sisters on a ice pond in front of our house. By eleven o'clock, warm temperatures had left a layer of water on the ice, so we quit skating. During the afternoon it started to cloud over. That evening my mother and older brother went into Crystal to visit another sister. While they were gone, the storm came up. My sister Ann and I were supposed to bring several sacks of coal into the house to be used for heating. Despite the high winds we were able to reach the tree, about 30 feet from the front door of our house where the coal was piled. We dragged the sacks of coal back to the house. We survived the rest of the night uneventfully, and my mother and brother remained in Crystal overnight.[2]

Douglas Ramsey and I studied history at the University of North Dakota. As North Dakota's centennial approached we talked about getting together for a project even though we had limited time for research and writing. A story about one of the most historic blizzards that hit North Dakota seemed natural. It was something North Dakota was famous for, but there were virtually no books on the subject.

After some preliminary research we had some questions that needed to be answered. Which area was affected most by the storm? Was this blizzard different than others? What kind of warnings were issued? Why were there so many casualties?

As time passed and more material was found, we had the makings of a good story. We tried to capture the "spirit" of the times. The blizzard setting was war. The violent background sounds of war and the pace of world events pushed the storm tragedy aside. There was a sense of uneasiness in the country. Headlines about the war overseas worried people in the United States. On October 29, 1940, the first peacetime draft in United States history began. Defense posters were a common sight in many factories in 1941. One of the common themes they stressed was "You Are a Production Soldier. . . . America's First Line of Defense is Here."[3]

The pioneer days were over by 1941, but many early settlers were still around. The automobile had changed rural North Dakota and Minnesota, and people fell in love with it, but still many farmers had teams of horses on the farm. Though modern changes made life less a struggle, many tasks still required non-mechanical force, lubricated by elbow grease.

In 1989, as North Dakota's centennial came and passed, our project became larger than we anticipated, but we continued our research and hoped to put the blizzard story together by the fiftieth anniversary of the storm, in March 1991. Daily work was our priority, but we spent our spare time reading newspapers from that time, talking to people who had experienced the storm, and writing our first draft. Time seemed to fly by; the fiftieth anniversary came and we were still editing our manuscript.

Most of our material was taken from newspapers. Reporters who had covered the aftermath of the storm had written articles about the strength, courage, and valor of people living on the northern plains. Many stories had tragic endings while others had remarkable tales of survival. The Fargo Forum conducted what it claimed was "one of the greatest newsgathering efforts ever thrown into a North Dakota story."[4] The Grand Forks Herald also gave the storm extensive research. Newspapers from small towns in Minnesota and North Dakota described how the blizzard affected local citizens. The Minneapolis Morning Tribune called the deadly blizzard the "Red River Valley Flash Storm."[5]

This story is about the people who lived through the Great Depression and World War II, and about one of the most famous blizzards they experienced. Children of the postwar baby boom have heard how their parents struggled through the hard times and the various types of chores that they did every day. They have listened to numerous stories about the tornadoes, floods, and droughts that their parents or grandparents witnessed. Oral histories are invaluable to the heritage of a region but are mostly forgotten as the years pass. A story about how ordinary people dealt with a sudden storm enhances the written history of a region. Their actions are the major focus of our manuscript. Here, the inhabitants' spirit and character is tested and usually shines. Just as many conversations begin by talking about the weather, so our story might serve as a start of a conversation and a bond between generations.

Our parents grew up in another era and had different daily routines. Folks, especially in rural homes, dreamed of having electricity, but most had to wait until after the war to realize this dream. Many farms had windchargers, generators, and large batteries that supplied electricity, but these were not dependable sources of power. Many people lit their homes with kerosene lamps. Today's conveniences, such as electric appliances and telephones, were present, but not commonplace, in 1941.

Americans loved their cars and trucks. The automobile had caused a revolution in ways of traveling. The Model T and the Model A were considered obsolete long before 1941. Every spring automakers introduced their latest innovations through new models in colorful full-page ads in popular magazines such as Life and Look.

An important centerpiece in many people's living rooms were large standup radios, Atwater-Kents, Philcos, and Motorolas. It was a time when many people looked forward each evening to hearing news and opinions from their favorite radio commentators, such as Lowell Thomas, Walter Winchell, and Fulton Lewis, Jr. People also enjoyed listening to music from such big bands as Glenn Miller, Tommy Dorsey, Artie Shaw, and Benny Goodman. Records made by these and other recording artists could be heard playing from jukeboxes (Wurlitzer, Seeburg, and Rock-Ola) located at taverns, candy stores, pool halls, and cafes.

Books and movies played important roles in people's lives. Prior to the blizzard the top films included Grapes of Wrath (John Ford), The Great Dictator (Charlie Chaplin), and Rebecca (Alfred Hitchcock). The most acclaimed movie of 1941 was Citizen Kane. Popular literature included For Whom the Bell Tolls (Ernest Hemmingway), Native Son (Richard Wright), and Abraham Lincoln: The War Years (Carl Sandburg). The popular songs were "You Are My Sunshine," "How High the Moon," "The Last Time I Saw Paris," "When You Wish Upon a Star," "It's a Big, Wide, Wonderful World," "Oh, Johnny," "South of the Border," "Blueberry Hill," and the "Woodpecker Song."[6] Before the coming of television, pictorial magazines were quite prominent. Included among these were Life and Look. True Romances was a popular magazine that women enjoyed reading. Although considered more news-oriented than pictorial, Time magazine gave people an up-close view of world events. Its editors sponsored an important newsreel, "The March of Time."

People, especially in rural areas, tended to take more of an active part in sports in the 1940s than they do today. Sports offered an emotional

X

outlet for a nation still recovering from the depression. Baseball was America's "national pastime"; every town had a team which battled for local honors. In 1940, Cincinnati beat Detroit four games to three to win the World Series, and Southern Cal defeated Tennessee in the Rose Bowl. Jack Dempsey retired, and the Chicago Bears trounced the Washington Redskins 73-0 to win the NFL championship. Tom Harmon, "Old 98," of the University of Michigan, won the Heisman Trophy. The 1940 Olympic games, however, were canceled because of World War II.[7]

When writing this book, we tried to capture the "spirit" of the times. For people who are interested in weather, we reviewed the forecasts and told how weather forecasts were made in 1941. We have copies of the weather maps that the newspapers published and a map that shows the track of the high and low pressure systems. For people who wanted information on their local area, we tried to tell what was happening in different places at the time of the storm. Sections are divided by individual towns in a geographical area. We looked to see what movies were showing at the theaters, what radio programs were heard, and which events brought people to town. For example, Gone With The Wind was playing in Fargo. In Grand Forks, people danced to the music of the Rhythm Aces Band at the Eagles Ballroom and to Ken Sutton's Orchestra at the States Ballroom. Bismarck hosted North Dakota's Class A basketball championship tournament.

The full picture also must include what was occurring on the world and national scene. On the night of the devastating blizzard, President

Franklin D. Roosevelt inspired millions of people around the world with his speech at the annual banquet of the White House Correspondents' Association. March 15 was the last filing date to submit federal income tax returns.

This book describes the path of the blizzard, almost an hour-by-hour report, as it advanced through the Canadian provinces, across the Drift Prairie of North Dakota, and then through the Red River Valley into the woods and lake country of Minnesota. Blizzard conditions subsided in northern Wisconsin, but record-breaking temperatures were set in the Great Lakes region and throughout the eastern seaboard. The storm caused seventy-one deaths in North Dakota and Minnesota; most of the fatalities occurred in the Red River Valley. Even with today's technology, meteorologists cannot always predict the direction a storm will take. We examined the information announced by the weather bureau and their operating procedures. We retold many of the stories, including some firsthand accounts. We believe this is the best method for explaining the feelings of isolation, desperation, and determination of individuals to survive a Saturday night calamity.

We placed an ad in the REC Magazine asking for personal accounts that involved the 1941 blizzard. In March 1991, we received several letters after an article in the Grand Forks Herald told of our intention of publishing a book on the blizzard. The letters mentioned such things as party phone lines, feather ticks, and milk wagons. We received a lot of information by asking the simple question: "Do you remember the 1941 blizzard?" People eagerly shared their recollections with us and we cherished their insights.

Our population figures for towns are from the 1940 United States decennial census and Canada's 1941 decennial census. All temperature readings are Fahrenheit.

Our title, <u>Looking for Candles in Windows: The Tragic Story of the March 15, 1941 Blizzard</u>, is not an original thought. "Candles in Window" was the headline of an editorial in the <u>Traill County Tribune</u> (Mayville, ND). In the aftermath of the storm, the editor mentioned how the pioneers placed candles or kerosene lamps in their windows during winter storms. He wrote, ". . . true to the training of the early pioneer, lights burned from every window and every home the country over, trusting that such service might be of value to unfortunate ones."[8] Many people spent Saturday night looking for candles in the window. By naming this book <u>Looking for Candles In Windows</u>, we wish to honor their spirit and achievements.

Larry Skroch

Grand Forks, 1992

INTRODUCTION

Over fifty years ago, a violent storm struck parts of Canada and the United States. On Saturday, March 15, 1941, a huge high-pressure system that originated in Alaska swept down on the east side of the Rockies and rushed eastward across the Prairie Provinces of Canada at an unusual velocity. Slightly ahead of this system, a fast-moving, low-pressure area moved eastward across the Dakotas and Minnesota. In Alberta, blizzard conditions developed early in the morning. As the day progressed, the provinces of Saskatchewan, Manitoba, and the extreme western edge of Ontario experienced a winter storm. In the twilight of the day, the storm continued south into the American part of the Red River Valley. See Figure 1. This illustration shows the progress of the storm.

The potential for a dangerous storm was high, but the outward signs—mild temperatures and light south winds in North Dakota and Minnesota—deceptively indicated something else. The weather, however, changed abruptly as the storm descended; the intensity and suddenness at which the blizzard struck is what made this storm unique and a killer. When the high pressure area came in contact with the low pressure area, winds of 40 to 50 mph increased to 75 to 85 mph. The Red River Valley, the region between the two centers, received the strongest winds of the blizzard.

1

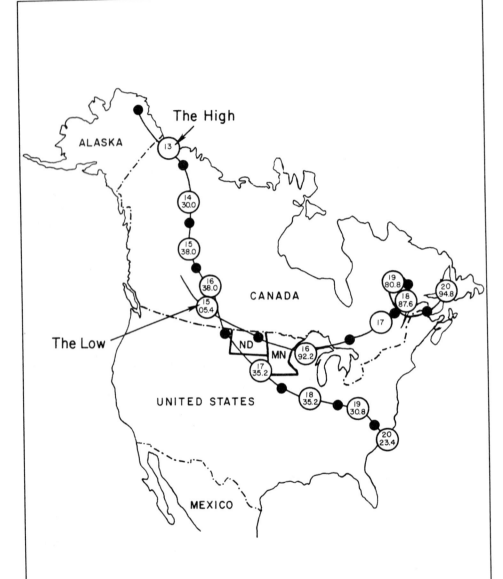

The small, dark circles give the positions of the high and low at 6:30 p.m. CST each day. The large, white circles provide the locations of the high and low at 6:30 a.m. daily (CST). The top number in the large circles indicates the day of the month for March 1941. The bottom number in the circle is the barometric pressure in millibars. For example, the 15 in a large circle means March 15, 1941, and the 38.0 below it is an abbreviation for 1038.0 millibars.

Source: <u>Monthly Weather Review</u> U.S. Weather Bureau, March 1941.

FIGURE 1: The track of the storm.

According to the National Weather Service, a blizzard, the most severe type of winter storm, is a combination of high wind, low temperature, poor visibility, and an abundance of snow in the air for an extended period. The characteristics are (1) wind speeds of 35 mph or more, (2) considerable falling and/or blowing snow, and (3) temperatures 20 degrees F. or lower. To be classified as a "severe" blizzard, conditions are (1) winds of 45 mph or more, (2) great density of falling and/or blowing snow, and (3) temperatures 10 degrees F. or lower.

Several types of winter storms occur on the northern plains that are fairly common, based upon where the storm develops. One of them is called an Alberta Clipper, so named because of its origin and speed. An Alberta Clipper is a fast-moving low system that sweeps into the Great Plains from the Canadian Northwest, usually from Alberta. In the 1800s, no other type of vessel could match the clipper sailing ships for speed. These unpredictable storms are accompanied by high winds, falling temperatures, and little precipitation. Light, powdery snow precedes these storms. Wind speeds can reach 40 to 60 mph with gusts that can go higher. Another type of winter storm involves low pressure systems moving out of the southwest, bringing large amounts of snow, strong winds, and lasting several days. The blizzard of March 15, 1941, was an intense Alberta Clipper.

The storm generally followed the normal west to east pattern of weather systems across the United States and Canada. Lows following highs usually resulted in unsettled weather. Lows average 20 to 30 mph over a 24-

3

hour period. Highs that follow them average 20 to 25. The speed of high and low pressure systems is generally faster during the winter months. Alberta Clippers usually travel at speeds up to 40 mph. Incredibly, this storm advanced at a rate of 56 mph.[1]

The high winds associated with the Alberta Clipper were due to the deep pressure gradient between the high and low pressure systems. Winds in a low pressure system circulate in a counterclockwise direction while they move clockwise around a high. Tornadic winds developed when the frontal winds of the high came in contact with the backside winds of the low. Although the approaching low can be seen on the March 14 weather map, it gave no hint of a drastic change in weather. (The weather maps for March 14-17 are for conditions in the United States as of 6:30 p.m. CST each day.) The March 15 weather map clearly shows the Alberta Clipper advancing across North Dakota. For the following day, March 16, the weather map indicates that the storm is now centered north of Lake Superior in Ontario. As can be seen in the March 17 weather map, the center of the low has moved into Quebec, and the trailing high now dominated the weather in the North Central states. See figures 2-5. The isobars on a weather map connect points of equal barometric pressure and can be expressed in millibars or inches. When isobars are compressed together, a large difference in atmospheric pressures prevails, as can be seen on the weather maps for March 15 and 16, 1941.

On March 18, the low circled around on itself in Quebec and then moved eastward through the Maritime provinces and out to sea. In the meantime, the high continued to slide in a southeasterly direction across the United States. On March 18, it was located in the Midwest. By March 20, it was centered in the Atlantic Ocean just off the Carolinas.

In terms of snowfall and duration, the 1941 blizzard would rate only as a minor winter storm. The combination of several factors, however, turned it into one of the most deadly on record. First, the suddenness of the storm's arrival and its intensity quickly put many people in a dangerous situation, especially outdoors or traveling out of town. In the span of one hour, the winds switched directions and increased to 50 mph. Second, the timing helped determine the number of fatalities in any geographical area. In the prairie provinces of Canada the storm occurred in daylight hours, enabling people to take precautionary measures. As the storm moved southeast, it picked up velocity. To complicate matters, it arrived on a Saturday, the day when farmers commonly brought their families to town for shopping and recreation, and it was payday for many people in the cities and towns. Most of the tragedies happened in places where the blizzard arrived between five o'clock and eleven o'clock Saturday evening. It was between those hours that most people were returning home from town. The death toll would have been much higher if the storm had lasted longer.

Each generation remembers one or two special winter storms. Pioneers of the Dakota Territory always talked about the January blizzard of 1888. Their sons and daughters mentioned two storms, the Armistice Day

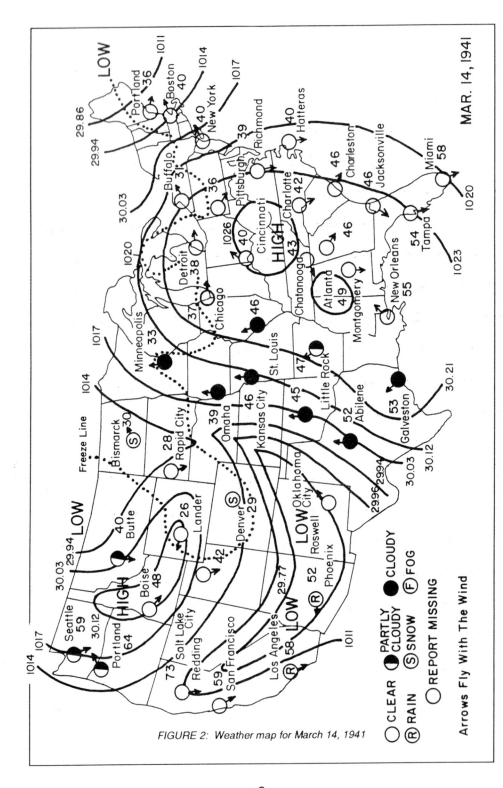

FIGURE 2: Weather map for March 14, 1941

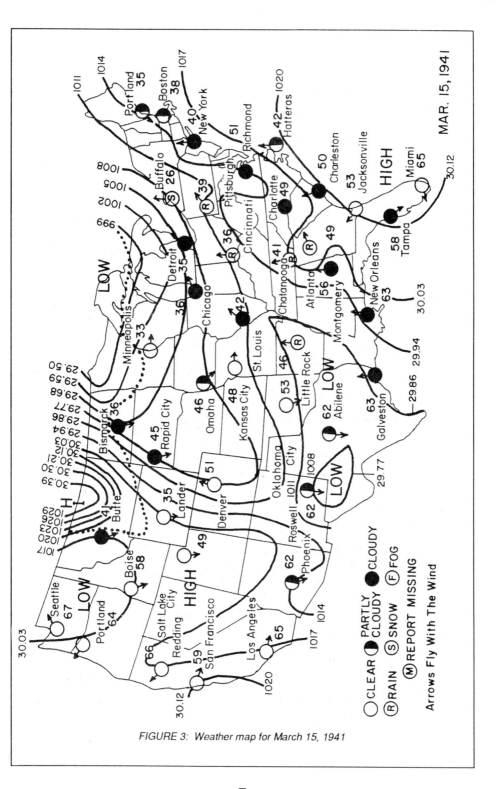

FIGURE 3: Weather map for March 15, 1941

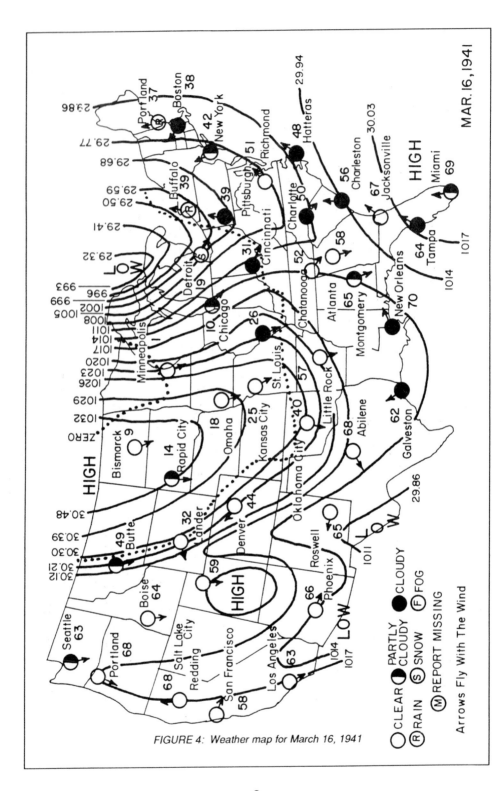

FIGURE 4: Weather map for March 16, 1941

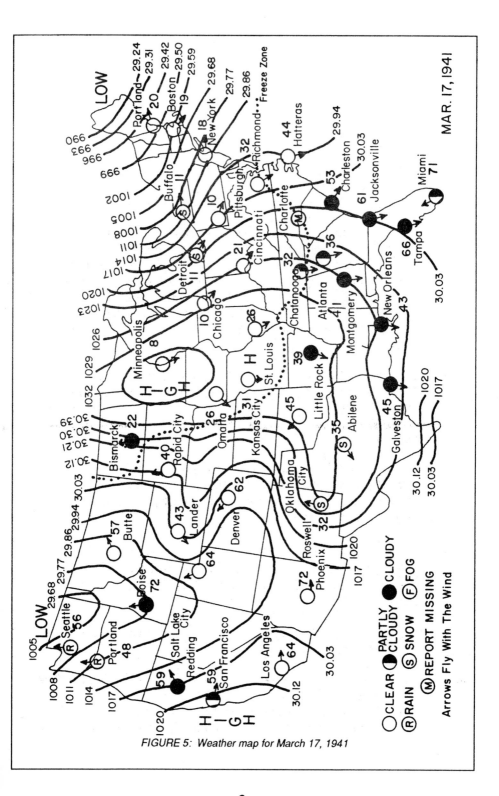

FIGURE 5: Weather map for March 17, 1941

blizzard of 1940 and the March blizzard of 1941. Postwar baby boomers recall the famous three-day blizzard of March 1966. It's hard to compare blizzards as a whole because storms usually affect an enormous area with different levels of intensity.

Other storms have been deadly. Here's a brief summary of the most lethal storms, not including livestock, for North Dakota and Minnesota:

1. On January 11, 1988, at least 200 people died, 109 of the fatalities occurred in the Dakota Territory when winds of 50 mph whipped snowfall across the upper Midwest. Many of the victims were teachers and students trapped in rural schools. The driver and passengers of a stagecoach that traveled between Bismarck and Washburn perished in the storm. In some places temperatures dropped fifty degrees in twelve hours.

2. On March 15, 1920, there were thirty-four casualties, including eight school children, in a storm that lasted for three days with 70 mph winds. This was the storm in which sixteen-year-old Hazel Miner sacrificed her life and saved the lives of her younger brother and sister.

3. On November 11, 1940, a snowstorm struck suddenly and killed fifty-six Minnesotans, mainly waterfowl hunters caught out in the field. This storm is known as the "Armistice Day" blizzard.

4. On March 15, 1941, seventy-one individuals (40 in North Dakota and 31 in Minnesota) lost their lives in a storm. That was one of the most deadly storm in North Dakota's history.

5. In February 1946, seven people died in a severe winter storm.

6. Between March 2nd and 5th, 1966, fifteen people died in a storm that stalled trains and left 30-foot-high snow drifts. The National Weather Service said this storm lashed towns and open country into a single "drifted wasteland."

7. On January 10-11, 1975, thirty-six inhabitants of

the area were killed in what the Weather Service called "the blizzard of the century," while others named it the "black blizzard."

8. On February, 1984, a winter storm claimed twenty-two lives in North Dakota and Minnesota.[2]

Weather forecasting came to the public attention around 1860 when scientific experts recognized the possibility of simultaneously collecting weather information from scattered locations and transmitting this information by telegraph to appropriate agencies. The daily weather map of the United States was first published by the government in 1871. An act of Congress dated October 1, 1890, created the United States Weather Bureau and made it responsible for the general weather service of the nation. On June 30, 1940, the Weather Bureau was transferred from the Department of Agriculture to the Department of Commerce. Since 1970, it has been known as the National Weather Service.[3]

It is important to understand the difference in how weather information is gathered and forecasts are made today as opposed to 1941. There were no weather satellites, weather systems were not tracked by radar, and the knowledge of the jet stream and the role it plays in determining weather was completely unknown in 1941. Up to and throughout World War II, weather forecasting was carried out by individual scientific experts who made the best estimates they could based on their personal knowledge and skills. The final outcome was as much a matter of expert opinion as of systematic knowledge. Since 1946, computers have brought about great changes in the science of meteorology. Remote sensing, beginning in 1960, enhanced the collection of weather data.

In 1941, the responsibility for making and issuing forecasts for states belonged to regional offices of the United States Weather Bureau. There were eight regional weather bureaus in the United States. The closest ones to the Red River Valley were at Chicago (the center that prepared forecasts for the north central states), Billings, Montana, and Kansas City, Missouri.

Field offices at the local level customarily issued a more detailed forecast, based on the state forecast, but with variations to meet local conditions. Meteorologists at the local level have authority to alter state forecasts and can issue special forecasts; in fact, have coresponsibility with Chicago in that field. Also, they have the authority to supply radio stations with special warnings.[4]

In 1941, like today, weather forecasts were made on the assumption that weather systems (high and low pressure centers, warm and cold fronts) move constantly. To keep track of the movement of these systems, the United States Weather Bureau maintained about 350 weather stations throughout the country. Each station recorded the barometric pressure, temperature, wind, and different amounts of precipitation at the surface of the earth. Readings from the atmosphere up to altitudes of several miles were taken at stations equipped with weather balloons and a radiosonde—a combination measuring instrument, or meteorograph, and an extremely lightweight radio that transmitted data. Radiosonde were first used in 1938 and by 1941 thirty stations were equipped with them. Weather balloons were used at 140 stations. Half of all the weather stations recorded only ground readings—the forecaster had a very limited view of the overall picture. Data was sent to the regional offices for analysis.[5]

Once the weather observations had been received, the information was charted and diagrammed. Information was charted daily at 7:40 a.m. and 7:40 p.m. This conversion process gave weather forecasters a principal (surface) weather map. The forecaster then calculated the speed and direction of movement of the weather fronts and the troughs of low pressure. Work was halted about 9:15 a.m. to allow the forecaster to analyze the map. A meteorologist dictated the forecasts around 9:30 a.m. or shortly afterwards. The forecasts were immediately telegraphed to the field stations in the states for which the forecasts were made. Copies of the forecasts were quickly furnished to the news media and radio stations. Evening forecasts were done in the same manner.[6]

Forecasts emphasized sky conditions, the chances of any precipitation, and any important changes in temperature. They used only general phrases in their predictions, for example, increasing cloudiness, little change in temperature, strong winds, etc.

The outbreak of World War II hindered the ability of the United States Weather Bureau to obtain weather information from Canada. (Canada declared war against Germany on September 10, 1939.) In September 1939, during a chance meeting in a United States Weather Bureau hallway in Washington, D.C., John Patterson, director of the

Canadian Weather Service, informed Lieutenant Wilburt M. Lockhart, head

of the aerological section within the Bureau of Aeronautics flight division,

that Canada would no longer issue weather broadcasts in the "clear."

Canadian weather reports that had been transmitted regularly by landline to

the Weather Bureau in Washington, D.C. were to be encoded for the use of

the Weather Bureau only.[7]

Lockhart convinced Patterson that such internal usage should be

given to the U.S. Navy and Army Air Corps. This would be done provided

these two service branches kept the weather information confidential and all

future weather transmissions were in military code. This of course had been

a worry for Lockhart—how the naval weather service was to send and

receive weather information once the navy fleet began observing wartime

radio silence.[8]

In 1941, the gathering of weather information was considered vital to

the security of the United States. Weather data received by the United

States Weather Bureau, whether by telegraph, radio, or cable, were in some

sort of code, mostly numerical. The reports were immediately translated by

a person who was an expert in such work.[9]

The blizzard of March 15, 1941, came out of Canada and

meteorologtists from Edmonton, Alberta, warned the Chicago Weather

Bureau about the strong winds in Canada.[10]

Two Northern Pacific locomitives and a caboose that were derailed in Griggs County near Moose, North Dakota on March 18, 1941. Photograph courtesy of the _Forum_.

Photo of a stalled car taken by a _Herald_ photographer after the storm. Courtesy of the _Grand Forks Herald_.

CHAPTER I

THE CANADIAN EXPERIENCE: A DAYLIGHT BLIZZARD

Yukon Territory

The 1941 blizzard began with a fast-moving high pressure system moving south and east out of Alaska following a fast-moving low system. It first passed through the Klondike Region and struck a small town in the Yukon Territory of Canada. See Figure 6. Dawson, located in the foothills of the Ogilvie Mountains, had been experiencing a dry winter up to March 1941. Local residents, 1,043 inhabitants in 1941, were worried about the lack of precipitation. While other areas experienced mild temperatures prior to the vicious storm, the area around Dawson had bad weather.

Beginning on March 9, Dawson received over six inches of snow in several storms that passed through the area. Strong northerly winds accompanied the snowfall causing considerable drifting. At 2:30 p.m. on March 14, Dawson reported a temperature of 3 degrees F. with clear skies and a strong north wind. By 2:30 a.m., March 15, 1941, the temperature had sunk to 23 degrees below zero. By this time, however, the front had passed and the wind had dropped to a breeze from the north. Skies remained clear

FIGURE 6: Yukon Territory.

with a steady barometer reading.[1]

Mayo, located approximately 100 miles southeast of Dawson, never experienced storm conditions but saw its temperature drop from 25 F. on Friday afternoon to 28 below on Saturday. The high continued southeast, parallel to the Rocky Mountains and towards the Prairie Provinces of Canada. See figure 7

On Tuesday, March 11, 1941, a pilot by the name of Kiteley left Dawson on a bush trip to Stewart with the expectation of returning the same day. But blizzard conditions developed and forced him to remain at Stewart overnight. The next morning he departed for Dawson but encountered more bad weather and was forced to land on a river. When weather conditions improved he continued his journey but was forced to make another river landing at an alternate landing point in Sunnydale because the airport at Dawson remained closed. Later that day he returned to Dawson. On Thursday, March 13, Kiteley left for the Blackstone country, but once again stormy weather forced his return to Dawson. He was grounded for the next two days. On March 15, he flew several passengers to Carcross so they could make connections with a northbound train.[2]

Alberta

The blizzard caught Canadian forecasters by surprise. The official

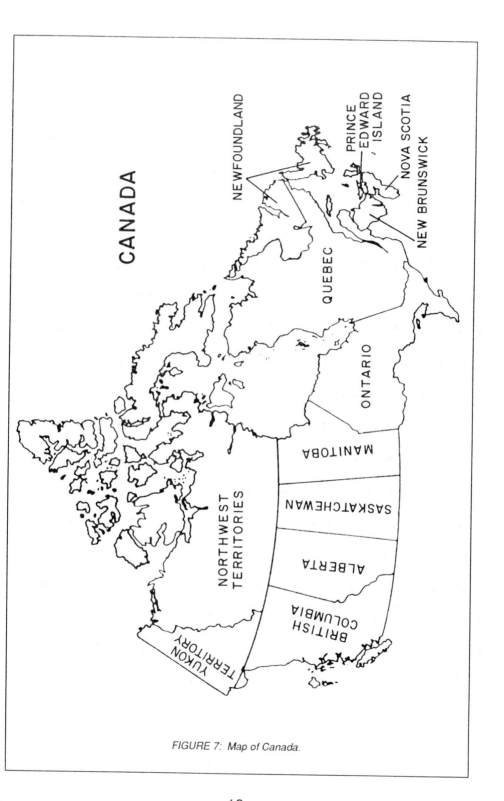

FIGURE 7: Map of Canada.

forecast for Alberta issued Friday, March 14, 1941, for that day and for

Saturday, March 15, called for "cloudy and slightly colder tonight and

Saturday, scattered snowflurries."[3] As soon as the meteorologists realized

that the change in weather would be more drastic than what they originally

had thought, they issued revised forecasts on March 15. The March 15

forecast called for "Strong northerly winds, and colder tonight and Sunday,

with light or moderate snowfalls in many districts."[4]

The high moved out of the Yukon Territory and headed into the

Interior Plains Region of Canada on the heels of a fast-moving low that had

developed on the eastern slopes of the Canadian Rockies. Together, they

would combine to form a deadly Alberta Clipper. Edmonton, Alberta, the

northernmost urban center of Canada, was the first major city in the path of

the storm. See Figure 8. The capital of Alberta had 93,817 residents in

1941. The weather had been pleasant earlier in the week for Edmonton but

colder weather was expected for the weekend. Despite the war hostilities,

there was a feeling of optimism in the air. Negotiations between United

States and Canada on a co-operative development and utilization of the

Great Lakes-St. Lawrence river basin were almost completed; the agreement

was signed March 19, 1941. Everyone waited eagerly to hear the live radio

broadcast of President Franklin Roosevelt's speech Saturday night, while

attending the annual banquet of the White House Correspondents'

Association.

In January 1941, the Administration introduced a bill that

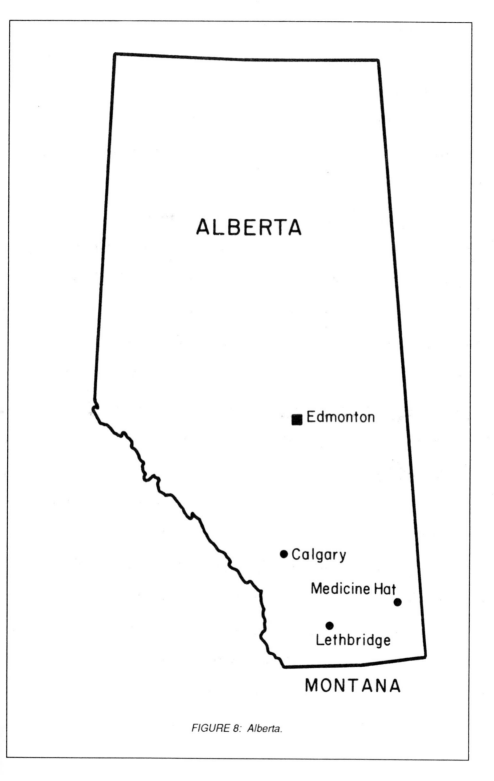

ALBERTA

■ Edmonton

● Calgary

Medicine Hat ●

● Lethbridge

MONTANA

FIGURE 8: Alberta.

authorized the President to sell, transfer, exchange, lend, lease, or otherwise dispose of war equipment and other commodities to a country whose defense he considered vital to the defense of the United States. The so-called lend-lease bill became law on March 11, 1941. President Roosevelt's speech was heard by millions and was re-broadcast in thirty different languages around the world.

The people of Edmonton enjoyed balmy temperatures on Friday, March 14, and at 2:30 a.m. Saturday morning a reading of 36 degrees was recorded. Then a violent wind skidded temperatures downward. One hour later the temperature had dropped to 18 degrees and at 7:30 a.m. reached zero. However, by midday the storm had passed and the skies were clearing.[5] The storm caused the inhabitants some discomfort, but it was quickly forgotten. The blizzard's impact was insignificant because most residents were sleeping when it roared in. People stayed inside or took adequate measures before they ventured out.

Southwest of Edmonton 180 miles lay the city of Calgary, Alberta. In 1941, it was the second largest city in Alberta, with a population of 88,904 residents. Geographically, the city is located at the base of the Canadian Rockies and is frequently subjected to chinooks, a warm, dry wind that descends the eastern slopes of the Rocky Mountains. On June 3, 1940, the city's artillery unit, 22-78th field Battery, Royal Canadian Artillery, had been activated into national service. Ernest Bevin, Minister of Labour and National Service of England, announced that women, married and single, of the ages 21 and 22 years, and men between 41 and 45 inclusive must register for national war service on March 16, 1941. For the first time in British history, women were conscripted into service.

The day before the storm arrived a high of 47 degrees was recorded in Calgary. But what occurred on March 15 was the opposite of a chinook. Wet snow and a strong northerly wind swept into the city at 6:25 a.m. Within three hours, blizzard conditions developed, the temperature dropped from 34 to 9 degrees, and winds reached 50 mph. Not enough snow fell from it, however, to hamper highway travel. The storm brought an abrupt end to the pleasant weather Calgarians had enjoyed the previous week. Residents continued planning for St. Patrick's Day celebrations on Monday.[6]

The blizzard advanced swiftly in a southeasterly direction. Without snowfall the strong winds created a severe dust storm in the southeast corner of Alberta. Medicine Hat, located approximately 160 miles southeast of Calgary, was struck by the blizzard about 8:20 in the morning. The community of Medicine Hat had 10,571 people in 1941. Big, bold headlines in Saturday's edition of the Medicine Hat News offered encouraging news on the war front, such as "LARGE BRITISH ARMY LANDS IN GREECE: Well Equipped Force Said To Number 100,000," and "Industrial Centres in West Germany Attacked." An article described Canadian efforts in the fortification of Gibralter, including the efforts of hard-rock miners whose expertise was needed at the gun-bristling rock cliffs. Medicine Hat received almost two inches of snow and winds averaging 44 mph. Conditions were harsh enough to ground planes and make highway travel difficult. By noon,

side roads had become blocked and visibility was reduced to one block. Train

No. 2 from the west arrived only fifteen minutes late. Fortunately,

temperatures remained above the zero mark, thus saving many lives,

including newborn livestock.[7]

Saskatchewan

The forecast for Saskatchewan on March 14 read: "Fair and

comparatively mild for Friday; Saturday, partly cloudy, a little colder in the

northern districts, with scattered snowflurries."[8]

After hitting Alberta, the storm rushed east toward the prairie

province of Saskatchewan. See Figure 9. The storm was moving at an

incredible speed. So far no deaths had been attributed to it, but that would

not be the case for long, as the storm grew in intensity. For Saskatchewan

on March 15, Canadian weathermen had issued an accurate revised forecast.

It stated, "Strong northerly winds, and becoming colder tonight and Sunday

with light or moderate snowfalls." However, the storm arrived early

Saturday afternoon instead of later in the evening. In the aftermath, it was

rated as "Saskatchewan's worst blizzard in twenty years."[9]

The first major city in Saskatchewan to be hit by the storm was

Saskatoon, the province's most populated northern city. In 1941, Saskatoon

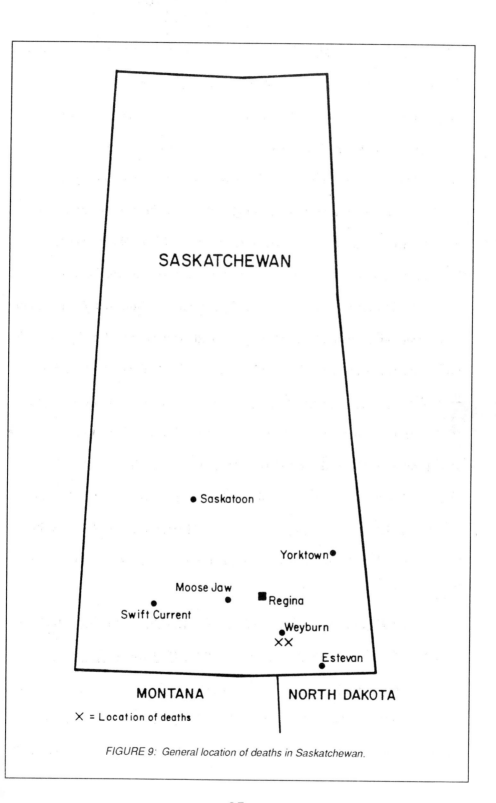

FIGURE 9: General location of deaths in Saskatchewan.

had 43,027 residents. The urban center is located about 155 miles northwest of Regina. On March 15, war news dominated the pages of the Saskatoon Star-Phoenix. Early in the afternoon, strong northerly winds, around 45 mph, quickly ended the springlike weather for the inhabitants. Out in the countryside the winds caused much havoc. Temperatures slightly above the freezing mark Saturday morning dropped down to about 20 degrees below zero later than night and early Sunday morning. Many of the smaller communities surrounding Saskatoon experienced similar conditions.

World events—the military and political situation seemed to change daily—created an aura of uncertainty. World news became front page stuff while local news was curtailed or placed on the back pages. The leading story of the Saskatoon Star-Phoenix on March 17 dealt with how the British and Indian forces recaptured Berbera, the British Somaliland port on the Gulf of Aden, and seized the Eritrean Heights overlooking the Red Sea. Their armies freed the long-besieged rail town of Cheren, the key to Asmara, Eritrea's capital (today a region of Ethiopia). Prime Minister Churchill's threat to tear Italy's African empire into "shreds and tatters" seemed to be coming true.

Canadian newspapers had accounts of the blizzard's effects but they came days later. For example, on March 17 the Saskatoon Star-Phoenix mentioned the terrible blizzard and it was put on page seven. The headline read, "47 DEATHS AS WIND HITS U.S.; Blizzard Claims Four Lives in Manitoba, Sweeps South; and Leaves Damage, Tragedy In Sections of North

Dakota and Minnesota." The newspaper ran a short article on the storm

from the Associated Press out of Grand Forks, North Dakota, dated March

17. Also, it carried a detailed story from the Canadian Press out of Winnipeg

which told of the deaths of the four Manitobans, reports of blocked highways,

and train delays in Canadian prairie provinces.

On March 18, the Saskatoon Star-Phoenix reported details about the

deaths of two Saskatchewan farmers: "Two Perish In Blizzard: Halbrite,

Crystal Hill Farmers Die In Snow On Saturday." The leading paragraphs

described the grim circumstances. Furthermore, it told how several

individuals came through the storm alive and only suffered severe cases of

frostbite. After these articles, there was no more coverage of the storm.

What happened in Swift Current was typical of the many small

towns of southwestern Saskatchewan. A key trading center located about

150 miles west of Regina, Swift Current, in 1941, had 6,379 residents.

Although it snowed early Saturday morning, road conditions remained good

and traffic was brisk. Merchants were busy waiting on customers.

Moviegoers watched two American westerns, Kit Carson and Stagecoach

War, the latest of the "Hopalong" Cassidy outdoor adventure stories. Folks

stopped at their favorite eating places. They talked about the play of the

local hockey teams as they made plans to watch the games later in the

evening.

Winds up to 50 mph rocked the area without much warning. Bitter

cold temperatures followed. Traffic slowed considerably as visibility deteriorated. Roads and highways became blocked with snowdrifts. The jubilant ride into town suddenly turned into a serious affair. Motorists became unexpected guests at farms located close to roads and highways. New friendships were made as the storm spread its wrath across the prairie. Ironically, city folks spent Saturday night on farms, while country folks quickly filled all the rooms at hotels and rooming houses in the city.

In Swift Current, the unexpected outbreak of bad weather affected two popular forms of entertainment. Describing the keen interest in the local hockey teams, a reporter for the Swift Current Sun wrote, "many braved inclement weather and uncertain roads Saturday night to support their team. Those who stayed home did so under compulsion and not very gracefully." Many rural individuals declined to venture into town to watch the Saturday night movies. The blizzard really surprised those who entered the show halls while the weather was pleasant and then faced a hazardous storm when they came out later.[10]

Regina, the capital of Saskatchewan, had a population of 58,245 in 1941. The day dawned cloudy in Regina and light, wet snow fell early in the morning. Temperatures climbed to 31 degrees from an overnight low of 12. On March 15, the following movies played in Regina: Virginia Road Show, The Villain Still Pursued Her, All This and Heaven Too, Father is a Prince, Three Cheers for the Irish, Tell No Tales, and Mein Kampf. As folks were going about their business, a loud, rumbling noise could be heard in the distance. About noon the clipper struck with a bang, with winds up to 50 mph. Blizzard conditions peaked in two hours and the storm was over in six. Although it lasted only six hours in Regina, The Leader Post called it the "worst blizzard in twenty years." Unlike Saskatoon, the blizzard was front-page news in the Regina newspaper. On March 17, large headlines reflected the tragedy of the storm: "TWO DIE IN STORM NEAR WEYBURN."

The grim blizzard had a considerable influence on the city and the vicinity. A farmer north of Regina became lost and froze his hands and face severely. A girl was involved in an automobile accident and required twelve stitches on her face. Streetcars and automobiles had their headlights on all afternoon. There were still thirty-four automobile collisions and two streetcars collided head-on, but nobody was seriously hurt. Several inhabitants suffered fractured limbs because of falls on icy streets. Regina's light and power company sent workers out to fix a couple of minor wire breaks during the storm. The noise of the storm completely silenced the sirens of the fire trucks responding to calls.

But some humorous stories involving hats were also reported from Regina. A man lost his hat in a gust of wind and when he retrieved it from a fence about 100 yards away he found an additional surprise, an air force officer's cap. A store manager lost his hat getting into his car when he went to pick up his wife downtown. He returned to the store and got another hat before he left. On his way back he saw a hat resting on the road so he stopped his car to pick it up. It was the one he lost an hour earlier, blocks away.[11]

Weyburn, located seventy miles southwest of Regina, experienced the worst evils of the blizzard, as it claimed the lives of two area residents. Weyburn was a key trading center because it was somewhat larger than the surrounding towns. Earlier in the week the Weyburn Rotary Club members had made final preparations for the annual Father-Son banquet on March 17. A local boy won a bicycle in a contest sponsored by a Vancouver manufacturing firm.[12] On March 15, people enjoyed the mild temperatures of Saturday morning. Chores were done hastily on farms. Although farmers had to be home for the evening chores, the trip to town on Saturday was a welcome relief.

Radio reports indicated Alberta had stormy weather but the mild temperatures gave the people around Weyburn a false sense of security. On March 15, 1941, the inhabitants looked outside early Saturday morning and discovered light snow had fallen as they slept. Although the skies were cloudy, the temperatures climbed to the thawing point. The happy mood was shattered by a howl. Winds of 50 mph swept in and hammered the area. It started snowing heavily. An "old fashioned" blizzard pulverized southern Saskatchewan, and temperatures dropped to 15 degrees below zero. The storm reached its peak Saturday afternoon. Winds continued blowing throughout the night, although they were less strong.

The inhabitants of Weyburn had their share of unfortunate experiences. Traffic in the area came to a complete stop. In a four-mile stretch south of Weyburn on Highway 35, fourteen cars were abandoned.

After thinking the situation over, motorists walked to nearby farms. Many travelers ended up at the Victor Windecker farmhouse. Mrs. Windecker entertained twenty people Saturday night. It was reported that, "many a yarn about blizzards in the old days was swapped." Ironically, her husband was stranded in town. A large wedding party was marooned at a farm home until Sunday. A man riding a horse was almost run over by a train he had neither seen nor heard. A few residents suffered minor frostbite after being caught outdoors. A Colgate farmer was badly frozen walking back to Weyburn after his truck smashed into a stalled truck on the highway.

At Halbrite, a small farming community near Weyburn, the storm claimed its first life, a Halbrite farmer. Fred Ebel, 57, a husband and father of eight children, walked to Halbrite Saturday morning and caught the morning train to Weyburn. He consulted a doctor regarding his ill wife at home and picked up some medicine. Ebel jumped on the noon train back to Halbrite. He started walking home but the storm charged in. Ebel missed his farm by one mile. He stopped and warmed up at a neighbor's farm. Against the wishes of the neighbors, Ebel headed out in the storm but failed to reach home. On Sunday, search parties were sent out and his body was found by one of his sons and the same farmer at whose house he had sought refuge during the storm.[13]

Arthur Baitan, a Crystal Hill farmer who had a wife and nine children, was the storm's second victim. He lost his life doing a routine chore. The violent winds spooked his cattle, so he left his warm home to

31

round up his herd and drive them to a nearby shelter.

Both deaths in Saskatchewan occurred in the southeastern part of the province. Ironically, on March 15, a search party discovered a victim of a previous storm. On February 22, 1941, Nettie Popowich had gone shopping in Yorktown, located 117 miles northeast of Regina, and was overtaken by a storm on her way home.[15]

Manitoba

Canadian meteorologists predicted the weather to change in Manitoba over the weekend. Manitoba's forecast for March 15 was, "Cloudy and becoming colder tonight and Sunday, with light snow and northerly winds increasing to fresh or strong on Sunday."[16] They expected winds between 19 and 24 mph, or stronger winds of 32 to 38 mph. However, a killer blizzard, with winds of 50 mph, smacked the western part of Manitoba Saturday afternoon. See Figure 10. In twelve hours, the dangerous Alberta Clipper scurried from Calgary, Alberta, to Winnipeg, Manitoba, a distance of 840 miles.

In Manitoba the cold, frenzied winds reached as far north as Dauphin, located 100 miles straight north of Brandon. The residents of Dauphin, totaling 4,662 in 1941, woke up to cloudy skies. Temperatures climbed to a high of 36 degrees. Everyone in town was charged up because the local midgets and bantams hockey teams were playing in the semifinal games of Manitoba's Midgets and Bantams championship tournament Saturday night at Portage La Prairie. Excited players jostled their way into a bus Saturday morning. For a short time, traffic in Dauphin was brisk as the parents and fans formed a caravan behind the team's bus. They started out for Portage La Prairie, located over 100 miles southeast of Dauphin.

The turbulent weather began around one o'clock in Dauphin. People scrambled for shelter as the bitter winds whipped snow and dirt into the air. At the Commonwealth Air Training School, several pilots on training exercises landed their planes in poor visibility.

Dauphin's hockey caravan was overtaken by the storm, but the group reached Neepawa, a town of 2,292 residents in 1941. Local officials let the group stay in a schoolhouse. On Monday, the teams reached Portage La Prairie and the youngsters played the hockey games which had been postponed.[17]

The storm's death toll continued in Manitoba. A search party found the body of an aged Indian woman late Sunday afternoon near Rossburn, located seventy-five miles northwest of Brandon. Mrs. M. Peewabic had been shopping in town on Saturday. Finished with her errands, Mrs. Peewabic began walking to her home, about three miles away. It started to snow heavily, and then the icy winds came. She struggled toward the faint lights in the distance but she failed to reach the farmhouse.[18]

Brandon, Manitoba, had a population of 17,383 in 1941, and is the principal trading center for southwestern Manitoba. On the weekend of

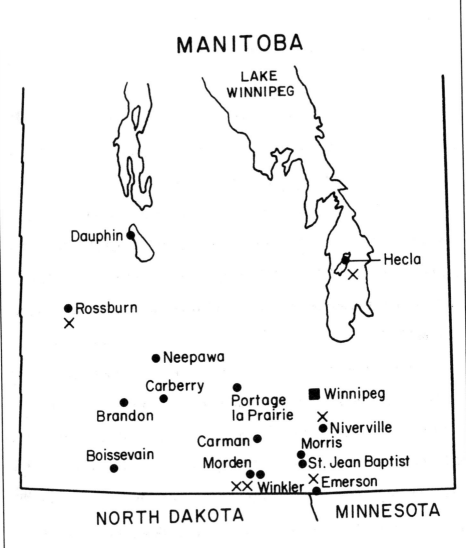

FIGURE 10: General location of deaths in Manitoba

March 15, Brandon was getting ready for the opening of Manitoba's Winter Fair on March 18. The fair was held in makeshift quarters because the arena buildings were being used by the military as a supply depot and training headquarters. Livestock, show animals and purebreds, from all over the province, began arriving on Saturday. Many competitors, however, did not reach Brandon until Monday because of blocked roads. The Brandon fire department received numerous reports of chimney fires and cases of overheated stovepipes caused by increased stoking and a strong draft. No major damage ensued.[19]

Small towns in southern Manitoba had similar storm experiences. The war effort and the sacrifices of the people at Boissevain and Carberry was typical.

Boissevain, a farming community, is located forty-five miles south of Brandon. One of the local businesses sponsored a "Patriotic Poem" contest. Everyone was urged to vote for their favorite poem. To raise funds for the war effort, a hockey carnival, featuring four rural teams, was scheduled for March 15. Already the central committee had $12,000 in honor pledges.

Light snow came down Saturday morning. The weather was pleasant, although temperatures fell one or two degrees an hour. Early in the afternoon, it started snowing heavily. Shortly thereafter, 50 mph winds bludgeoned the area. The blizzard stunned the large crowds at the rink, and the chairman of the carnival committee warned everyone not to travel until the storm let up. He instructed people about where to find shelter.

Boissevain residents opened their homes to their stranded neighbors who spread quickly around town. Volunteers prepared hot meals and beverages.

The crisis was handled efficiently in town, but everyone worried about what was happening out in the countryside. A reporter for The Boissevain Recorder wrote, ". . . great concern was expressed for those who had left town just before or after the storm broke. It was a relief to all when it was known they reached their homes safely. Several had very close calls and had an experience they would not like to have again."[20]

The story was the same at Carberry, located thirty miles east of Brandon. Preliminary organizations were being set up for the "Drop Your Scrap Iron On Berlin" campaign in Carberry. Citizens were urged to bring scrap iron to the local elevators and from there trains would haul the iron away to war factories. Freight charges were paid by the Patriotic Salvage Corps. On March 15, the war effort was curtailed. The blizzard and an outbreak of measles in the school suspended a charity program for the Manitoba ambulance fund which regularly donated food and clothing to the Red Cross, stocked ambulances with necessary medical supplies, and provided mobile kitchen units for overseas.

The Carberry News Express stated that, "one of the worst March storms ever recalled in this district struck with startling suddenness here Saturday afternoon at 5:00 and kept up for five hours." Many farmers who had left town for home came back. Others were caught midway and they barely made it home. Near Carberry, John and Charlott Dennstedt, a farm couple, lit a fire in the shelter of a bluff to keep from freezing. Their four-mile journey lasted five hours. James Muirhead, while walking home, was tormented for several hours by the strong, cold winds. Everyone reached home safely, although many suffered minor cases of frostbite. Nearby at the Royal Air Force airfield, a pilot, undertaking his first solo flight, landed the plane perfectly in very difficult weather. Along No.1 Highway many cars went into the ditch, but a bus carrying twenty-nine passengers arrived in Carberry only a few hours late.[21]

Hundreds of people were completely unprepared in Portage La Prairie, in 1941 the fourth largest city in Manitoba with 7,187 inhabitants. It is located halfway between Brandon and Winnipeg. On Saturday, Portage La Prairie hosted the semifinals of Manitoba's Midget and Bantams Tournament. Anxious officials postponed the games. People were relieved to hear that the teams from Dauphin were safe in Neepawa. Fans were stranded throughout the area. The Royal Canadian Mounted Police rescued three women. Local police searched for five children who had failed to return home after watching the afternoon movie. The kids had split up and were playing at their friends' homes about the time the Alberta Clipper brought the subarctic winds. Word was never sent to their parents. Around 9:00 their nightmare ended when they received information their children were safe. Fire brigade workers answered five chimney fire alarms between 6:20 and 10:30 p.m.

The community had a power shortage, causing several blackouts.

Utility man ventured out in gale winds to repair the damage. Commenting on the loss of electricity, a reporter wrote, "As far as most householders were concerned, the break happened at an inopportune time as many were listening to President Roosevelt's smashing denunciation of dictators and promise of aid to nations gallantly resisting aggression. Most, however, heard the rebroadcast Sunday." Farmsteads near Portage La Prairie had guests until the roads were cleared on Sunday.

In all the cities, intense cold followed blizzard conditions. On Sunday, Portage La Prairie's fire department worked for four hours in 15 degrees below zero to put out a fire at the Jesse Goodale farm. They struggled with frozen hoselines and encountered a shortage of water; the capacity of the water tank on the fire truck was only several hundred gallons.

Dauphin's hockey teams reached Portage La Prairie on Monday and they played in the semifinal games that evening.[22]

> On Saturday, Steini Erickson left home by dogsled to raise his winter fish nets. He had a fishing operation on Lake Winnipeg near Hecla Island. Out on the ice he was blinded by whirling snow and lost his way. As the storm raged, his family and friends waited for him to return. The storm ended, but Erickson did not come home. A search party from Hecla spent two days looking for the fisherman. On Monday night they found their friend, frozen to death. His dogs were found alive, standing faithfully by their master.[2]

Manitoba: The Red River Valley

The <u>Minneapolis Tribune</u> called this blizzard the "Red River Valley

Flash Storm." Geographically, the Red River Valley is unusual. It is about 300 miles lone and varies in width, from a few miles in the south to over eighty miles in the northern part. A remnant of glacial Lake Agassiz, the Red River Valley, with few exceptions, is flat and treeless for the entire length and width. The headwaters originate near Browns Valley, Minnesota. At this continental divide, one stream flows south to form the Minnesota River, which flows into the Mississippi River on its way to the Gulf of Mexico. The other stream flows north into Lake Traverse, a long, narrow lake that separates South Dakota and Minnesota. Here the valley is only a few miles wide. Leaving Lake Traverse, the stream flows north and takes the name of Bois de Sioux. At Wahpeton, North Dakota, the Bois de Sioux joins the Ottertail River, coming from the east to form the Red River. The valley is forty miles wide near Wahpeton. It continues to widen gradually as it flows north. By the time it reaches the Canadian border, it is at least sixty miles wide. In Canada, the valley widens sharply and is about eighty miles wide south of Winnipeg. The soil is very rich in the valley, making it some of the best farmland in the world. The Red River Valley is heavily populated, compared to surrounding areas.

The storm in Alberta, Canada, had begun from a fast-moving high pressure area. Winds circulate clockwise in a high pressure system. The northerly winds that struck the prairie provinces were frontal winds of the approaching high. Slightly ahead of this system a fast-moving low pressure area had moved across the Dakotas and Minnesota. In a low pressure system, winds turn in a counterclockwise direction. On Saturday the mild temperatures, and southerly winds that North Dakota and Minnesota were experiencing were frontal winds of the low. The most unfavorable situation had developed Saturday night. The low pressure system had moved eastward so the backside winds of the low combined with the frontal winds of the high. When you have two fast-moving and opposite pressure centers, the result is extraordinarily strong winds. The people in the Red River Valley were in a precarious position as the area between the two centers received wind gusts exceeding 80 mph. Without any major geographical obstacles to slow down the winds, the flatness of the valley acted as a funnel to increase the velocity of the storm winds. The daylight storm, unruly and headstrong, roared into the night.

Ironically, a short article in the evening issue of the Winnipeg Tribune on Saturday had the following caption: "Winter's Last Kick is Still To Come." The article stated, "Winter is not giving up without a struggle, and light snowfall has occurred over most of the prairies, accompanied by lower temperatures in Northern districts. Strong north winds are expected to bring cold here and some light snow." Many Winnipegers probably chuckled that night after supper when winds of 50 mph hit the city. It was a deadly "last kick."[24]

The storm thundered into Winnipeg about 6:00 p.m. Not much snow, about seven-tenths of an inch, accompanied the blizzard. Winnipeg had a temperature reading of 25 degrees at 6:00 a.m., but twelve hours later it was

15 below zero. The capital recorded little damage. Traffic slowed down considerably but persisted. The Northern Pacific train was eighteen hours behind schedule into Winnipeg. The Great Northern ran eleven hours late, while the Soo Line was five hours late. A bus en route to Winnipeg was delayed eight hours near Crookston, Minnesota. The Winnipeg-Emerson bus, with a full load of passengers, was snowbound six hours between Letellier and St. Jean, twenty miles north of its terminal. The St. James Canadians, a Winnipeg midget hockey team, and fifteen loyal fans bound for Carman, Manitoba, retreated to a school in Oak Bluff.[25]

Four people died in Manitoba's Red River Valley. The tragedy farthest north was that of a teacher from Niverville school district. Niverville is located twenty-five miles south of Winnipeg. About seven o'clock Saturday night, Isaac I. Fast left town and walked toward his house out in the country. The storm had just begun but Fast believed that he could make it home to his wife and six children. The blizzard steadily grew worse. A search party found him dead, crouched beside a telephone pole a half-mile from his home.[26]

Mrs. John Jenzen and her six-year-old daughter Marie lived on a farm between Morden and Winkler. On Saturday they visited her brother's home, three miles away. Some light snow had fallen late in the afternoon, making the countryside white and beautiful. They left for home around six o'clock in their enclosed cutter, a light sleigh pulled by a horse. Minutes later the blizzard struck in full force. They were within a half-mile of home

41

when their horse wandered off the highway and became entangled in a fence. The top of their cutter was blown off by winds exceeding 50 mph. Visibility was nil and it was getting colder by the minute. Mrs. Jenzen failed to free their horse so they used the cutter as a windbreak.

Sunday morning, a farmer discovered their frozen bodies huddled together beneath the cutter. It was the only multiple-death incident in Canada.[27]

An elderly Indian died out on the open prairie near Swan Lake, located ten miles north of Emerson, Manitoba. He was identified as Nahwaykeesick of the Swan Lake Indian Reserve. His body was found tethered to his pony, the lines wrapped around his waist.[28]

Many people faced death but survived the ordeal. Here is what happened to some residents from Morris, located forty miles south of Winnipeg. The blizzard caught a family that was returning home after attending a funeral. Their carriage went off the road near Morris. C. K. Kroeker, in his 70s, left the rig to get a bearing but never returned. The rest of the family waited there an hour but they had to move on. In the morning Kroeker was found crawling along the ground and was rushed to the hospital. Kroeker remained alive because he kept moving as much as possible. His determination and will to survive was amazing. He suffered a severe case of frostbite.

A Winnipeg family and a friend, originally from Morris, were heading for Morris to visit relatives, but the weather turned much worse before they could complete their journey. Unable to see the road, they ended up in the ditch. The motor quit, depriving them of the use of the car heater. Their twelve-hour ordeal was less grueling because they had groceries and extra clothes along, but it was still a shocking experience. During the night a bus from Winnipeg, on its way to Emerson, failed to see their distress signal and passed the stranded group. The bus already had rescued a number of people along its route. Early Sunday morning, they walked to a corner gas station near Morris and later took refuge at the home of friends. On Monday their car was pulled to town and fixed. They returned to Winnipeg later in the day.

Returning to Morris from Winnipeg, H. W. Sanders and his son Eddie ran into trouble when their car went into the ditch. Unable to get it out, they started walking to the nearest town, Silver Plains. Sanders ended up carrying his son the last part of the way.[29]

The storm also hit the southwest corner of Ontario but had little impact on the province. Kenora, the largest community to be affected, reported no incidents related to the storm. Besides Kenora, there are only a small number of communities in the area, and the Lake of the Woods occupies much of the region. The highway between Kenora and Winnipeg was blocked in several places, though the highways that ran south and east from there were open for travel.[30]

The blizzard killed eight Canadians. Alberta suffered no deaths because it was storming when the people woke up in the morning and before the residents ventured outside they took appropriate measures. The blizzard caught many people in Saskatchewan by surprise because the weather was pleasant earlier in the day. In Saskatchewan, two farmers died from exposure. In the twilight of the day, the Alberta Clipper reached the southern half of Manitoba. It claimed six lives in Manitoba. Hundreds survived the blizzard by seeking shelter as quickly as possible and many delayed their travel plans. In Canada, there was no outcry against the national weather bureau. Canada was at war, and weather information was considered vital to its national defense.

CHAPTER II

THE AMERICAN EXPERIENCE:
A NIGHT OF TERROR FOR NORTH DAKOTANS

North Dakota: The Place, People

The month of March is a special time for the people of North Dakota.
The weather starts to warm up and thoughts of spring emerge. Children
played on their sleds until the sun melted all the snow. Farmers had high
expectations in the spring of 1941. The year before there had been ample
rainfall, record crops, and high farm prices. Farm life changed with the
arrival of automobiles, tractors, and electricity, but farmers still had to be
self-sufficient.

The week of March 15 was exceptional for North Dakota sports in
1941. On Saturday night, three basketball teams were crowned state
champions—Class A high school boys and the consolidated high school boys
and girls. During the week of March 15, the stage for North Dakota's Class
B state high school basketball tournament, today the leading sporting event
in the state, was finalized, and the field for North Dakota's Class B
independent championship tournament was set.

Overall, North Dakota is a plains state and lies at relatively low elevation. See Figure 11. The state has three topographic regions (excluding the Turtle Mountains in north central North Dakota and the Little Missouri Badlands in the southwest). The surface level of the state rises in three broad steps from the Red River Valley in the east through the higher Drift Plains of the central region to the Missouri Plateau. The eastern part of the state is generally about 1,000 feet above sea level, and the southwestern part of the state is generally about 3,000 feet.

Throughout North Dakota's history, agriculture has been the primary source of income. The state has three general farming areas coinciding with the topographic regions. There is a general farming region, a wheat region, and a wheat-cattle region, all based on the type of soil and amount of precipitation.

The Red River Valley, a general farming region, is the best agricultural area in the state because it is suitable for specialized crops such as sugar beets and potatoes. The rich soils, flat terrain, and more precipitation than the rest of North Dakota makes the valley a prosperous economic region. In 1940, as today, the Red River Valley had a greater population density per square mile than that of the Drift Prairie/Missouri Plateau region. The boundary between North Dakota and Minnesota is formed by the Red River. The two dominant trading centers of the Red River Valley have been Fargo-Moorhead and Grand Forks-East Grand Forks. In North Dakota, Cavalier, Grafton, Mayville, and Wahpeton have attracted a

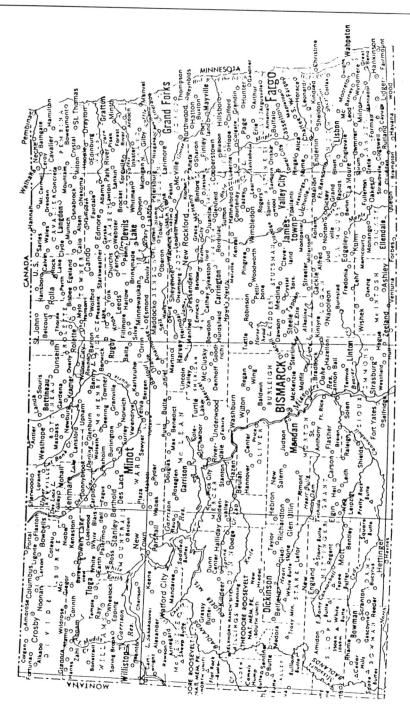

FIGURE 11: A Map of cities and towns of North Dakota.

great deal of business from the surrounding communities. In 1940, small farming operations prevailed, but the farm depression of the Twenties, the Great Depression, and the drought of the Thirties caused a rural exodus. Many farmers were forced to seek employment elsewhere—hundreds headed to defense plants on the west coast.

The Drift Prairie and Missouri Plateau, except for the Slope Region, are predominantly a wheat region. The soils are good but there is marginal precipitation. This region averages only 17 inches of annual precipitation—the Drift Prairie receives more precipitation than the Missouri Plateau. It has less than half the population density of the Red River Valley. One dominant feature of the wheat region is the large number of towns with fewer then 750 residents. Minot (north central), Devils Lake (northeast), Bismarck (south central), Jamestown and Valley City (southeast) are the chief trading centers. Bottineau, Rugby, Carrington, Harvey, and Langdon draw business from neighboring communities.

The center of the March 15 storm was 200 miles wide. It passed through the southern half of Alberta and Saskatchewan Saturday morning and afternoon. It missed all of Montana, except for the extreme northeast corner. One of the few small towns in Montana that was affected was Plentywood. The snow that accompanied the storm was wet and heavy but the flurries lasted for just a little while. Winds of 50 mph brought frigid temperatures for the weekend, but a bright sun warmed things up on Monday. No accidents were reported, and some local residents canceled their weekend trips.[1]

Weather Forecasts For

North Dakota Prior To The Storm

On the northern prairie one looks at the type of clouds in the western sky, a change in wind direction, and temperature fluctuations as hints for a change in weather. If slight, however, these clues can go unnoticed. In 1941, for more advanced warnings of oncoming weather, people listened to weather reports broadcast on radios or read forecasts printed in newspapers. Most of the local radio stations, including Bismarck's KFYR, Fargo's WDAY, and Grand Forks' KFJM, came on the air at 6:30 in the morning. The first official weather forecast was sent over the air around 7:30 a.m. Radio stations had times scheduled for weather information. For example, KFJM had reports at 7:30 a.m., 11:30 a.m., 12:30 p.m., 6:00 p.m., and the last report at 7:30 p.m. WDAY's broadcast times were listed as 7:35 a.m., 9:30 a.m., and 10:15 p.m. The stations often repeated and added reports based upon the situation.

On Friday, March 14, 1941, the United States Weather Bureau forecast for North Dakota was as follows:

> North Dakota: Increasing cloudiness Friday followed by occasional light snow at night and on Saturday and possibly in extreme west Friday; no decided change in temperature.[2]

This weekend forecast seemed typical for mid-March. Weather

49

earlier in the week was mild, a good percentage of last winter's snow had melted. It was good news for farmers who planned on taking their families to town on Saturday. Basketball fans who had to travel were pleased by this information.

Quite often small-town weekly newspapers are published on Wednesday or Thursday. The weather of the past week is reviewed and they carry forecasts for the weekend. These reports are based on information gathered earlier in the week and are sometimes wrong by the weekend. Besides reading the local paper, people turned to the larger newspapers of Fargo, Grand Forks, and Minneapolis for regional and national news. In 1941, the major newspapers published morning and evening editions, except no Sunday evening editions or Monday morning editions. People in the rural areas received the morning edition.

On the day of the tragic blizzard, March 15, 1941, the morning editions of the Grand Forks Herald, The Fargo Forum, and the Bismarck Tribune carried the following obsolete forecast: "North Dakota: Considerable cloudiness with light local snow Saturday and Sunday; colder Sunday." On Saturday morning many people read this forecast or heard it on their radio station and made their plans accordingly.

Chicago, the regional center for the north central states, had reports of snow and high winds from northern Canadian points at 1:00 a.m., March 15. They took no action at this time but monitored the situation. Later reports indicated the conditions were conclusive enough to issue a different forecast for North Dakota. At 6:30 a.m., the weather bureau issued a revised forecast, one that meant trouble. It was changed to "Light local snows tonight and Sunday with cold wave and strong northerly winds." The Fargo-Moorhead bureau acknowledged the difference and passed the information on to the public.[3] The revised forecast was printed in the evening editions of The Fargo Forum and other major newspapers on March 15.

The Fargo-Moorhead weather bureau, located at Hector Airport in Fargo, issued a forecast for North Dakota on March 15 at 9:45 a.m. that was similar to the forecast issued by the Chicago office and predicted strong winds Saturday night. "Occasional light snow tonight and Sunday; cold wave with strong northwest winds tonight and Sunday." At this time the forecast was made available to the local media, radio stations and newspapers.

One hour later a "stockman's warning" was issued: "Stockmen are advised to protect their herds by driving stocks to shelter and housing young stocks." E. J. Fox, meteorologist in charge of the Moorhead bureau, called Fargo-Moorhead business firms that shipped perishable goods and warned them of the approaching cold wave. This was one of the services provided by the local weather bureau.[4]

Williston, Dickinson, and Bismarck

The examples of Williston (northwest), Dickinson (southwest) and Bismarck (south central) illustrate the effects of the storm in western North Dakota. These areas of North Dakota experienced robust winds and a cold wave, but the winds were not as strong as those further east. The acute change in the weather took place in the afternoon, reducing some of the terror.

By mid-afternoon on Saturday the storm arrived in northwestern North Dakota. The county first affected was Divide County. Crosby, the county seat, had a population total of 1,404. Earlier in the week the weather had been mild, and on Saturday the weather appeared to be the same. Folks went about their business as usual. In the middle of the afternoon it stopped getting warmer, and the light southern winds died down. Then 40 mph northwest winds with snow flurries descended on the area. The drastic change in weather astonished everyone, but the squall lasted only several hours. Temperatures continued to drop the rest of the day and throughout the night. The people of Divide County felt the raw winds, but they suffered no hardships.

The people of Williams County to the south had dreams of glory for the Williston boys high school basketball team. North Dakota's Class A boys high school basketball tournament was the most prestigious in 1941. Throughout the week everyone talked about the chances of the local team at the Bismarck tournament. On Thursday, March 13, the Williston Coyotes lost to the Fargo Midgets in the opening round. On Friday, Williston defeated Grafton to get into the consolation championship game on Saturday afternoon.

Williston reached a high of 35 degrees F. on Saturday before the weather took a turn for the worse in the afternoon. At three o'clock the light southern winds switched to the north, with gusts over 40 mph. Very little new snow accompanied the storm. The wind packed what snow there was on the ground into rock-hard drifts. Williston's local weather observer "expected some kind of a storm for the area but never expected the winds to reach the proportions it did in the eastern part of the state."[5] The piercing winds did not dampen the spirit of the town, however, because the Coyotes won the consolation championship game by beating the Bismarck Demons 36 to 33 on their home court.

Williston's basketball fans in Bismarck had a scare driving home. After watching their exciting victory, some fans headed back to Williston. On their way they ran into hard winter winds and snow flurries that made the countryside appear totally white. Whirling dust and dirt blackened the skies most of the time. Fortunately, the fans took U.S. Highway 10, the first hard-surfaced highway across North Dakota, which had been completed in 1938. This eased their burden somewhat, and everyone made it back safely.[6]

In the wake of the intense storm, a strong high pressure system descended upon the Northern Plains. Williston was in the center of the high. At 6:30 p.m. Sunday, Williston recorded a barometric reading of 30.54

inches of atmospheric pressure. This was the highest barometric reading observed in the United States associated with this high pressure system as it followed the deadly low across the United States.

Although the center of the storm rushed through the southern half of Saskatchewan and Manitoba in the afternoon, it was powerful enough to affect Dickinson, several hundred miles south of the Canadian border. Dickinson, located in Stark County, had a population of 5,839 in 1940. The windstorm arrived at 4:30 p.m. Only a trace of snow fell but wind gusts topped 40 mph. Temperatures dropped from 33 degrees to 7 below zero in a couple of hours. The Dickinson Press called the storm the "worst storm of the 20th century." The following is what the local reporter wrote:

> Coming in the wake of mild weather, the terrific storm caught thousands unprepared. Its severity was felt in Dickinson, 300 miles west of the death area. As sudden as the dropping of a curtain a black fog of churning dust and snow blinded the prairies for a thousand miles. . . .
>
> There were few persons in the northwest who did not mourn the loss of a relative or friend for the winter tornado covered a vast area. With trepidation, northwest citizens kept close to their radios and exhausted newspaper supplies as they sought to hear or read of the fate of communities and persons with whom they were familiar.[7]

The residents of Dickinson escaped serious injuries and property damages from the storm.

In the aftermath, The Dickinson Press mentioned the storm but did not follow up in its coverage. Friends and relatives in the eastern part of the state sent copies of their local papers. The leading stories concerned the decisions to pave 30 blocks in the city limits and the upcoming annual spring concert, sponsored by its public schools. This event was expected to attract more than 1,200 music lovers to hear 250 musicians from Bismarck and Glendive, Montana, besides the local talents.[8]

It was championship week in Bismarck. It was a special time because people yelled loudly for their hometown team. In Bismarck all the lodging places were filled to capacity, including the Hotel Patterson. In 1940, Mandan defeated Bismarck to win the Class A basketball tournament. Bismarck defeated Mandan in the opening round of the 1941 Western Sectional Playoff. Throughout the week the Bismarck Tribune and many other newspapers in the state showed pictures of the players, cheerleaders, and crowds. Stories described the keen competition.

The opening games of the tournament were held on March 13. Grand Forks defeated Grafton and Fargo outscored Williston. Wahpeton, the tournament favorite, won impressively over Jamestown and Bismarck lost a close game to Minot.

On Friday, Fargo, a team many people picked to upset Wahpeton, was surprised by Grand Forks. Wahpeton sneaked by a determined Minot team. The pairing for the championship game was set. The Grand Forks team was peaking and Wahpeton lost some of its aura of invincibility in its narrow victory.

The Bismarck Tribune headlines on Saturday read, "British Ready to fight for Greece," and "Special Train Brings Wahpeton Rooters." KFYR broadcasted the title game and Fay Brown did the play-by-play analysis; he had announced the championship game for the last eleven years. Williston

won the consolation game Saturday afternoon.[9]

In the days prior to the storm, Bismarck enjoyed fairly mild

temperatures. On Thursday, March 13, the thermometer topped the freezing

mark at 33. At 6:30 p.m. that evening skies were clear in Bismarck and the

barometer was very high at 30.49 inches of atmospheric pressure. As the low

started to approach Bismarck, the barometer started to fall. A high of 31

degrees was recorded in Bismarck on Friday. That evening it snowed and

the barometer fell to 29.93 inches. Temperatures were even higher in

Bismarck on Saturday. After an overnight low of 21 Saturday morning,

temperatures rose to 40 above that afternoon. The barometer continued to

drop all day, reaching 29.69 inches at 6:30 p.m. just as the storm approached

Bismarck.

Warnings were somewhat ignored because warm temperatures added

much excitement to the atmosphere of the tournament. F. J. Bravendick,

meteorologist in charge of the Bismarck bureau, called KFYR at 3:00 p.m.

and informed the radio station that a storm was moving towards North

Dakota and was increasing in intensity. Storm warnings were repeated

several times during the afternoon, discouraging some spectators from

driving to Bismarck for the championship game. But most of the fans were

already in Bismarck. At 6:30 p.m., KFYR was notified that a dangerous

storm was quickly approaching the city. Bravendick requested that storm

warnings be broadcast immediately and a special weather bulletin be sent to the auditorium.

The tournament director hastily announced the special bulletin. He urged the large crowd not to travel. As the Fargo and Minot teams battled for third place honors, Bismarck experienced 30 mph winds and one-eighth mile visibility. By the time the championship game started, high winds had jolted Bismarck. Occasional snow flurries made it treacherous. The winds peaked in Bismarck at 47 mph at 8:30 p.m. Wahpeton's dream team won the championship game.

Bismarck reported no property damage. Despite the onslaught of bad weather, there was a large crowd at the auditorium. Fans and teams from the eastern part of North Dakota returned home on Monday because many roads still were blocked on Sunday. In the next few days, as the horrors of the blizzard became known, the luster of the Class A tournament was diminished and attention shifted quickly as the death toll mounted. On Monday, the stark headlines of the Bismarck Tribune read, "59 Dead as Storm Screams Across Dakotas, Minnesota; Many Missing," and "Storm Came on 21st Anniversary of Hazel Miner's Heroic Death."[10]

A hit-and-run accident took place on a Bismarck thoroughfare late Saturday night. Police found Gilbert Schulsan, a WPA laborer, at eleven o'clock and rushed him to the hospital. Near his body the authorities discovered bits of a broken car headlight. There were no witnesses to the accident. On Sunday, Schulsan died. His death was not attributed to the tragic blizzard, though it was indirectly related.

After the storm passed, the temperature dropped to 2 below on Sunday morning. At 6:30 that evening it was partly cloudy in Bismarck, and the barometer had rebounded to 30.50 inches.

As it turned out, there was only one death recorded in the Missouri Plateau region. It happened in the northeastern part of Burleigh County, near Wing. On Saturday, Emil Erickson, a farmer who lived two miles west of Wing, walked to town. Upon meeting a neighbor there, Erickson accepted a ride part of the way home. He was strolling home when the storm broke with a vengeance. The piercing cold took his life. His body was discovered 200 feet from his farm home.[11]

Minot, Bottineau, Rolla, Rolette, Rugby, and Cando

On Thursday, March 13, Minot beat Bismarck in the first round of the state Class A basketball tournament. The Magicians almost pulled off the upset of the year on Friday by outshooting Wahpeton, which was undefeated with a twenty-two game winning streak.

The team's sparkling play was the talk of the town on Saturday. Minot's KLPM announcers graphically recalled the match. That evening folks waited to hear the result of the third place game with Fargo. Hotels, cafes, and restaurants were getting ready for the upcoming North Dakota Class B High School Boys Basketball Tournament in Minot on March 20-22. The Chamber of Commerce had a busy week answering questions about the facilities and resources available for the tournament. Teams from Oberon, Underwood, Mott, St. Mary's, Mayville, Cavalier, Mohall, and Rugby would be competing.

Spring was in the air. At noon the people of Minot enjoyed 35 degree weather, but KLPM was repeatedly advising its listeners of a cold wave warning with strong winds on Saturday, along with stockman's warnings. Racing down from the northwest, the Alberta Clipper arrived late in the afternoon. Winds peaked around 6:00 and by midnight it was 6 degrees below zero. Minot did not receive any new snowfall as a result of the storm. It was nothing more than a bad windstorm.[12]

KLPN covered President Roosevelt's speech Saturday night. Roosevelt outlined what steps the United States was taking for its defense and provided details of the lend-lease program. Fans were disappointed again as the Minot Magicians lost another close battle to Fargo.

The blizzard paralyzed some areas in north central North Dakota, but other areas were unruffled. Minot fans in Bismarck stayed overnight, though U.S. Highway 83 between Minot and Bismarck remained open throughout the storm. Afterwards, in the political fallout, E. J. Fox stated that "Minot received storm warnings twelve times during the day" in a report to the chief of the United States Weather Bureau at Washington, explaining the actions of the weather officials at the local level. Ironically, one of the places that was best prepared for the oncoming blizzard did not get hammered.[13]

Throughout the morning and into the afternoon the weather in Bottineau, located in the Turtle Mountains, was mild and pleasant. The Turtle Mountains are really hills, rising about 400 to 800 feet above the surrounding plain, and are a heavily wooded island of timber and lakes in the otherwise treeless prairie. Although the Turtle Mountains region extends into Manitoba, it occupies much of Bottineau and Rolette counties in North Dakota.[14]

In 1940, the two largest communities in Bottineau County were Bottineau, with 1,739 inhabitants, and Willow City, with 524 residents. Antler, Kramer, Landa, Lansford, Maxbass, Newburg, Omemee, Overly, and Souris are other towns located in the county.

The clear blue sky gave no indication that "Bottineau County's worst blizzard in many years" was only hours away. In the afternoon the sky clouded over and turned gray. In Bottineau, it started snowing heavily, but the big white flakes appeared harmless until winter winds swatted the area at four o'clock. Within an hour, a full-scale blizzard erupted and continued for six hours. The temperatures dipped sharply, from a high of 30 degrees to 15 below early Sunday morning.[15]

Bottineau County residents reacted quickly to the arrival of the storm. Local hotels, motels, and boardinghouses rapidly filled up. But there were not enough accommodations for everyone. Folks rushed over to the homes of their friends. The popular gathering places, such as the town bar or cafe, remained open all night. Card parties and all-night pool games were

60

organized. Radio broadcasts helped ease some of the confusion. Telephone operators worked way past their normal business hours so people could hear the voice of a loved one.

Out in the country, countless motorists were trapped at farmhouses and roadside filling stations. As the storm dished out its violence, a light from a farmhouse meant relief and comfort on a restless night. The warm cookstove in the kitchen and a hot cup of coffee were all one wanted. Chicken soup and beef stew were heated up and served. The smell from bacon, ham, and side pork woke up visitors who spent the night. One farm, three miles west of Bottineau, had twenty-nine snowbound guests.[16]

Snowplow operators worked throughout the night, but they failed to keep the roads open. On March 16 at 5:00 a.m., Ernest Piquette, a snowplow operator, found a partially buried car about five miles west of Bottineau, on State Highway 5. He heard the motor running and assumed everyone would be all right in the car. He dug the snow away from the car door and opened it. A quick glance with a flashlight revealed that everyone was dead. The victims were later identified as Mr. and Mrs. Paul J. Nordberg from Mohall, North Dakota, and their son Ralph, a resident of Minot.

On March 15, Andrew Bjork, a farm hand, left his employer's farm to get a cow at a nearby ranch, three-fourths of a mile away. The storm winds swept in and Bjork disappeared. Sunday morning search parties were organized and sent outt look for him. Late Monday his body was discovered about three miles from his own home. Bjork had walked over a mile past his destination before he collapsed and died.

One man's courage was remarkable, but it almost caused his death. As the snow swirled about Edwin Berentson of Newburg, he jumped on the front fender of the car to help guide the driver. In the dark turbulence, another car struck their vehicle and broke Berentson's leg. The drivers took Berentson to the nearest clinic where his broken leg was splinted.[17]

Rolla is located in Rolette County and in 1940 had 1,008 residents. On March 11, Rolla's independent basketball team upset Hannah, the 1940 Class B state champions with four returning stars and heavily favored to repeat in 1941. Rolla looked forward to playing in the North Dakota Class B Independent Basketball Championship tournament at Harvey, North Dakota, on March 17-19. The cagers' victory over Hannah was brought up again and again in the local cafes by those who regularly met each morning for coffee and freshly baked caramel rolls. Alexander, Sanborn, Stanley, Hoople, Linton, Mohall, and Rolla would be competing for the first time at this level of competition. Last year's runner-up team from Velva was back and was tagged as the new favorite. Reporters covered the event, and the box scores were carried in the major newspapers.

The weather in Rolla was mild on March 15 but radio warnings, beginning around noon, mentioned an approaching storm. Going to town on Saturday afternoon was more than a ritual—farmers sold their goods to the local creameries and grocery stores. Light snow fell as many families traveled to town. Rolla learned that its first-round opponent in the upcoming tournament would be Velva. Just before 6:00 p.m., the bleak winds settled in. Rolla, however, was lucky because wind velocities were lower than in surrounding areas. Livestock losses were light and no individuals died out on the prairie.[18]

The deadly storm blocked the roads and highways throughout much of northeastern North Dakota. The Class B Independent Basketball tournament was postponed and rescheduled for March 2-26. Everybody in the community knew somebody who had died in the storm. Rolla's regional win seemed less important, and on March 24, Velva defeated Rolla. Velva went on to win the tournament.

Mrs. Willard Young, a resident of Rolette, had a terrifying experience. She was all alone in a stalled car a mile south of the Grand Forks airport. Her ordeal lasted from 6:30 Saturday night to Sunday noon. Young survived but her legs were frozen badly.

Rugby, located in Pierce County, is near the geographical center of North America. In 1940, Rugby, the county seat of Pierce County, had 2,215 residents. A. C. Larson had a crew of men renovating the Farmers Union building, and he expected to open a grocery store shortly after the first of April. Improvements to the old John Deere Implement building were completed and final preparations for opening were underway. The Gronvold Motor Company continued the extensive alterations to their downtown plant. Rugby had won the 1940 North Dakota Class B high school boys basketball championship. On March 8, the Rugby Panthers won the district title by beating Rolla and they earned the regional title with their victory over St. Leo's of Minot the following week.

As the defending champion, Rugby received a great deal of publicity prior to the tournament, but the tragic blizzard overshadowed it. Rugby successfully defended the Class B title in Minot on March 20-22 by beating Mohall, Cavalier, and the St. Mary's Saints in the championship game.

There were no deaths in the vicinity but the community mourned the loss of a former Rugby resident. Miss Harriet Coger, a Grand Forks (Winship) school principal, met her death near the Northwest School of Agriculture near Crookston, Minnesota. Miss Coger was a sister of Albert E. Coger, pioneer lawyer of Rugby who resided in Los Angeles, California, and Mrs. Elizabeth Wenzel who lived in Bismarck, North Dakota.

Caught out in the rigorous storm, individuals from Pierce County had noteworthy experiences. Returning from Devils Lake, the mayor of Rugby, C. N. Knudson, rolled down his car window and attempted to follow the road by the weeds along the ditch. He became stuck six miles east of Leeds. In a few minutes, a car with five passengers from Fillmore ran into the back of his car. The Fillmore bunch joined Knudson in his car and they stayed there for the next six hours. Floyd Meyers, near Fero, heard several cries for help as he trudged his way to the barn. Investigating further, he came across an exhausted man crawling in waist-deep snow. Collecting his breath, the man directed Meyers to his friend who had collapsed earlier in an open field. An hour later the trio warmed up by the kitchen range in Meyers'

64

home. The Peter Bischoff family, stranded at a neighbor's farm until midnight, lost about $200.00 worth of stock and poultry because the doors on his barn were not open. Ingvold Teigen, Leo Aafedt, and Bischoff shivered throughout the night as they looked for the farm animals. Jesse Romine, a truck driver for the Rugby Bakery, took shelter overnight in a barn belonging to John Critenson. Romine furiously banged the front door of the farmhouse, but nobody was home and the house was locked up. There were many hogs in the barn and Romine later joked he had "only pigs for company and he didn't mind if the pigs didn't." C. P. Hanke, manager of the Otter Tail Power Company in Rugby, had business in Fergus Falls, Minnesota. Ernie Haeuser was waiting for nice weather to pick up his car in Fergus Falls, and when his boss headed there, he took advantage of the wonderful opportunity. On his way back, Hanke ran into the storm near Petersburg at 8:11 p.m. and at 10:30 his motor stalled. Hanke wrapped himself up in an extra coat and for the next thirteen hours he wrestled to keep awake. On Sunday morning, Hanke struggled to a farmhouse a mile and a half away, despite the fact that the wind kept blowing his feet out from under him. Haeuser made it back as far as Crary when poor visibility forced him to pull over on the side of the road. Staring at the treacherous snow, Haeuser had seen a glimmering light. Meanwhile, inside the house the farmer and his brother-in-law caught a glimpse of a headlight. They quickly grabbed their coats and went outside to help. It was storming so bad that when Haeuser turned off his car lights the rescuers lost sight of the car. Meanwhile, Haeuser stepped outside, ready to seek shelter. He heard rasping voices in the breath-taking winds, but could see no faces. Overjoyed, Haeuser turned on his car lights and the farmers headed toward the flickering lights. Getting back to the farmhouse was just as big a challenge. The farm owner knew there was a fence about 15 or 20 feet away and it led to his house. Haeuser had a rope and they tied one end to the car and by trial and error they located the fence and returned to the farmhouse. It was a pleasant evening for all. Haeuser had to wait for another nice day to get his car at Crary.[20]

Cando, located in Towner County, is in the heart of durum country. In 1940, the city had 1,282 residents and served as the county seat.

Saturday night, Mrs. William Baumgartner, Edith Engstrand, and Curtis Carlson left Cando for the Herman Engstrand farm, where Baumgartner was employed. The trio had stopped at a rural schoolhouse about one mile from the Engstrand farm, when the weather deteriorated. Although Mrs. Baumgartner had eight children, her thoughts centered on her youngest child at the Engstrands. She probably figured her son would be frightened by the storm and she wanted to be there to comfort him. Against the wishes of the young couple, Baumgartner stepped out of the schoolhouse and headed for the Engstrand farmhouse. She froze to death 300 yards from the farm. Tracks in the snow indicated that at one time she was close to the farmhouse but had turned. Edith Engstrand and Curt Carlson stayed in the school the rest of the night and went home unharmed the next morning.[21]

Cavalier County:

Langdon, Sarles, Hannah, Munich, Loma, and Clyde

In the aftermath of the storm, many exhilarating and deplorable stories came out of Cavalier County. Some of the larger towns along the Great Northern tracks included Langdon, 1,546; Milton, 310; Sarles, 302; Osnabrock, 269; Hannah, 261; and Munich, 216 in 1940. Alsen and Loma had 312 and 256 residents respectively and were located beside the Soo Line.

Langdon hosted the annual Class A Independent basketball tournament March 12-13. Teams from Grand Forks, Langdon, Minot, and Fargo were first-round winners. In the next round Grand Forks defeated Minot by one point and Fargo beat the Langdon Aces in a close game. Grand Forks's Pepsi Cola defeated Fargo's Powers Coffee Shop for the championship.

On March 7, the Langdon boys won the District 12 championship by topping Milton, 32 to 26. In the regional title game on March 14, the Cavalier team beat Langdon, 28 to 25. Langdon merchants were happy about the extra business and the boom continued on Saturday when local residents came to town. Everyone was in a festive mood.

About 5:00 p.m., radio reports indicated a storm had moved into north central North Dakota from Canada. The dangerous blizzard grew more violent as it approached Cavalier County. Two hours later it roared into Langdon and lasted until daybreak Sunday morning. High winds, 40 to

80 mph, whipped snow and dirt into the air, creating a "blinding obstacle for motorists which drove cars into ditches, confused horses and then blinded, froze, or suffocated those who tried to walk to safety."[22]

"I'll never quit telling about the people up here," was the statement of Hannah Swanson of Minneapolis after she and her brother's family, Mr. and Mrs. Gunnar Swanson and their children Glen and Carla, were rescued from the storm after eight grueling hours. Four miles west of Sarles their car stalled on the open prairie amid callous winds. Soon afterwards, out of the darkness, a man wearing a light overcoat suddenly opened the car door and hurled himself into the auto, too exhausted to talk. The Swansons gave him a massage to get his blood circulating. Regaining strength, he identified himself as Warren Tewksbury of Towner. Tewksbury told the group that his car had stalled earlier and he started walking at 5:45 p.m. It was 7:30 when he reached the Swanson's car. Meanwhile, Clifford Barke, John Swanson, Dick Barker, and Walter Martz were stranded in Sarles and they learned that the Swanson party never made it home Saturday night. Around 10:00 they left Sarles with a team of horses during a lull in the storm. They soon encountered snow-blocked roads. Barber and Martz started walking, stopping at a farmhouse to warm up. They continued on and came across Tewksbury's car, but found nobody. A short time later they reached the Swansons. After reassuring the group, Barker and Martz went to a nearby farm to get a team. No one was home so they broke into the house to get blankets. They started a fire and then returned to the stranded party. The group cuddled up in the blankets and walked to the nearby farmhouse. Snug and warm, they spent the night there. Meanwhile, Mrs. Martz, thinking her husband was safe in town, fretted for their livestock. After the storm eased, Mrs. Martz and the family dog drove the cattle, horses, and sheep to shelter.[23]

The tragic blizzard attracted nationwide attention. Local newspapers printed stories about how the storm affected its residents. These articles later appeared in the larger newspapers in the storm area. The process continued when major newspapers in the United States contacted North Dakota and Minnesota editors for information about the storm. The nation drew strength from the courage and fortitude of the people in the small towns of North Dakota and Minnesota.

One particularly sad event took place near Hannah. Two children who were cousins, Kenneth Nickerson, eleven, and Louise McLeod, twelve, attended a 4-H meeting at a country schoolhouse. At 5:45 p.m., after the meeting was over, they started toward their homes, about two-and-a-half miles north of the school, on a toboggan drawn by a horse. About 6:15, the full-fledged Alberta Clipper reached Hannah. As soon as the storm hit the area, their parents started looking for the children. Family friends joined the search. Sunday morning at 3:00 they found their bodies about a half-mile southeast of the school. The horse was still alive about a quarter of a mile away. Apparently the horse refused to face the terrific winds so the children unhitched the horse and attempted to ride it home. However, the horse drifted with the storm. Fortunately, thirteen children and two supervisors remained behind to visit a bit after the meeting and were still talking when the ferocious winds arrived. They bundled around the stove and passed the time.

A Langdon farm family had a very cruel experience. Mr. and Mrs. Harold Weiner, their eight-year-old daughter and nine-month-old son, made it back to the driveway to their farm. However, the road was still blocked with snow and, as usual, they parked their car several hundred yards away. In the aftermath, the reporter wrote, "As they stepped out of the machine, the daughter was swept away by the wind and rolled along a field much like a small barrel, with her parents, the mother clutching the baby to her bosum, in pursuit." Their eyes remained focused upon their daughter as they scrambled toward her. They grasped their daughter gratefully but in the mad dash lost their bearings. After a while, the Weiners stumbled upon a fence which Mr. Weiner recognized as his own. Leaving his family there, he scouted ahead. Mr. Weiner followed the fence and soon discovered their sheep barn. He returned to get his family but his wife was unable to move. Half dragging and carrying her to the shelter, Mr. Weiner and his family stayed there for the remainder of the night. In the morning he hitched up a team of horses to a stone boat and took her home. After making his family as comfortable as possible, Mr. Weiner walked to a neighbor's farm. His neighbor hitched up a team of horses and went to get the doctor at Langdon. Upon their return the doctor treated Mrs. Weiner and her son at home.

Later they were taken to the Langdon hospital. The boy recovered his health, but his mother died two weeks later.[25]

A similar incident happened to a family who lived near Munich. Mr. and Mrs. Jacob Hoffman, their four-year-old daughter Ervone, and a neighbor, Henry Friesen, were returning from Devils Lake. Because the road to their home was blocked with snow, Mr. Hoffman parked the family car along the highway. Their farmhouse was located about 220 yards away. Leaving their car, they walked toward the farm and were within 50 feet of the house when they became exhausted and dropped to the ground. The frigid cold temperatures and biting winds took their breath away, but Mr. Hoffman was able to stagger home. Once inside his house, he telephoned several neighbors and explained the desperate situation. Going back outside, Mr. Hoffman searched for the others. Hoffman's friends quickly assembled and started their search. At 1:30 Sunday morning they came across three casualties. Inching further along, they discovered Mr. Hoffman who was barely alive.[26]

The will to survive is strong. Three men from Loma, Joe Stamm, Gerald Ballweg, and Charles Hamann, left Langdon a few minutes before the storm rolled in. Their car stalled, and without a heater they realized the dreadful possibility of freezing to death. They burned a can of furniture polish and a couple of small boxes for heat. After running out of handy fuel, one of the men drained the oil from the crankcase of the car. The oil lasted only several hours and then they were out of fuel again. They burned the fan belt next. It was enough to carry them through the night. Early in the morning they walked to a nearby farm and were made comfortable. The car, however, was damaged beyond repair.[27]

Many individuals survived the storm by staying in their vehicles. In Cavalier County, for example, LaVerne and Henry Dick, brothers from Clyde, spent ten hours in their stalled car in Highway 5 between Langdon and Calvin. They had plenty of gas to keep their car running at intervals, and the heater kept them from freezing.

The March 15 blizzard blocked all the roads in Cavalier County and caused some damage to property. On Monday afternoon, snowplow operators opened Highway 5 east of Langdon and on Tuesday morning they had opened the highway west of town. A caravan of cars followed the plows into Langdon. By Tuesday night the roads had drifted shut again and remained blocked until late Wednesday night when the snowplow operators cleared them a second time.

In Loma, stout winds ripped the entire front end of a pool hall loose and the debris knocked down telephone lines, halting phone service for most of Loma. The pool hall owner worked hard to save his equipment but the storm was too much. On Sunday, friends helped him move the damaged furniture to a building across the street, and they shoveled snow out of the demolished building, which included the barber shop. Near Loma, at Ted Kjos's farm, a windcharger was twisted off the house. Kjos, a school bus driver, kept the bus at his farm. It was tipped over in his yard.[28]

Ramsey County: Devils Lake,

Webster, Edmore, Brocket, and Lawton

Devils Lake experienced a sudden gale, reaching a speed of 48 mph, at the height of the storm at about eight o'clock Saturday night. It stopped snowing about 11:30 and five inches were recorded overall. The westbound Greyhound bus was stalled near Petersburg; about fifteen passengers spent the night in a farmhouse. Between Devils Lake and Churchs Ferry, twenty cars were abandoned, but most of the occupants made their way to farmsteads. Those who waited out the storm in their cars had a frightful night. Great Northern Train No. 3 was seven hours late Saturday night, but the Empire Builder was only one hour late on Sunday.

Every generation remembers one or two blizzards more than all the others. Odin Bremseth, from Devils Lake, wrote about the 1941 storm in March 1990.

> I hadn't heard the forecast. The Empire Builder had pulled in and was still standing there at the depot when we [Bremseth gave an older woman who was his neighbor a ride into Devils Lake] left town. We just got out a quarter of a mile when the wind hit, sounded like someone stood there with a blow torch. . . . I had a Model A Ford and they don't get wet very quick. I knew just about where there was an approach. I turned around and got back in town and we kept warm. . . . There was a fellow hauling cream for the creamery about 60 miles west of here [Devils Lake] and he called his wife and told her he didn't think he could make it home. She thought he was kidding but in about an hour she found out

73

what was going on. The old lady that was with me, their youngest girl was home with her dad. When he didn't come in from the barn she attempted to tie some twine together and go out, but good thing she didn't make it, because he got to the chicken coop just when the wind hit and he stayed there so she wouldn't have found him in the barn. They [the people around the area] seemed to think it was sort of a tornadic storm. It had such a suction, my neighbor couldn't hold the stove down and if he shoveled in fuel it would have thrown it all out. . . . The people that died, their lungs were full of dirt.[29]

The sudden and violent blizzard created a lot of uncertainty but the telephone offered reassurance at a time when it was needed most. Although many households did not have the use of a telephone, they knew where they could take advantage of one. At Devils Lake, all plant facilities of the Central Electric and Telephone Company were used to capacity for the first time since the exchange opened. Between seven o'clock and nine o'clock the telephone company estimated that 3,000 calls were completed. Joe C. Crookhan, district manager, figured every telephone in town was used on an average of at least six times during this period[30]

Sparks flew and the smell of smoke was strong at the home of E. W. Griswold. The owners hurriedly placed a call to the fire department. Loud winds muffled the clanging fire alarm in Devils Lake. However, firemen left the station during the brunt of the storm and worked their way very deliberately to the site of the alarm. Meanwhile, at the Griswold's, the panic subsided and things calmed down when the chimney fire died out. They welcomed the rescue crew into their house and told them the good news. The fire chief inspected the stove, the pipes, and the chimney, and he agreed that the chimney fire had burned itself out and the house was no longer in any danger.

Each gust of wind vibrated windows in Devils Lake. Anybody who has lived on the northern prairie for any length of time knows that howling noise. Radios blared away as the people hankered for storm news. The telephone rang constantly, sometimes breaking the tension or adding to it. Party lines were busy and word of those in trouble spread fast, but in many cases a considerable amount of time passed before the fate of loved ones was known.

In Devils Lake, friends of Mr. and Mrs. Melvin Reep received word that Melvin's brother Sever had been found frozen to death near Michigan, North Dakota. They were asked to relay the message but they failed to contact the Reeps. They learned only that the couple had left Devils Lake and their whereabouts was unknown.

Search parties began looking for Mr. and Mrs. Reep on Sunday morning, but without any luck. Hope faded. On Monday, Mr. Tiegen, a local farmer, noticed his cattle milling around something in the pasture. Walking over to it, he discovered two dead bodies. Authorities concluded the Reeps, who had been married less than two years, were on their way to a farmhouse in Noonan township, fourteen miles northeast of Devils Lake, where Mrs. Reep taught school. They parked their car at the roadside corner and started walking the final two miles. It was cold; the winds came up. They drifted southeastward with the storm. Tracks indicated that Melvin had carried his wife for a short distance before he staggered and collapsed. Their lungs were full of dirt.[31]

Mr. and Mr. Joe Lange of Webster, a town located thirteen miles north of Devils Lake, were rushing their small son John to the hospital in Devils Lake Saturday night. The boy had almost cut his toe off with a double-bitted axe. The distressed parents encountered the ill-timed blizzard. Hitting rock-hard drifts, they continued on in the swirling snowstorm. They collided head-on with another vehicle driven by two men from Derrick, located a mile south of Webster. Mrs. Lange suffered a badly sprained ankle in the collision. Both parties were marooned until 2:30 Sunday morning, when they were picked up by other travelers.

The Edmore Herald News described the March 15 blizzard five days later:

> Following two hours of beautiful snowfall in comparative calm, the wind came up in a gale in a moment's time at about 7:00 Saturday evening to usher in the worst and most disastrous blizzard that the community has experienced in years, and measured by its fury was probably as bad as the one of March 12, 1922.
>
> Wind velocity at Grand Forks at the height of the storm was fixed at the weather bureau at 74 mph from the north, northwest, and was hardly less here, and so dense was the storm that the visibility was zero or at best ten to fifteen feet. Temperatures were about 10 above, which caused the snow to melt on one's face and clothing, but the driving winds drove dampness through the protective outer garments.[32]

At Edmore, Mr. and Mrs. Ernest Sanderson, their three children, and Mrs. Sanderson's physically-disabled brother were on their way home when the blizzard winds sprung up. Their car stalled near the coulee bridge west of the city. Mr. Sanderson and the oldest boy, Vaule, left the others and walked home, about a half-mile away, to get blankets. They called the authorities in Edmore and asked for help. Charles Ingersol, the fire chief, W. H. Johnson, the chief of police, Elmer Melland, and Paul Knutson formed a rescue party about nine o'clock. The volunteers bundled up and tied a sturdy rope around their waists. Fighting their way foot by foot through the blinding snow, they reached the stranded party. They guided everyone back safely to town. Mrs. Sanderson suffered frozen limbs. They were a sight to see. Their faces were soaking wet and their outer garments frozen stiff.

Right after they had returned to town, another distress call came in. Mrs. Ralph Kuchar and Ralph Jr., a high school senior, were in trouble east of town. Johnson and Ingersol courageously volunteered to lead another rescue party. Nine men offered to go on the dangerous mission. Obtaining more rope and extra clothing, they were soon prepared for the excursion. Locating the Kuchars two miles east of Edmore in their automobile, the rescuers handed them warm clothes. On the way back to town the gallant men formed a protective circle around the Kuchars. It was about 1:30 Sunday morning when they returned the second time. Johnson and Ingersol could barely stand after battling the elements.

Unfortunately, another report of a missing person came in. This time it involved Lawrence Melland, the brother of the man who had risked his life saving the Sandersons. Elmer's condition was such that he could not help search for his brother. Lawrence Melland, Art Fjalstad, and Svale

Egeland had driven Nels Elshaug to his farm Saturday night and were returning to town when the storm broke. They encountered car trouble close to the Malmin farm. Melland stayed in the car for a few minutes, and then insisted he had to go home to do his chores. He departed. Sitting close together, Fjalstad and Egeland covered their heads with a blanket and stomped their feet to stay warm. Three or four times they made a desperate attempt to reach the Malmin home but were driven back by the fierce winds. The cold was so intense that at 4:30 a.m. the two men decided on one final all-out effort. They succeeded. Egeland suffered only frozen toes, but Fjalstad's feet were badly frozen. They experienced terrific pain and medical aid was impossible because of blocked roads. Early Sunday morning fifty men combed the area for Lawrence Melland. The hunt for the Edmore farmer continued all day Sunday and Monday. On Tuesday the search party grew to sixty men, but there was little hope that Melland would be found alive. Alfred Danielson, a farmer east of Edmore, sighted the body lying in a field while getting a load of straw around noon on Tuesday. Lawrence Melland had roamed six miles after leaving his companions. Lawrence Melland was the last victim to be discovered in the aftermath of the storm in North Dakota.

On Monday, a plane from Langdon flew to the Malmin farm and took Fjalstad to the Langdon hospital. Egeland was taken to Edmore in Harold Hurst's snowmobile.

C. E. Strand, the local telephone manager for Edmore, visited the dial exchange building on the night of the storm. He said, "everything was working, with calls coming through in an endless clicking." Strand answered criticism from impatient residents who complained about telephone services by explaining "there really wasn't any interruption of service, but rather the system was unable to handle calls as fast as they were made." He reported that 1,400 telephone calls were completed between Saturday night and Sunday morning. In the next 24 hours there were 3,300 calls registered and only 40 were uncompleted.[33]

Brocket, located in the heart of the Durum Triangle, had 291 residents in 1940.

Mr. and Mrs. Alvin Thompson and their two-year-old son were within sight of Brocket when everything went wrong. Their car stalled. They decided to walk to a nearby sheep shed and wait out the storm. They searched in vain. Visibility was down to zero. Holding hands, the Thompsons changed course and headed toward Brocket. They struggled. Frightened, the Thompsons turned back toward their car. They wandered aimlessly until they stumbled across a corn shock, a big pile of stalks shaped like a tepee. Mrs. Thompson clutched her son while Alvin dug a hole in the corn stalks. They huddled together and used the snow and corn stalks as a form of insulation from the harsh winds. At 5:30 the next morning, Mr. Thompson walked to the V. F. Beavar farmhouse and brought help to his wife and child. Mrs. Thompson was badly frostbitten and their infant suffered from exposure.[34]

Another story from Brocket was told in a letter to the <u>Grand Forks Herald</u> by William J. Vasicek, a highway worker:

> I got lost in the blizzard coming home from work and stayed
> out all night, but faith which gave me courage kept me
> fighting for my life. I'm thanking God that I am still here,
> only with frost bitten hands, feet, and face, and stiffness
> through my whole body. It's an experience I will remember
> the rest of my life.
>
> I was well dressed . . . and was soaking wet clear to the skin
> when I reached Vendal Skalicky's farm by following the fence
> which my team brought me to. I unhooked the team and let
> them face fate, but they survived. I turned my sleigh over me
> and dug in under it to keep from freezing. I stayed there
> eight hours before I dared follow the fence which even then
> was hard because my face kept freezing over with ice and it
> was hard to breathe. I had to work with my shovel and keep
> moving every second of these many hours to keep my blood
> circulating.[35]

A similar tale of courage happened just down the road. Joe T. Bina from Lawton had been in Brocket earlier in the day. He was returning home when the strong winds peppered the area. Bina's freight wagon offered no shelter from the bitter winds and snow slashed his face. Sitting high on the wagon seat he heard the horses snorting. It was so cold it hurt. Decision time. Bina turned the team of horses loose and tipped the wagon box over himself. The wait was sheer agony but he survived the prairie storm and endured minor frostbite.[36]

In 1940, Nelson County had 9,129 residents. Population figures for the small towns were as follows: Lakota, the county seat, had 907; McVille, 548; Aneta, 509; Michigan, 491; Petersburg, 285; Pekin, 229; and Tolna, 172. The Great Northern Railroad linked the farming communities together. Although different nationalities settled in Nelson County, the majority of foreign-born residents were from Norway.

Nelson County had the most fatalities in North Dakota. Nine deaths occurred in that county and two long-time residents died nearby in Ramsey County. For some reason this area, especially from Michigan to the Niagara Corner, has a long history of receiving the brunt of many winter storms. On March 20, The Lakota American devoted its entire front page to the storm's horrifying effects. The dark black headline was shocking: "11 From Nelson County Die In Storm." One town, Michigan, had seven deaths, including Mr. and Mrs. Melvin Reep who resided in Devils Lake.

It was a pleasant day for Lakota residents on March 15. After a long, cold winter, the warm temperatures seemed special. Early in the afternoon the temperature reached 33 degrees. People were shopping and visiting friends and relatives. Farmers brought their families to town after the chores were finished. Parents had a hard time calming their children—they were looking forward to having a soda pop and watching a movie at the cinema.

At 7:40 p.m. the frightening blizzard arrived in Lakota. A reporter for The Lakota American described the beginning:

> With a 30 above temperature and a breeze from the south, two flashes of lightning which streaked across the sky seemed to act as a signal for the storm to start its work of death and destruction, and without any warning the winds switched to the northwest, and the storm hit as quickly as if someone had dropped a blanket over the state. Later in the evening, the temperature dropped 30 degrees in two hours, and reached around 12 below before morning.[37]

The Capitol Theater in Lakota was crowded with people enjoying the movie Knute Rockne—All American when the blizzard conditions exploded. After seeing the initial punch, M. A. Zimmerman, the manager, started making arrangements. Zimmerman kept all the children in the hall until their parents picked them up. Others stayed overnight at the hotel across the street or in the apartment buildings nearby.

Saturday night, Mr. August Carlson of Lakota, an elderly gentleman, left home to buy some tobacco at a nearby store. Mrs. August Carlson expected her husband to return any time. But the blizzard came up. She looked out the window, hoping to catch a glance of her husband. There was no word from her husband as the storm blew through the region. Dawn broke. People ventured out and looked around. Mr. Carlson was found dead, in a standing position, leaning against a light pole only 50 feet from his home.

Local residents were caught out in the storm and experienced car trouble. For example, Agnes Olson of Lakota, a teacher at Southham, and a group of Southam women were returning from Devils Lake. They were roughly a mile and a half from home when their car became stuck in a deep snowdrift. In one hour the gale winds had forced wet snow under the hood, killing the motor. All of a sudden they had no heat. Furthermore, their car had a broken window letting in the icy winds and snow. Inspecting the car, the women found a piece of canvas and they used it to break the wind. To stay warm they rubbed their arms and legs and moved around as much as possible. Each minute seemed like an hour. Wind gusts up to 80 mph jabbed the car. They waited and waited. After eleven hours had passed, one of the women walked to a farmhouse a half-mile away and brought help back. They came through the ordeal without any serious effects.

As the storm raged Saturday evening, Mrs. Jacob Geritz, Jr. gave birth to a baby girl at the Wallum hospital. The proud father and his dad arrived in Lakota only a short time before the storm broke.

Illinois township, located southwest of Lakota, suffered no fatalities, but some of its residents had cruel experiences. Mr. and Mrs. Gene Gordon and their daughter-in-law Mrs. James Gordon were stranded in their car east of the Arthur Howser farm. They kept warm by wrapping their feet in bath towels and making leggings out of yard goods they had purchased in town earlier in the day. The Gordons had bought a can of kerosene. They burned the oil a little at a time, tearing strips from a robe for wicks. Mr.

Howser and Paul Gasper came to their rescue at 6:00 Sunday morning. Neighbors took care of their stock while they rested at the Howser farmhouse. Their car was pulled home by a team of horses Monday afternoon.

A farmer and his wife from Dodds township, located south of Lakota, had a narrow escape. Charles Ward was doing chores in the barn when the blizzard struck. He was unable to return to the house, so he stayed there. His wife, after several hours of worrying, lit a gasoline lantern and started toward the barn, but became lost. Crawling on her hands and knees, she reached a fence and followed it to the sheep shed and from there to the barn. Hours later the couple made it back to their farmhouse. Mrs. Charles Ward suffered two badly-frozen ears and a pretty sore body for several days.[38]

Bernice Smaage, 14, and Rosalie Anderson, 15, lived on farms south of Michigan. The girls were best friends and spent a lot of time together. On Saturday, Bernice walked over to the Anderson farm and visited Rosalie. When it came time for Bernice to go home, Rosalie started out with Bernice because the Smaage farm was located one mile to the west. Strong northwest winds put the girls in a terrible situation. They were within 220 yards of the Smaage place but turned back because the cold winds became unbearable. They wandered off the road and became lost. For two days their parents worried about their fate and approximately 100 men searched the area. On Monday afternoon the missing girls' bodies were found close to the Melvin school. Mr. and Mrs. Severin Smaage and Mr. and Mrs. Mortinus

Anderson arranged a double funeral and the girls were put to rest in a double grave.

Peter Smiley, a farmer who worked on the John Yoney farm south of Michigan, became lost in the storm while attempting to go from the house to the barn. On Monday morning they found his body a mile southwest of the farm.

On Saturday, Sever Reep, a farmer near Michigan, had business in town. Being a good neighbor, Reep gave John Kallestad and his two sons a ride into Michigan to greet Mrs. Kallestad, who had been visiting her sister in Mayville. Later that evening, they were on their way home. The Kallestads got out on the highway near their farm just as the storm hit. As the family walked toward the farm, Mrs. Kallestad became too exhausted to walk. Mr. Kallestad wrapped his coat around his wife and took his sons home. He returned with a team and picked up his wife. However, she died shortly after being taken into the farmhouse.

Sever Reep continued on his way home but his car stalled. He tried walking home but never made it. Sever had a wife and five children at home.

In 1941, church steeples dotted the countryside. The tragic blizzard had dire consequences for a country church in Nelson County. Members of the Center Lutheran church helped the T. J. Reep family after the deaths of their two sons and a daughter-in-law. Triple funeral services were held for the Reeps at the Center Lutheran Church on March 20. Two days later, the church held double rites for Bernice Smaage and Rosalie Anderson.

Dahlen, located in the northeastern part of Nelson County, experienced the death of a local man. Andrew Hentjium, 55, went to Dahlen on Saturday with Lars Brudahl, his employer. Brudahl brought his three sons along. That evening around six o'clock the group left town in a sleigh drawn by two horses. The storm frightened the horses and the whirling snow hindered their progress home as the blizzard gained intensity; they were forced to walk. Brudahl and his sons held hands while Hentjium walked right behind them, but they became separated. Brudahl and his sons trudged to their home, but Hentjium did not make it back to the farm.

On Friday, March 14, young residents from Tolna put on a three-act play entitled "Old Crusty Takes the Air." The auditorium was packed and a dance was held after the show with the Martin Baldwin's orchestra providing the music. A food sale, sponsored by the Catholic Altar Society, was held at the C. E. Anderson store on Saturday. Many farmers ended up staying overnight in Tolna after the devastating winds hit. Oldtimers called the storm "the most severe blizzard in many years." Mr. and Mrs.. Leland Steinmann were trapped in their automobile with their baby until three o'clock Sunday morning. The Steinmanns walked briskly as possible to the Lloyd Gulbro home in 12 below zero weather. The parents suffered minor frostbite, but their baby came through without any ill effects. Another couple also had a terrifying experience. Vernon Haas and Ione Thorson took Mrs. Clarence Halvorson to Cummings, North Dakota, on Saturday and were just outside the town limits of Pekin on their way back when their car stalled. The young couple remained in the car until the storm subsided. Sunday morning they staggered into town and their arms and legs were badly frozen.

Mrs. Maria Christianson, 64, residing on the Mrs. Gusta Brude farm near Pekin, failed to make it back home from Pekin. Reports indicated that she had left town just prior to the start of strong winds. Mrs. Christianson tried to follow a fence but turned the wrong way. She crawled until her strength was gone and she died.

A farmer near Aneta, Carl Hillisland, 72, was on his way home after spending some time in town. Driving a team of horses, he encountered trouble when the weather turned worse and a pole in his rig broke. He walked behind the horses but the wind was at such a velocity that it made breathing difficult. Hillisland became exhausted and dropped to the ground. He tried to keep going but failed. The horses found their way home. A search party found his body Sunday morning.[39]

Something amazing happened on the Nels Boostrom farm near McVille on March 23. Wallace Boostrom, 14, was playing with his dog near the turkey house when he broke through a snowdrift. He worked his leg out and a moment later out popped the head of a live gobbler. Boostrom had lost six turkey hens in the March 15 blizzard and the gobbler had been missing. The gobbler had lived on water for eight days.[40]

Sheridan, Wells, Eddy, and Foster counties did not have any deaths
attributed to the storm. Griggs County, however, had one fatality.
Residents organized search-and-rescue parties, and in the aftermath
experienced sorrow and happiness.

For example, August Hass and Walter Christe from New Rockford in
Eddy county spent Saturday night at Jul Farr's home. They had walked to
Farr's place after their car ran into a big snowdrift. On Sunday, Hass and
Christe walked ten miles to reach their New Rockford homes. New Rockford
reported winds of 50 mph during the storm.[41]

Folks in Foster and Griggs counties became concerned when two
truckers from Carrington were reported missing. A large search party of at
least seventy-five men from Glenfield, Carrington, and Cooperstown, began
looking for A. N. "Bud" Graves and Lester Engberg on Sunday. The process
was slow and hard. There was a seven-mile stretch on Highway 7 that had
drifts 15 feet high. Before snowplows rammed the snowbanks, men probed
each drift with long rods for the missing truck and men. The operation
continued on Monday. Search crews received a message stating that Graves
and Edberg were safe. They had run into the ditch after the storm broke and
walked to a nearby farmhouse. The farmstead had no telephone. They
remained there Saturday night and Sunday. On Monday, the truckers took a

sleigh to Sutton and jumped on a Great Northern train. The men got off at Glenfield and encountered a large number of men from Carrington who, to Graves' and Engberg's surprise, were looking for them.[42]

Griggs County was not as lucky, as one death was recorded near Cooperstown, the county seat since 1882. Cooperstown is located fifty miles east of Carrington and had 1,077 residents in 1940. The Saturday blizzard swung into Cooperstown at eight o'clock. One hour later wind gusts reached 75 mph and tapered off a little before midnight.

A story of heroism and tragedy that came out of Cooperstown involved Bob Miller, who made his usual trip from Valley City to Cooperstown bringing goods from his father's bakery. Originally, Miller's bakery was located in Cooperstown. Raymond "Whitey" Johnson had the day off, so he went along with Miller to visit his parents in Cooperstown. Johnson had grown up in Cooperstown and had worked for Miller in both places. They began their return journey, but when it appeared that a bad storm was developing they decided to go back. They planned on turning around at the first corner, about a quarter of a mile out of town, but missed the corner. The men continued to the next corner, but before reaching it their truck slid off the road. Unable to get their truck out of the ditch, they locked the cab and started walking back to Cooperstown, about a half-mile away. After going a short distance they realized they would never make it. Returning to their truck, they became lost. When they left town the wind was from the west, so they turned and walked with the wind at their back.

They did not realize that the wind had switched to the north and instead of walking towards Cooperstown, they were heading away from it. Holding hands they plodded on, each step becoming a greater effort. The icy wind made it hard for them to breathe. They yelled to ease the tension. Moving on, they walked blindly into a fence and their hopes shot up. Following the fence, Johnson soon collapsed. Miller helped him stand up and they staggered on. Johnson went down again, totally exhausted. Miller carried him until he fell against the fence which ripped his trousers and cut deep gashes into his flesh. Miller dug two snow trenches and laid down beside Johnson. However, he did not stay there very long. He stood up and dragged Johnson until the strain was too much. After resting, Miller went for help. Several hundred yards away he stumbled upon a sheep barn. After regaining some of his strength, Miller kicked the walls and hollered for help. Upon hearing a dog bark, he headed towards the sound. Miller found no dog but came across a house. It was empty and there was no telephone. Miller took off his wet clothing and quickly put on the dry clothing he found there. Miller then went back out into the storm and worked his way back to Johnson. To inspire his friend, Miller told him there was a house only a few feet away. But Johnson was worn out. Miller tried carrying him but was too weak and he reluctantly crawled back to the house. Peeling off the ice and snow that was frozen to his clothing caused slight tears. He lit an oil burner and warmed up. When the storm had let up, Miller started for Cooperstown. After the moon broke through the clouds he realized he was going the wrong way. He changed directions and wobbled into the Exchange hotel at 5:15 Sunday morning. Miller's eyes were almost swollen shut and his hands and feet were frozen. A rescue party left immediately but Johnson was found dead, lying by the fence. Under a doctor's care, Bob Miller recovered and a week later went home.[43]

The sounding of the fire alarm in Cooperstown during the storm, forced the fire department to send its fire truck out in the storm. Men walked in front of the fire truck, keeping it on the road. The truck stalled, however, before it reached the Nels Sandvik home where a chimney fire had been reported. Fortunately, the Sandviks were able to put the fire out. Upon returning to the station, firemen noticed that Jim Christianson, a member of the fire department, was missing. A frantic search developed but Christianson was found safe at the Art Edland home. He became separated from the others and at the first opportunity took shelter.

Another man from Griggs County had a harrowing experience in the storm. E. Tracy, a businessman from Cooperstown, had a meeting in Devils Lake and his wife was accompanying him. He left town and went to a nearby farm to pick up the babysitter. At the farm he found out that the girl was not home. The storm came up when he was returning to town. His car stalled. Tracy had seen a fence and decided to follow it, figuring it would lead him to a farmhouse, but he missed it. Luckily, he found his way back to the car. Tracy's car had a spotlight and he shined it on the fence. He focused his attention on the light and walked backwards toward the fence. This time he reached the fence. Tracy followed the fence to an open gate and he recognized it. Familiar with the farm, he used snowbanks as guides. He thought about making a dash for the place where he thought the house was located, but he decided against it. Afterwards he stated, "I had a terrible time to hold myself down. But I knew that if I missed the house, the result would be fatal." Crawling on his hands and knees, he gradually reached the barn and took shelter. Since the barn was terribly cold, He tried six times to reach the house. But he did not dare to let the barn out of his sight. About midnight, he caught sight of a windmill. Keeping it in sight, Tracy headed in the direction where he thought the house ought to be. Suddenly he saw a glimmer of light! He ran to the house and was soon cuddled up to a warm fire.[44]

The storm caused a major problem for the Northern Pacific Railroad in Griggs County. Parts of the Valley City-McHenry branch line were covered with huge rock-hard snowdrifts, especially between Cooperstown and McHenry. A work train was made up in Dilworth and two train crews were called out of there on March 18. The train consisted of a Russell snowplow, a large wedge plow, and two locomotives, along with some boxcars and a caboose. Section men from Rogers and Binford were picked up by the train to help in the clearing operation. The process was slow and hard. With the Russell plow ramming the snowbanks the workers would clear the snow from the tracks. Unfortunately the plow derailed two miles east of Mose a small town located twenty-five miles west of Cooperstown. The train slammed into a drift, and the big plow turned and broke a rail. The Russell plow and the locomotives lay wildly crisscrossed on the tracks, but the rest of the train stayed on the tracks. Engineer E. P. Qualley had a broken leg and Fred Lewis, the fireman, had cuts and bruises. The engine crew in the second unit escaped harm. Riding in a boxcar, a section hand, Robert Moore, suffered a concussion when he was thrown about in the derailment. After the accident he walked into Mose and collapsed. Twelve other section men had minor injuries.

The Northern Pacific Railroad called in a wrecker from Dilworth. Relief crews were called in from Valley City and three doctors joined the relief train.

By Thursday night the wreckage was cleared but the branch line was still closed. The Northern Pacific Railroad sent a rotary plow to finish the job of opening the branch line. Business resumed later on in the week.[45]

The storm passed briskly through Steele County, leaving some lasting impressions on its residents. On Saturday, Finley, 677 residents in 1940, hosted a basketball tournament for junior high school teams. Teams came from McVille, Hope, Kloten, Mayville, and the consolidated schools of Lindaas and Logan Center. Throughout the day, people cheered for the boys from their home towns. The tournament was winding down when the storm raced into the area. Many adults, and at least fifty children, were stranded at the auditorium. The folks from Finley were quick in offering their hospitality. Most of the children stayed in private homes while the majority of the adults passed the time in the auditorium.

The Hope basketball team had finished its games and departed from Finley, but the storm brought them to an abrupt stop one mile south of Finley. Being trapped in the car and hearing the wind blow outside made the tournament seem insignificant. It was a night the players would never forget. The parents had a stressful time when their children never came home, and their anxious telephone calls offered no relief. On Sunday morning, Superintendent Easton, who also was in the car, walked back to Finley and summoned aid.[46]

The Finley Press believed that the weatherman put up a "weak sales talk" in the aftermath of the storm. The newspaper thought adequate warnings at 6:00 or 7:00 p.m. could have saved many lives. A resident of Finley learned about the storm when he called a friend out in Williston.

Folks in Hope had only a warning of 45 minutes before the storm hit. One frantic telephone call from Lakota started a frenzy. Some people had a hectic time. For example, Mr. and Mrs. Oliver Vierkant were in a cafe when their children called and told them to come home. They were two blocks from the cafe when the wind roared in. The Vierkants went two blocks and turned back. Mrs. Vierkant stayed overnight at the Henry Jakes home, the first house they came across. Using a flashlight, Mr. Vierkant fought his way home in the storm. He walked in circles, ending up at the same cornstalk five times before he finally made it home.

Arthur Kerkow went up and down the street in Hope seeking shelter for those stranded in the crowded movie hall. He brought food back for the people staying in the theater overnight.[47]

The following is R. D. Larsen's recollection of the 1941 storm:

> I was seven years old and lived west of Hope, in Steele County. I had been outside that day, in shirt sleeves. After the blizzard hit, my dad opened a door on the downwind side of the house and hardly any snow swirled in. There was just a white wall of snow moving past the door. My dad stuck his hand into it and it just disappeared. I wanted to do it so dad hung onto me. It was like putting your arm into a very fast moving stream of water. The next day there was a snowdrift between the house and barn. Standing on top I could see over the house and looked right at the big hay mow door.[48]

Jamestown, Dazey, Rogers, and Valley City

The violent storm was moving diagonally across the northern part of the Red River Valley and heading toward Wisconsin. Regions south and west of the main path of the storm had wind gusts of 55 mph, instead of 75 to 85 mph.

Jamestown, located in Stutsman County, had 8,790 residents in the 1940 census. In 1939, the Jamestown high school boys won the Class A state championship basketball tournament. Jamestown lost to Wahpeton on March 13 in the opening round of the 1941 tournament and the consolation game the following day.

Stutsman County reported little damage from the blizzard, despite 55 mph winds. Jamestown's radio station broadcast a warning of approaching 40 to 50 mph wind eight times during the day. Travel was difficult in and around Jamestown. Peace officers were stationed at various city exits to warn motorists and they halted traffic out of Jamestown until the storm had abated. Some folks were caught out in the storm, but there were no fatalities.[49]

Suddenly the blizzard swept into Dazey, located twenty-five miles northwest of Valley City in Barnes County, with a population of 215 in 1940.

Growing up on a farm close to Dazey, the Taylor brothers looked forward to Saturday night when they could go to town. Leo, 17, and Donald, 15, took their ten-year-old twin brothers Dickie and Robert roller skating March 15. After skating, they left for their home, which was located four miles southeast of Dazey. Their car stalled and they decided to walk home. Mr. and Mrs. Warren Taylor became worried when the boys did not return. Word of the Taylor's plight spread rapidly. Starting at midnight, Ralph Bender and Beaument Stowman from Dazey walked approximately 15 miles in their search for the boys. At 7:45 a.m., Leo and Donald were found frozen to death. Digging into the snowbank, Vernon Jacobson, a neighbor, saw the feeble wave of an arm. It was Dickie Taylor's last gesture because he died a few minutes later. He had protected his twin who was found alive. Robert was taken to the hospital in Valley City and he survived the storm.[50]

A farmer near Rogers, located sixteen miles northwest of Valley City in Barnes County, took a dangerous chance in the blizzard. Mahlon Bonzheimer walked three miles back to Rogers after his car came to a standstill. He waited in the car until the storm let up somewhat before setting out and arrived without suffering any injuries.

A couple of turkeys emerged alive from a snowdrift after being buried for twenty-three days on the Robert Grindler farm near Rogers.

North Dakota's Winter Show took place in Valley City on March 11-15. Gaylor Walker won the second annual sheep-shearing contest. Between 500 and 600 buyers attended the two-day livestock auction sale. Henry Hamann, from Washington, D.C., conducted a federal egg-grading class, and 60 people took part. Temperatures climbed to 33 degrees Saturday afternoon in Valley City. The farm exposition was a big success. The last scheduled events for Saturday night included vaudeville entertainment from the Twin Cities and a dance with the Litchville and Davenport bands providing the music. But a violent storm scurried into Valley City at eight o'clock. Within one hour snow had blocked the underpass on U.S. Highway 10 and other roads and highways. By Sunday morning it was 11 degrees below zero. Snowplows and wreckers were busy clearing the roads and pulling out cars.[51]

Incredibly, a live sheep was uncovered in a snowbank on the Fred Schroeder farm near Valley City seventeen days after the storm.

Fingal, Litchville, Fort Ransom, Oakes, Ellendale, Forman, and Gwinner

In the aftermath, two stories came from Fingal, located twenty-one miles southeast of Valley City in Barnes County. In 1940, Fingal had a population of 300 people.

On Saturday, Newell Nelson of Fingal left the A. J. Lee farm at 8:30 p.m. Blizzard conditions developed. After his car stalled, Nelson ventured out into the hostile storm. He stumbled across a ploughed field and came upon a fence. He followed it until he struck a machine. Working his way over the contraption, Nelson discovered it was a mower. Amazingly, he recalled that such a mower stood close to a gate leading into the Gerhard Olson farm. Nelson continued on, and sure enough, he came to a gate. Tired and gasping for breath, he saw a flicker of light. Bucking the winds, Nelson made it to the house and banged on the door. Olson opened the door, and he was shocked. Standing there was a shivering, worn-out man, his face and head encased in ice. To their surprise, the man was their neighbor.

Two sisters from Fingal, Albina and Delphine Stangler, 28 and 14, were returning home after attending church. Their car stalled and they decided to wait out the storm. Their trust in God gave them confidence during the lonely and cold vigil. The sisters were severely frozen and later admitted to the Valley City hospital.[52]

A family from Litchville, located twenty-five miles southwest of Valley City, had quite an experience. Mr. and Mrs. Albin Aune and their two daughters were traveling west on Highway 46 when the storm whipped in. They became stranded and the couple carried their small children three miles to a filling station. Mrs. Aune and her daughters required medical aid

98

and were taken to the hospital in Valley City.

The storm was still deadly as it was accelerating away from North Dakota. It killed Albert Jacobson, 73, and his son Albert Jr., 11, near the town of Fort Ransom, located approximately thirty miles south of Valley City in Ransom County.

The following account was written by R. D. Larsen in 1990. Larsen talked to Haakon Holm, who participated in the search for the Jacobsons and Paul Olson, who was the son of Oscar Olson, one of three men who had discovered the bodies. Larsen has written many stories about the early pioneers in Ranson County. He wrote:

> March 15, 1941 was an unseasonably warm day. Water was running into the Sheyenne River and people were in their shirt sleeves. Shortly after 7:00 p.m. the temperature began to drop, snow began to fall, high winds began driving the snow in its path.
>
> Albert Jacobson, 73, and his son, Albert Jr., 11, were in town. Before leaving, they stopped at Henry Martinson's garage where Haakon Holm put air in a low tire for them. They left, saying they would stop at the Olson's store for a salt block. A short time later Mrs. Jacobson called the garage. She asked Haakon to try and catch them if they were were still in town and tell them there was a terrible blizzard on the prairie and not to try to come home. Haakon drove to Olson's store and found they had left. They called Mrs. Jacobson. Her husband and son had not returned. Haakon Holm, Oliver Nelson, and Chet Highness set out to find them. They drove until their car stalled, then tying themselves together with rope they set out on foot. They found the Jacobson's car farther on—empty! The three men walked an estimated 18 miles from shortly after 8:00 p.m. until 4:00 the next morning. They found three other persons trapped in their cars and took them to safety. When the bodies of the father and son were found the next morning the tracks of the searchers were found to have passed within 10 feet.

The Jacobson's car stalled about two miles from Fort Ransom. As near as I can tell, the storm ended in this area by 1:00 a.m. Three men who lived within a mile or so had been keeping in contact by phone. When the storm let up the three, Ole Olson, Art Anderson, and Oscar Olson set out to search for the Jacobsons. The moon was very bright and the temperature had dropped to way below zero. They found the bodies about 6:00 a.m. After the storm an account in the Fargo Forum stated, "Tracks In Snow Tell How Boy, 11, Fought in Vain to Save His Father." But Oscar Olson told his son Paul that it appeared the boy had collapsed first and the father had put his gloves under his head and went on another 50 feet where his body lay.

A stormy day in the winter will still bring up the subject. To this day one thing is apparent, it was not just a Jacobson family tragedy, but a community tragedy.[53]

It was tragic in the worst way because Orville Larson and Mr. and Mrs. Lloyd Helm of Fort Ranson came across the Jacobson car stopped along the road. They looked in the car but it was empty. By estimating the time factor afterwards, they guessed that the Jacobsons had abandoned the car just about 15 minutes prior to their arrival.

One unusual victim of the storm was J. E. Bunday, who was a seventy-five-year-old civic leader in Oakes, located sixty-files miles south of Valley City in Dickey County. It its early history, Oakes had three railroads and in 1940 had 1,665 residents. Bunday suffered a heart attack in front of the First National Bank where he worked for many years. Bunday's physician believed that overexertion brought on the heart attack.[54]

On December 29, 1990, Mrs. H. J. Gronbeck, a resident of the Oakes area, wrote a letter to the authors. She wrote:

The March 15, 1941 blizzard is something I am sure I will never forget.

My husband was in the hospital in Oakes. The Noonan home, now known as the "House of Twenty-nine," was being used for a hospital. He had an appendectomy March 12. While the surgeon was removing the infected appendix, it burst, sending the infection into the stomach.

In those days there was none of the miracle drugs, such as sulfa drug, to fight the infection. By March 15 he was burning with fever. We had friends that lived in town, and they had seen my husband and decided I had better come to town to be with him. Our farm was seven and a half miles out and they came for me . . .

When my friends came for me it was a mild winter afternoon. There were no weather forecasts so we had no advance information . . .

I stayed at the hospital. About ten or eleven o'clock it sounded like the building was struck by some force. The lights went out and a window in the hospital bathroom was blown in. The nurses became very frightened and were doing their best to find something for lights. A few candles and flashlights were found. the hospital had quite a number of patients.

At that time the Otter Tail Power Company had an auxiliary plant that could carry the town and in a while that seemed like an eternity, the lights came on. Our rural areas did not have electricity but rural electricity came a while later. My husband recovered but he was hospitalized for 14 days. . . .[55]

Ellendale, located seventy-five miles south of Jamestown in Dickey County, had 1,517 residents in 1940. Ellendale experienced mild weather on Saturday but as the day progressed the weather turned slightly colder and snow began to fall. This was followed by rain turning to sleet and later to snow as the wind became more violent. The storm arrived in Ellendale about 8:30 p.m., but winds reached only speeds of 35 to 40 mph. The storm was not as dangerous as in other areas because there was very little snow on the ground in the vicinity. By Sunday morning the temperature slipped to 6 degrees below zero at Ellendale. Western Dickey County "felt only the fringe of the blast and a few persons were forced to leave their stalled cars and continue on foot."[56]

Sargent County is located east of Dickey County and in the southeastern part of North Dakota. Sargent County experienced no casualties. The Sargent County News described the storm as "the worst blizzard of this winter," and said it "followed a day of bright sunshine which raised the temperature way above the thawing point and hardly a cloud could be seen in the sky a short time before the storm struck." Trees were blown down and outbuildings damaged by 60 mph wind. A call from William Jentz of Gwinner rallied local residents as he reported his wife and two small sons missing. Forman and Gwinner residents organized rescue parties, and the search began on Sunday at two o'clock in the morning. They went home in good spirits at 9:30 after learning that Mrs. William Jentz and the boys were safe at the George Cartier home. No word was sent because the Cartier household did not have a telephone.[57]

A Summary of Deaths Recorded in the Missouri
Plateau and the Drift Prairie Regions of North Dakota

The blizzard of March 15, 1941, affected most of North Dakota's Missouri Plateau and Drift Prairie regions. The Missouri Plateau had one fatality, which took place in Burleigh County. However, there were five deaths recorded in Bottineau and Towner counties, located in the north

central part of the Drift Prairie region. Meanwhile, the Drift Prairie

counties bordering the Red River Valley experienced horrendous

consequences. In Cavalier County, six people died while in Ramsey County,

three lost their lives. The county with the most deaths in North Dakota was

Nelson County with a total of nine. Griggs, Barnes, Ransom and Dickey

counties accounted for seven more deaths. Overall, North Dakota had a total

of forty fatalities and of these thirty occurred in the Drift Prairie.

Pembina County: Walhalla, Neche, Pembina, Hamilton, Cavalier, Glasston, St. Thomas, and Drayton

Pembina County, named for the high bush cranberries which grew

wild in the area, had a population of 15,671 residents in 1940. The largest

towns along the Great Northern tracks included Walhalla, population 1,138;

Cavalier, 1,105; Neche, 565; St. Thomas, 503; Crystal, 428; Bathgate, 312;

and Hamilton, 255. Two major towns serviced by the Northern Pacific

Railroad were Pembina, 703, and Drayton with 688 residents.

The war overseas was getting closer to home. The United States,

although not officially at war, was mobilizing its forces and supporting the

allied powers. In January of 1940, three large bombers from the Lockheed

Manufacturing Company were flown to Pembina, North Dakota. Two pilots

remained with the planes at the airport south of town while the other two crew members took documents to the custom house where their papers were immediately cleared. Upon their return, the pilots flew the planes to a hastily prepared airfield north of Pembina. A team of horses pulled the planes across the border to an adjacent airfield. This was done so the United States would not violate neutrality laws.[58] Starting on October 30, 1940, men were being drafted into service. Many people signed voluntarily. On February 10, 1941, the 164th Infantry Regiment of the North Dakota National Guard entered federal service. The 188th Field Artillery was activated on April 1, 1941.[59]

The blizzard rushed into Walhalla, located about forty-five miles northwest of Grafton, shortly before seven o'clock Saturday night. The Walhalla Mountaineer reported that winds were "so intense in the city that driving was almost impossible even in the shelter of the buildings." Also, the neon lights from local structures, "looked like a lighted match at a block's distance." Firefighters braved the elements and put out a chimney fire at the Joe Dumas place.[60]

James Johnson of Neche and John Dahl of Grand Forks lit a fire in the trunk of the car and kept reasonably warm until the car started on fire. They put the fire out and endured the cold. They were in a near coma when a farmer came along and rescued them.

At 7:24 p.m., the wind in Pembina was at 36 mph, but ten minutes later it jumped to 58 mph. Pembina immediately warned the Fargo airport station of the drastic change. This was the first report Fargo had received that a dangerous storm had arrived in northeastern North Dakota.[61]

Afterwards Mrs. Frank Cummings of Pembina praised KFJM, the Grand Forks radio station, for a 4:00 p.m. weather report Saturday that kept her family home.

On Saturday, Mr. and Mrs. Mike Howry went to Pembina while their oldest girls babysat at home. When the storm came up, the couple decided to wait it out in Pembina. Meanwhile, back on their farm three-quarters of a mile south of town, Katherine, 19, and Florence, 14, figured their mother was out in the storm and was having trouble making it home. Leaving the younger boys at home, they walked over to the railroad tracks which ran along their farm and headed for town. On Sunday, Mr. Howry returned home. To his horror, he discovered that his daughters had gone out into the blizzard. He quickly returned to Pembina. In the meantime, a Northern Pacific engine, unknown to its train crew, dragged a body into town on its cow catcher. The locomotive that dragged the body into Pembina had been sent from Grand Forks to replace an engine that was damaged. During the storm, the gale winds blew a boxcar off one of the industry tracks in Pembina onto the main line and a short time later the passenger train from Emerson hit the boxcar, damaging the engine. Word of the tragic death spread fast and a crowd gathered at the depot. Hearing of the commotion, Mr. Howry went to the depot where a tragic sight awaited him. He identified the body as one of his daughters. Search parties walked along the railroad tracks and discovered the body of the other sister a mile south of Pembina near a

105

railroad trestle.[62]

Roy Fee of Hamilton, a representative of a school supply company, was on his way home from Neche, located fifteen miles northeast of Cavalier. South of Neche, his car stalled and with snow drifting in through the cracks, he devised a way to keep from freezing. Fee burned rags and a bundle of paper in a tin pail that was in his car. He had sixty matches which he used sparingly. Burning rags and newspapers at intervals, he was able to stay warm. Early Sunday morning, he walked back to Neche.[63]

Temperatures had been mild in Pembina County on March 14 and 15. Cavalier, located about thirty-two miles north of Grafton, had a high reading of 32 degrees for both days. On Saturday, Cavalier received .76 of an inch of precipitation, about 7 inches of snow. During the storm the wind speeds were estimated at 58 mph in Cavalier and the town had an overnight low of 14 degrees below zero. According to the Cavalier Chronicle, "many pioneers can recall storms lasting two and three days, but they fail to remember when a storm of such intensity hit this county so suddenly."[64]

In the aftermath, reporters wrote about people facing death. The Cavalier Chronicle, however, let a local farmer write his own tale of his ordeal in the storm. On Saturday night, Herbert Schlucter wanted to take his family to Cavalier but Schlucter's vehicle became stuck in a snowbank one-half mile from his farm. He walked home to get a team of horses to pull his vehicle out. Schlucter wrote:

> After harnessing my team, I started for the car. Just after
> leaving the barn, the storm was upon me, and I could not see

106

anything. It was just like a solid wall of snow, and then I began having trouble with the team. The horses would not face the storm, and I worked with them for some time. I know that I had crossed one barb wire fence because I heard it scraping on the sleigh. Then the horses became entangled in another fence, and I tried to lead them over the fence and finally got the team loose from the wire. I then realized that it would be impossible for me to get the team to the car, so I unhooked them from the sleigh and separated them and turned the horses loose.

I began to wander, and at that time I was certain I was walking in the direction of my stalled car, but I now realize that I was far off my course. I believed that it was about 8 o'clock when I turned the horses loose. After walking and crawling for what seemed like hours, I found a fence. I had no idea where I was at this time or where the fence might lead me. I held onto the fence and kept walking. It was very hard to stand up because of piled up snow, ice, and dirt. Many times I fell while following the fence and I realized that if I sat down and rested that I would fall asleep, so I kept on moving and fought the urge to stop and rest.

After following the fence for what seemed to be hours, I ran into some small willows and hit a post. At this time it was about three in the morning, I had my flashlight with me and I looked at my watch. I did not at this time have any idea where I was because the storm was still very blinding and it was still dark. I hung onto the post and fought against sitting down and resting, realizing my only chance to keep from freezing to death was to keep awake until daylight. Thinking of my family, I was able to withstand the cold and the storm and kept hanging onto that post.

Just before the break of day the storm subsided for a second, and I saw the outline of some buildings. But I still had no idea whose farm it was at this time. After thinking for a few minutes what was best to do, I crawled on my hands and knees toward the buildings and just before reaching the house, I recognized the place to be the George Schroeder farm, one and one-half miles south of Cavalier. I knew the house was vacant, so I forced my way into the house, it was pitch dark and very cold. I used my flashlight and began searching for something dry to wrap myself in as my clothes were wet and frozen. I jammed some old rags that I found between my underwear and body as my clothes were frozen to my body. I was terribly cold and wet. After slipping on an old pair of overalls, I started to walk to another farm where I knew Pete Fossum lived. Knowing that my family was still out in the storm, I realized that I must rescue them as soon as possible.

I walked the one-half mile to the Fossum farm with little difficulty as the storm had subsided somewhat and the wind was blowing on my back. Mr. Fossum got his car out and we drove to where my car was stalled. We reached it without any trouble. After placing my family in the car and starting back to the Fossum home, we ran into the ditch a short distance from our destination. We walked to the farm home and remained there the rest of the morning.

My wife, believing that I would have little chance to survive the storm, got out of the car and was going to look for me, but the children began to cry and she got back into the car. Her clothing was wet and frozen, but she was able to keep the children from getting frostbite by wrapping some clothes she found in the car about the children. My wife's legs were quite badly frozen.[65]

After resting a while, Schlucter helped Fossum with his chores and then walked home and did his own work. Schlucter delivered milk to a neighbor and hired someone to do his evening chores. Relatives heard about their troubles Sunday morning and they drove out to the farm at 10:00. They brought their kin to Cavalier and Herb Schlucter sought medical attention.

David Sterling, the eldest son of Mr. and Mrs. John Sterling of Glasston, walked over to the James Littlejohn farm to get some milk Saturday night, one of the chores he usually did for his mother. Sterling picked up the milk at the barn and chatted with his neighbors before he left for home, about a quarter of a mile away. Talking it over, the men decided to make sure the Sterling boy had made it home safely because the weather was changing. They left the barn only a few minutes after the boy had departed. The neighbors reached the Sterling place but David was not there. Mr. Sterling and his friends looked for the boy until the storm forced them to quit. The search continued on Sunday but he was still missing that night. On Monday, the body was found two miles south of the Sterling place.

On Saturday, Mr. and Mrs. Nicholaus Heuchert of St. Thomas traveled to Hensel and visited their three daughters. The Heucherts left for home about 15 minutes before the blizzard descended on the area. They were almost home, but their car slid off the road. They abandoned their car and attempted to walk home. Their sons found their bodies a quarter of a mile away from home on Sunday morning.[66]

Mrs. Fred Shear and her daughter Kathleen of Drayton were stranded in their car sixteen hours south of Drayton. The following account was written in 1991 by Kathleen Shear Bellamy of Drayton:

> Dawn on March 15, 1941, promised a beautiful spring day. My mother and I decided to drive from Drayton to Grand Forks to shop as it was Saturday and I was not teaching school that day. Before we left Mother said to my dad, "Don't worry if we don't come back tonight—we may stay in Grand Forks." Why she said this I'll never know—we had no intention of staying overnight. The man I was engaged to was coming to see me that evening so surely I planned to come home!
>
> After shopping all day we stopped to visit my dad's sister in Grand Forks for a few minutes and then started home. It was snowing big soft flakes—making it a little hard to see the road. I was driving on the left side of the two way traffic highway because it was easier to see that edge of the road.
>
> About 8:30 the snowfall lessened and I commented that I thought the snow was ceasing when suddenly the wind

changed from the south to north bringing such heavy snows that it seemed as if a solid white blanket had been thrown over the car leaving absolutely no visibility. I started to turn the car to the right side of the road but because I couldn't see a thing, I stopped diagonally across the highway. Mother was fearful that another car might come along and hit us in that position. I reasoned that if we couldn't see to move, no one else could either. However, she felt she should get out of the car to see how, exactly, we were situated on the road. She tied my scarf on her head (she had been wearing a new spring hat!) and stepped out of the car. With her hand on the door handle, she could not see the car beside her. Fortunately, she did not let go and was able to get back into the car. In the few seconds she was outside, she was covered with a thin coat of ice as the north wind brought chilling temperatures. My scarf was wet and had shrunk to a smaller size.

We turned off the motor for we were afraid of exhaust blowing into the car. Temperatures kept dropping during the night and before morning were well below zero. We jumped up and down, climbed from front seat to the back seat and back again, and sat on each other's feet to try to warm those extremities! We sang songs, told jokes, and prayed to keep awake. We were both tired and could have easily fallen asleep and soon would have frozen to death. Because of all the whiteness outside, it seemed lighter inside and we could see each other dimly. Occasionally, we would see sparks near the rear view mirror, probably static electricity—but this did not add to our comfort and fear of fire was another reason for not running the motor.

Although the car was new and quite tight, snow still blew in the front and back seats. We tried to keep active all night and at eleven o'clock the next morning we paused to take stock of our situation. We were hungry—we hadn't eaten since noon the day before. The wind was not abating and if this should be a three day blizzard, we could not spend another night in the car.

We decided to try to find shelter while it was daylight. We could see the edge of the road right beside us, so it seemed prudent to make the move right then. I managed to get to the trunk of the car where my dad kept an old shirt and a pair of pants to don if he had car trouble when he was wearing his best suit. I was wearing my usual heavy clothing—snow pants and two pairs of mitts—she had been wearing only thin gloves. She tied several handkerchiefs together and tied her spring hat with them. She put on my dad's pants but because she was larger around the waist than he, the pants couldn't be buttoned! We took string off packages and tied the pants on. I tied the old shirt around my head.

We had a big old fur robe, and we held this in front of us as we headed out into the wind. Even with this bit of protection it was difficult to breathe with the strong wind blowing in our faces. Because our feet were so cold walking was difficult—our feet felt like heavy stumps. After a quarter of a mile we could see trees in the distance. Since there were deep snowbanks between the road and the trees, we decided to stay on the highway rather than chancing going to the trees only to find no buildings. (We learned later there weren't any buildings there.) We kept walking about another quarter of a mile where there were more trees, and we could see a house! We walked across the snow filled ditch and over a fence covered with snow. Mother caught her toe on a wire and fell down. I got her on her feet again just as a dog started to bark—a welcome sound that indicated there were people living in the house. Just as we got into the yard, the string on mother's pants broke and the pants began to slide down. Mother tripped and could hardly get up As we were laughing so hard—partly from the pants falling down and partly from relief as help seemed so near. Just then the door opened and the lady of the house, Mrs. Altendorf, said, "Oh, bring that lady in—she's dying!" Mother was not dying, just laughing too hard to get up.

We were welcomed into the home and provided with a delicious chicken dinner, and we were ready for it! The home was small, two rooms downstairs with a stove in each room. I sat in all this warmth with my coat on all afternoon and just could not get warm. Towards evening I walked to their neighbor's house just across the highway. These folks had a telephone. I told the woman of the house what I wanted to say, she repeated it to another neighbor she could reach on the party line, who in turn related the message to the Grafton operator who could reach the Drayton operator, who called my dad. All my dad knew was that we were safe and he thought we had been at the farm house during the storm. He had not worried about us during the night because of what mother had said about the possibility of our staying in

Grand Forks. When we had not called by Sunday afternoon, he phoned his sister in Grand Forks only to find we had left there a short time before the storm broke. Then he did worry until I was able to get my message through to him. His sister called the highway department to report us missing and they agreed to do some searching when the storm was over. About 4 or 5 days later they called our house in Drayton to see if we had ever arrived home.

Sunday night Mrs. Altendorf apologized for not having an extra bed for us. We assured her we were fine—only too happy to just be inside. A bit later she said the boys had decided to sleep on the floor and we could have their bed. We snuggled between two big feather ticks, and it was only then that I finally got warm!

Monday morning we took a team of horses and pulled my car to the yard. When we lifted the hood no motor was to be seen—just a big mound of solid snow! After melting the snow, we got the car started and headed for home. Another car with two men and a boy were also headed for Drayton to take the boy to school. They drove first—hitting the snow banks on the road until the car could go no further. Then we all got out with shovels and pushed their car through first, then ours. We got to the curves in the road about 2 or 3 miles south of Drayton., Then there was a 6 or 8 foot high wall of snow all through the curves. We walked to Hedman's house nearby and called my dad. He got the Drayton policeman, Mr. R. Newans, to drive his car out to the snow blocked curves and we walked down the railroad tracks to meet him. Finally, we reached home Monday night. It was several days before the road was cleared so we could get my car home.

This was an experience I will never forget. I hope never to be that cold again. However, we were fortunate not to have frozen or even to have frostbitten toes or fingers. Many others lost their lives while were were unharmed—truly an answer to prayer.[67]

During the blizzard, snowplow operators rescued many people but in Drayton something different happened. Saturday night, Phil Saumur and Arthur Kolstad left Drayton in a truck to relieve Pete Smith and Barney Swenseid who were running a rotary plow on Highway 29 west of town.

Their truck stalled and they did not dare leave it until Sunday evening. Saumur and Kolstad walked over four miles back to Drayton and suffered from frostbite. Smith and Swenseid operated the plow until it ran out of fuel. They remained in the plow until the storm ended and afterwards walked into St. Thomas, arriving about noon on Sunday.[68]

Walsh County: Grafton, Adams, Park River, Lankin, Pisek, and Fordville

In Walsh County, the residents of Grafton, 4,070 in 1940, were excited about the Class A basketball tournament in Bismarck. The community whooped it up and supported their players. On March 13 the cagers played Grand Forks, their arch rivals, in the opening round but were defeated 24-18. In the consolation game the next day they faced Williston and lost another close game.

The wind had been blowing from the south at Grafton when the storm blew into the area at eight o'clock Saturday night. The Walsh County Record described the arrival of the storm:

> The wind switched from the south to the north in the time it could take to throw a switch. Snow and dust, lashed by the thundering wind that resembled a tornado in its intensity, choked to death many victims or caused them to drop exhausted, far from their intended paths, and there to slowly freeze to death as the snow swept in a grave-like sound over their bodies.[69]

Bennie Molde of Grafton captured the spirit of the times in the following account he wrote fifty years later:

> I was safe at home when the storm hit. I was a Saturday nite
> employee of the Basell Bar, and we lived abut 6 blocks from
> uptown, but I did not venture out to report to work.
>
> Also, I was an employee of the Grafton Milk Company as a
> routeman. At that time we used a horse and enclosed rubber
> tired milk wagon for our routes, in those days we went out 7
> days a week. We would go down to the barn, about 7 blocks
> to the north of where we lived, to get the horse and wagon
> about 5 a.m.
>
> Sunday morning by that time the storm had abated
> somewhat and I got there ok. I harnessed the horse and put
> a blanket under the harness, on cold days the horse would
> handle better if we kept him warm. When I took the horse
> out of the stall to the open door he stuck his head out then
> pulled back and would not go outside. It was still stormy but
> by 7 o'clock we tried again and managed to get him hooked to
> the wagon. We made our route, if I remember right it was
> about 10 below—they didn't use windchill then. In those
> days we thought we had to go and jobs were hard to come by.
> Today, I am sure we would have waited it out and not
> attempted going out.[70]

Ed Nelson, a truck driver for Johnson's stores, was stranded east of
Adams, located about thirty miles west of Grafton. Wearing light clothing,
he was not prepared for the winter storm. After his motor quit, the truck
compartment became terribly cold. Nelson crawled in back of his truck
which was enclosed and he moved fifty 10-gallon cans, full of cream, from one
end to the other to keep warm.

Park River, located approximately twenty miles west of Grafton, had
1,408 people living there in 1940. On March 10, Park River opened a
recreation hall and ping-pong tables were set up. Small children could play
games there early in the afternoon. School children had use of the facility at

114

4:00 p.m. and adults used it late in the evening.

On Saturday, Mrs. Nancy Charon and her son William were returning to their farm near Park River. They were a half-mile away when their car slipped into a ditch. They attempted to walk home, but Mrs. Charon tired quickly, so they returned to their car. They were unable to get back into the car. Mrs. Charon lay down beside the car and Willie covered her with blankets. Willie went for help but became lost and wandered much of the night. Though he finally made his way to the home of his brother Thomas Charon, by the time they returned with assistance, his mother had already died from exposure. William Charon was badly frozen.[71]

Lankin is located approximately twenty-five miles west of Grafton in Walsh County. In 1940, the town had 283 residents. There were hundreds of motorists stranded in the storm, but A. W. Harazim, a man from Lankin, wrote a running account of his experiences the night of the storm. He later wrote a letter to the Grand Forks Herald that explained his feelings concerning his ordeal very well.

> As I was driving toward Whitman on Highway No. 35, it was snowing quite heavily. I drove only three miles when the storm struck all of a sudden. A terrific gale hurled thick snow ahead, and I could not see a thing. It was exactly 7:25 p.m. as I looked at my watch. I ran into a snow wall on the side of the road, backed the car out and started again. Time after time the same thing occurred until I just couldn't back out any more.
>
> There I was, helpless and all alone. I opened the door to see which side of the road I was on, and the wind took the door and me out with a jerk. Finally I managed to get back into the car but the snow wet the seats and the blankets covering them. I kept the motor running to keep the heater going, and

turned on the radio, listening to reports of the storm and heard a warning to motorists not to leave their cars.

I heard at 10 p.m. a radio report that winds were blowing at 72 mph. That was enough for me. I was horror stricken, believing that it might take the car and me. The wind was howling more and more, and I figured it must of reached a velocity of a hundred miles an hour. The car was almost lifting off the ground and shaking terribly.

At 11 p.m. the motor stopped, and the gas gauge showed empty. There was nothing to do, so I talked to myself until I got tired of that. I cannot think of the words to describe my mental condition at that time.

I was thinking of my family, as they did not suspect I was out in the storm, which probably was a good thing. I figured I could last until Monday morning if the temperature did not drop too far, but that if the storm should last three or four days with such intensity and much colder temperature, such as the reported blizzard of the pioneer days, I would certainly freeze to death.

It was growing colder right along and I did not have heavy clothing on, but I had a shopping bag of soiled clothes I was taking home to be washed so I went to work putting on the soiled clothes.

I sat there thinking what might happen next. Believing that should I sooner or later freeze, I thought it would be a good idea to get out a piece of paper and pencil and make notations as to what I was doing from time to time and how the storm was progressing so my family and friends would learn just how long I lived and what was going on before I died, in case I did die. That kept me busy so I did not go to sleep.

Along about 4 a.m. I took my mind off the possibility of freezing and discovered that outside the wind seemed to be diminishing, which gave me courage and I quit making further notations.

I finally became satisfied that I would live and then must have dozed off, for I was awakened suddenly when someone rapped on the window and said, "Are you alive or dead?"[72]

Clarence Sobolik knocked on Harazim's car window. He was heading to the Pete Bina farm to get help for his wife and three small children who were stranded about a half-mile away. They also had spent the night in their car. In a little while everyone was rescued. The farm couple took good care of their visitors and gave them a ride into Whitman Sunday night.

Pisek is located six miles south of Park River and the town had 242 residents in 1940. Mr. and Mrs. Charles E. Maresh and a neighbor, Joe Kribs, started for the Maresh home a short distance away but they became lost in the storm. However, they followed their own footprints back and were able to reach shelter. The trio remarked afterwards, "We were not cold, but were almost choked by the driving snow."[73]

Vic and Rose Potulny of Fordville, located fifty miles northwest of Grand Forks, saved the March 18, 1941, edition of the <u>Grand Forks Herald</u> for over fifty years. The <u>Herald</u> interviewed the couple on the fiftieth anniversary of the storm. In 1941, the couple and Vic's mother and Rose's sister went to Grand Forks to trade in their 1936 Ford for a 1940 Plymouth. Fifty years later Vic said, "I don't ever expect to see something like that again," and "That's one in a lifetime. I never saw a storm hit so hard and fast. I didn't think it was possible." They were three miles from home when the storm hit. "It was like somebody threw a blanket over the windshield and I had to put on the brakes because I could not see anything." "The gravel was hitting the car so hard, I said there'd be no paint left on it," he remembered. They had two blankets in the car because it was cold riding in the 1936 Ford, but the Plymouth was much warmer. Rose explained, "Vic's mother wouldn't let us go to sleep. She was afraid we would freeze to death," and "We sang songs, and talked and prayed." Sunday morning Vic Potulny went to the John Dryburg farm for help. They returned with a horse and sleigh and took the women back to the Dryburg home. Vic helped Dryburg haul his cattle to his barn with a stoneboat. "We had to practically roll them into the barn. None of them could walk. They were that far gone." Half of Dryburg's cattle died from pneumonia afterwards. Meanwhile, the women spent the day trying to hear radio reports of the storm. Rose said, "They were listing people that were missing but the static was so bad we couldn't make much of it."[74]

Grand Forks, East Grand Forks, Manvel, Kempton, Northwood, Hatton, Mayville, Portland Junction, Kelso and Hillsboro

In March 1941, it seemed like spring had arrived early in the Grand Forks area. At the beginning of the month there was 15.3 inches of snow on the ground but by March 14, only 2.1 inches remained. The first robin was sighted by Anna Marie Carl on March 9 in East Grand Forks. Easter hats and spring coats for women were on sale. J. C. Penney had a sale on men's clothing—Marathon hats, $2.98; Towncraft shirts, $1.98; Spring Top coats, $14.75; Town-Clad suits, $19.75; and Towncraft oxfords, $3.98. Farmers were busy getting ready for spring planting.[75]

On March 10, the 7th annual city bridge tournament opened at the

Dacotah hotel. The final round was scheduled for March 18, and all funds raised were to be donated to the British-American Ambulance Corps.

North Dakota's state legislature passed a bill calling for an increase in tax on wine from 7 to 11 cents and from 8 to 12-1/2 cents on whiskey, and on March 10 it became a law when John Moses signed it. The legislature also put $3,000.00 in a special fund to pay rattlesnake bounties, 25 cents a snake.

Spring plays were announced and performed throughout the area. On March 14, the Hoople junior civic group presented The Eighteen Caret Boob at the Hoople hall. In Grand Forks, the Central High School students put on a comedy named What a Life on March 21 at the auditorium. At Northwood, area residents saw Down on Abbey's Farm on March 21.

Basketball fever was in the air. East Grand Forks hosted Minnesota's District 31 championship tournament. On March 12, in the opening round, Thief River Falls, Crookston, Warren, and East Grand Forks were winners. The following day, East Grand Forks and Thief River Falls won their games. Thief River Falls and East Grand Forks met in the championship game on March 14 and the Thief River Falls Prowlers prevailed.

On March 12, Grand Forks's Pepsi Cola won the North Dakota Class A Independent Basketball title in Langdon. The next day they headed for the All-Dakota Independent Basketball Championship tournament in Aberdeen, South Dakota. On Saturday night they faced Aberdeen's Freshy

Bar for the title.

Grand Forks defeated Grafton in the first round of the Class A basketball tournament in Bismarck on March 13. They following day they played the Fargo Midgets, the team many picked to upset Wahpeton.

On Saturday morning, March 15, folks in Grand Forks enjoyed reading the Grand Forks Heald. The front page had a bold headline: "Central, Wops Clash Tonight For State Class A Cage Title." The story mentioned how Glenn Hubbard's team defeated Fargo and what to expect against Wahpeton. In Grantland Rice's column, people read that Frank Leahy was named head football coach at Notre Dame.[76]

But the war overseas cast dark shadows in the United States. People watched the fall of France in 1940, British and German armies marching away to battle, and air raids on London on big screens at their local theaters. They heard Hitler and Mussolini talking on their radios. The deadly conflict was rapidly approaching home because on March 11, eight county men were inducted into the army. Other stories and headlines conveyed the sense of urgency: "Franklin Roosevelt Addresses Nation Tonight on Aid Program," "Yugoslavs Stiffen Attitude Towards Germany's Demands," and "German, British Continue to Swap Heavy Air Blows." KFJM broadcast Roosevelt's speech live at 8:30 Saturday night.

Grand Forks received a half-inch of heavy, wet snow Friday. On Saturday the Herald summarized it as "typical blustery March weather." The one-paragraph article said, "More snow is forecast today and Sunday with a drop in temperature predicted Sunday." Temperatures were mild Saturday afternoon in Grand Forks, at one o'clock it was 30 degrees. At four o'clock it was still 29 degrees outside and south winds were about 9 mph.

It was payday for many city folks. March 15 was the last filing date for tax returns and the post office was busy throughout the day. Couples looked forward to several dances Saturday evening. The Rhythm Aces Band was playing at the Eagles Ballroom while Ken Sutton's Orchestra provided the music at the States Ballroom. It was "Local Entertainment Nite" at the Dacotah Hotel. Movies showing at the local theaters included Dr. Kildare Goes Home, starring Lew Ayres, Lionel Barrymore, and Loraine Day; This Thing Called Love with Rosalind Russell; and Tom Brown's School Days, featuring Sir Cedric Hardwicke, Freddie Bartholomew, and Josephine Hutchinson. Kids enjoyed the afternoon matinee Junior G-Men with the Dead End Kids. On Saturday nights there was roller skating at the city auditorium.[77]

People were out shopping and having a good time. The talk of the town was the play of the Central Maroons and everyone speculated on the outcome of the championship game. Rural families came to town; the kids went to the movies while mom and dad shopped. Farmers would make a special trip to the car lots and farm implement dealerships to look at the new vehicles and farm equipment. Valley Motors' Big "10" sale was in process—a ten-day sale with free trial usage for ten days. It was a typical Saturday.

KFJM broadcast a special warning at 5:15 p.m. It warned of

approaching 40 to 50 mph winds and low to zero visibility. Every 15 minutes the warning was repeated until the blizzard struck.[78] At 6:30 the barometer read 29.60 inches and was falling, but no one gave much thought to the weather. At 8:45 it was still 26 degrees outside and the big, white snowflakes fell innocently to the ground.

Around nine o'clock President Roosevelt had finished his inspiring speech. "The American people," the president said, "recognize the extreme seriousness of the present situation. That is why they have demanded, and got, a policy of unqualified, immediate, all-out aid to Britain, Greece, China, and all governments in exile whose homelands are temporarily occupied by the aggressors. From now on that aid will be increased until total victory has been won."[79]

Thoughts shifted quickly to Bismarck where the Maroons of Grand Forks Central and the Wahpeton Wops were warming up.

As the storm blew into Grand Forks between 8:45 p.m. and 9:00 p.m., the temperature dropped 12 degrees. Temperatures continued to fall and by midnight it was down to 2 degrees below zero. At nine o'clock the bitter cold winds reached 70 mph, and several times the weather station recorded wind gusts at 85 mph. One hour later winds were measured at 68 mph and after that the wind gradually subsided. But they were still very dangerous—54 mph at 11:00 p.m. and 52 mph at midnight.

The Grand Forks Herald described the onslaught:

A light snow and temperatures hardly under freezing had
marked the early evening in Grand Forks. A southern breeze

gave promise of a pleasant evening, except for the warning of the weather bureau that a "much colder" wave was due in the night.

Then, suddenly, the storm struck. Through the falling snow the wind shook itself with sudden energy, twisting from the south to the north As though a switch had been thrown in some gargantuan tunnel where winds are made. And with it all temperatures dropped sharply to below zero in two hours.

Out of the north the howling wind came, first like some distant roar of airplanes, blasting its way with mounting intensity across northeastern North Dakota and northwestern Minnesota as it swept down from the Canadian border.

It was only a matter of minutes before visibility was nil. Anyone in the open found breathing difficult, so great was force of the dirt and snow laden wind. Automobiles on highways choked up with snow, their ignition fouled, gave up and generally were abandoned.[80]

Casimir Grace, weather observer at the airport, headed out in the storm to take a temperature reading in a box about twenty-five feet away from the building. Grace said, "The wind knocked me down and with visibility near zero, I was lucky to get back to the buildilng." He remained on duty eighteen hours because the roads leading to the airport quickly became blocked with snowdrifts and his replacement could not make it out there.

As it turned out, people in the Grand Forks area were listening intently to their radios Saturday night. First they heard Roosevelt's address and then everybody wanted information on the violent storm. Basketball scores became less important. Grand Forks Central Maroons lost the championship game. In Aberdeen, South Dakota, Grand Forks's Pepsi Cola lost the title game in the All-Dakota Independent championship tournament.

Hundreds of people were caught in downtown Grand Forks when the blizzard swept into the city. Darell Olson, a clerk for the Burlington Northern, heard a couple of stories about the blizzard of 1941 when he was growing up. He said:

> A father went to pick up his daughter at an S & L clothing store in downtown Grand Forks. When he went by the store his daughter was not outside yet, so he started to go around the block and that's when the storm hit. He could not see to drive and he did not get around the block again. The car sat on the street until the storm was over. Everyone was ok.

People stayed in cafes, restaurants, and bars during the storm. Others took shelter at gas, bus, and railroad stations. Children were kept at the movie theaters, city auditorium (roller skaters) and other amusement places. Churches and stores were safe havens for folks who wanted to get out of the storm. Farmers stayed overnight at hotels, inns, and rooming houses. Stalled motorists by the University of North Dakota stayed at fraternity and sorority houses In most cases, people remained where they were when the storm broke.

About twenty women and children stayed in the East Grand Forks fire hall. The firemen served them lunch at midnight.

Traffic came to a halt; bus and taxi operations were suspended. All Great Northern trains were held in the city until it was safe to proceed. James Kennedy, division highway engineer in Grand Forks, estimated that highway crews rescued at least sixty persons from stalled autos. He reported fourteen stranded motorists were taken to Hillsboro. Kennedy figured there were about 150 to 175 cars stalled in the Grand Forks area. A WPA bus was requisitioned in Manvel and some refugees were taken to Minto.

There was some minor wind damage reported in Grand Forks. A door was blown off the Dacotah Pharmacy. The Berg building on South Third Street had a large plate glass window blown in. The front metal plates on the old hangar at the airport were ripped off in the storm, and the planes were almost buried by snow that drifted in. A WPA shack ended up on the highway near the ballpark. Power companies reported minor circuit breaks and street lights in some sections of town were out. Telephone lines were slightly damaged. Teletype and telegraph receptions were erratic. The Grand Forks fire department received only one call during the storm and that concerned a chimney fire. As there was no damage from it, and the residents of the house said the fire presented no danger, the fire department chose not to respond to it.

Frank Meyers, an elderly farmer who lived six miles northwest of Grand Forks, became lost in the storm when he left his home to feed his stock in the barn. His neighbors became alarmed when they did not see any smoke from his chimney Sunday morning. A search party was organized and Meyers was found near a haystack one-half mile away. A lantern and a shovel were found near his body.

Miss Harriet Coger and Mr. and Mrs. Elmer Ellington were found frozen to death near the Northwest School of Agriculture, about a mile north of Crookston. Miss Coger was the principal of Winship School in Grand Forks. Mr. Ellington was a salesman for the Paramount-Publix Film

Company and his wife had taught at the Belmont school in Grand Forks for twenty-five years.

Mrs. Edith Thompson, society editor of the Grand Forks Herald, and Mrs. Frances B. Kannowski, Grand Forks' city park superintendent, had a test of fortitude. They spent eleven hours stranded on the highway near Ardoch, North Dakota. Edith Thompson wrote about the experience.

We had no idea that the snow that was falling gently was any different than the one the night before until we turned the corner leaving Ardoch. The wind began to blow a little but nothing to be alarmed about. When we reached the corner a mile beyond, Mrs. Kannowski who was driving said, "I can't see a thing." The storm hit us like a clap of thunder. We were on the turn besides the post and there were times when I am certain that the bank on the turn kept us from being blown into the ditch.

When the car was stopped, I opened the door to see if I could glimpse the edge of the blacktop and found that the car was rolling backward. We kept it in gear and the emergency brake set from then on. The snow which was as fine as fog hit the windshield, seemingly from the bottom and streamed up toward the top, like water running reversed, over an apron of a power dam. It got on my nerves, that and its persistent shrill whistle at the corner of the frost shield.

I am not sure what our first reactions were. I remember my teeth chattering for 15 minutes from the shock of finding the car rolling backwards and Mrs. Kannowski's shocked surprise when I told her that there was no doubt that we were there for the night and hoped not any longer. Tales of early day blizzards that I had heard when a child raced through my mind, and I knew that if we were there much longer than morning, we would not care.

The car was new. There was no robe, not even a sack to cover the grill in front, although I never could have stood up to get to the front of the car, the wind was so terrific. Going out for the weekend we had taken our best clothing, thin housecoats instead of warm ones. I used a nightgown for a headshawl all that night and the next day, but we joked all night about saving the bluebird on Mrs. Kannowski's hat.

We could not run the motor continuously and the heater did not get very warm in that wind, but it helped and it cheered us up. We wrote a log, taking turns every hour and listing every foolish thing we could think of. The struggle to keep warm was hard.

We had nothing to cover our laps but the housecoats, and we kept our circulation up by trying to climb into the little space behind the seats every little while all night. As the night wore on, it was harder and harder to find something to laugh at. We played "bean porridge hot" by the hour, rubbed one another's legs and feet to keep up the circulation. and each tried to keep the other from knowing what agonizing stomach aches we had from nervousness.

It was comparatively light for the moon was nearly full, and at 4:15 by the log, we saw a patch of blue sky. We moved the car a little then without turning on the lights for they only reflected from the snow. Neither of us could remember a single line of poetry, not a song, but it being Lent, Mrs. Kannowski could remember the Litany. At that the night did not seem as long as you might think.

In the terrific wind, even at 6 a.m. it was hard to turn the car around for the wind would catch it and whirl it where we did not want to go, the ditch. But we finally made it and started back to Ardoch. We did not quite make it, the gas ran out. We tied our robes around heads and ran for the nearest house. All the fright of the preceding night, and the wind, took us over the fence and through the drifts, with a speed neither of us will ever make again. It seemed an interminable time before we got any response from the W. J. Drew family who could scarcely hear us above the howl of the wind. That five minutes did us the only harm, we frosted our legs.[82]

Manvel, 209 residents in 1940, is located ten miles north of Grand Forks. On March 15, Manvel hosted an independent basketball tournament. Teams from Fisher, Oslo, Key West, and Inkster participated. Here the blizzard trapped at least 100 people, fans and basketball players.

Olger (Ole) Hoverson, Alfred Thiede, and Art Morgan were stranded in Manvel. Around midnight they heard there were several cars stalled just east of town, and the passengers were slowly freezing to death. The trio talked over the situation while keeping an eye on the storm. At one o'clock they left Manvel in Hoverson's sedan. Keeping his head out of the car door window, Hoverson drove cautiously along. They ran off the road many times, but Hoverson was able to back out of the ditch while Thiede and Morgan pushed. A mile out of town they came across the first stalled car. Hoverson, Thiede, and Morgan found the occupants to be from Forest River and they were numb with cold. The Manvel men helped them into their car. They continued on and discovered another car. These people were from Gilby. They took the motorists in and continued on. Hoverson's eyes flinched as he strained to see the road. Thump. They hit a car that was stopped close to a large drift. Now thirteen people were marooned. After resting for a little bit, Hoverson and Thiede headed towards the James Mulligan farm. Morgan stayed and reassured the storm victims that his friends would be able to get help. Hoverson and Thiede came across another stalled car with its motor running. They jumped inside and met David Espie, a man from Kentucky. Espie said, "They were so stiff and bundled up they looked like mechanical men. A sheath of ice obscured their faces." They stayed in the car for one hour and warmed up. Then Hoverson and Thiede went out in the cold. Upon reaching the Mulligan farm they discovered that the barn doors were almost covered with snow. It was impossible to get the horses out. Mulligan advised the men to keep the others in their cars until the wind let up.

Hoverson and Thiede fought their way back to Espie's car. Ole told Espie,

"I'll walk ahead of the car and try to lead the way and you follow until we get

to the big drift. Then we'll get the people out of the cars ahead and bring

them back to yours." Espie said, "although he was only a foot or two in front

of the car, Ole was just a shadow," and "I'll never know how we reached the

drift." Ole and Alfred left again. An hour passed and they came back,

leading eleven individuals that were half frozen. Espie had kept his car

running and it was fairly warm inside. Four women and nine men piled into

the car. They weren't out of danger yet. Espie's gas gauge read only one-

fourth full. Ole suggested that "we'll turn around and try to make the farm."

It took them a half hour to get the car facing the right direction. They drove

until the car ran out of gas. It wasn't longer after that Mulligan appeared.

He told them, "You better try to make it to the house." They plowed their

way through the knee-high drifts and made it to the Mulligan farmhouse.

Espie remarked, "They were wonderful people. Mrs. Mulligan had oatmeal,

coffee, and sliced oranges. They even joked about it then, but every one of

them knew they'd been looking right at death. They might talk about Adolf

Hitler conquering the world, but after seeing the bravery of North Dakotans

in the storm, I'm convinced he'll never conquer these people up here. And as

long as I live, I'll never forget a man named Ole and his companions from

Manvel."[83]

On Saturday night, a 27-ton Great Northern empty B-2 boxcar that was spotted at Kempton, located seven miles south of Larimore in Grand

Forks County, became a runaway. The boxcar started moving when 70 to 85

mph winds hit the area. It rolled through the mainline switch and

amazingly did not derail there. Once on the mainline it quickly gained

momentum. Before long it was moving approximately 60 mph. Northwood,

located six miles south of Kempton, had 1,063 residents in 1940. In near

zero visibility, the out-of-control boxcar roared through Northwood without

incident. The next town on the branch line was Hatton, located eight miles

south of Northwood in Trail County. The steel boxcar almost crashed into an

automobile that stalled very close to the railroad tracks there. Located

fifteen miles south of Hatton is the town of Mayville. The wildly-careening

boxcar sped through Mayville at about ten o'clock on the wings of hurricane-

like winds. Gerhard Strom was walking on the railroad tracks and stepped

off to take a shortcut to his house. A few seconds later the runaway boxcar

whizzed by him. At Blanchard, the next station sixteen miles south of

Mayville, C. B. Froke, a Great Northern agent, saw the car shoot past the

depot. He tried calling the elevator man at Preston, located five miles south

of Blanchard, but there was no answer. Froke contacted Bruce Smith, the

agent at Hunter, ten miles south of Blanchard, and told him there was a

runaway boxcar. Smith rushed out into the blizzard and threw the derailing

switch. A minute later the boxcar derailed there and was not damaged.

Overall, it had traveled about fifty-five miles and went through the middle of

four towns.

The streets in Mayville that Saturday night were crowded with people. Local residents, 1,351 people in 1940, talked excitedly about Friday night's Class B high school boys regional overtime victory against Casselton, their arch rival. Approximately fifty cars carrying 200 fans escorted the team back from Fargo. This victory sent Mayville to the state Class B tournament in Minot on March 20, 1941. Children sipped a coke while they watched the picture show at the Delchar Theater. Cafes and restaurants were busy. People lingered in and out of stores. It was a pleasant event; at eight o'clock the temperature was around 30 degrees.

Mayville's youngsters belonging to the national organization of Future Farmers of America hosted a basketball tournament Saturday. FFA members from Casselton, Cooperstown, and Hunter high schools took part in the event at the auditorium.

Little thought was given to the weather. Shortly after 9:00 the northwest winds came so suddenly that shoppers had almost no chance to return home. Afterwards, B. W. Condit, editor for the Traill County Tribune, wrote:

> It's going to be a long time before anyone tells you that the storm of the past week end was a joke. It's going to be hard to convince most people that the pioneer had to endure sufferings in storms we know nothing about. When a blizzard is so bad that lights in store buildings across the street are not visible, when a person can see no farther than a few feet ahead, and when an 80 mile wind whips wet snow and dirt as well as articles of every nature through the air, and temperatures drop from freezing to zero in an hour and a half, well you got something.
>
> Only last fall the nation was shocked when it was learned

that an Armistice Day blizzard had claimed the lives of a
score or more of hunters in the southern Minnesota
communities. It seemed so strange to think that a storm of
such intensity could trap so many people with such tragic
results, but the people can understand the situation this
week.[85]

Mayville residents opened their homes for those seeking shelter from

the icy winds. Stores and restaurants remained open all night, giving

customers a warm place to stay. More than seventy youngsters were

stranded at the high school. Girls from the four high schools prepared large

pots of steaming coffee and made tidbits out of a half loaf of bread, a little bit

of butter, and some corn syrup. They served the hungry athletes and "the

whole affair turned out to be a most delightful party, as thoughts of what

might be happening out of doors was dismissed from mind."[86]

A fellow from Mayville made a few quick trips about town and

dropped local residents off at their homes as the weather turned worse. He

returned to downtown and parked his truck by the main street restaurant

where he was going to wait out the blizzard. Leaving, he noticed an

inebriated man sleeping in the back of his pickup. He quickly woke the man

up and they hurried out of the storm.

Mayville almost lost their doctor in the March 15 blizzard. Dr. L. O.

Swanson, returning from Hillsboro, was near the Freeland farm when the

storm erupted. He pulled over to the side of the road when the wall of snow

descended upon him. Recognizing the danger, Swanson turned his car

around so the rear end faced the bitter winds and he carefully inched the

back wheels of the car over the edge of the highway to help hold it in an upright position. His car ran smoothly for about fifty minutes, but then the float in the carburetor froze open. The motor raced for ten minutes and consumed the rest of the gas. Hours dragged by. Swanson ripped the seat covers from the car and wrapped the material around him to keep warm. Alone in the car, the doctor struggled to keep awake. Several times he caught himself dozing off. Shaking his head to stay awake, Swanson thought about many things, including writing his will. Meanwhile, in Mayville, the party lines were extremely busy and before long the town knew the doctor was missing, and he was somewhere between Hillsboro and Mayville. At dawn rescue workers manned a snowplow and began searching for him. Swanson was picked up at 6:00 a.m. and the crisis ended.[87]

At least four Mayville residents spent Saturday night in stalled cars. K. M. Hill, Eldred Dormacker, and a hitchhiker were marooned between Finley and Cooperstown. Dorothy Safford and Jo Ann Condit were returning to Mayville. Miss Condit said, "We were traveling down the highway about 50 mph when a wall of dirt and snow driven by a fierce wind swept us off the highway and into the ditch."[88]

The blizzard caused much property damage in the area. At the State Teachers College the roof of the auditorium was almost blown off and the windows in the library building were shattered. Snow drifted in and caused more damage in both places. Also at the campus, the large chimney on the main building collapsed, sending tons of bricks to the ground. The Grinager store and Mayville Furniture, located downtown, had large plate glass windows blown in. The neon sign at the Times Cafe was busted.

Homeowners reported private damages. In the Hatton area a barn and a hog

shed were demolished.

Many sparrows were found dead on the streets and alleys in Mayville

in the following days as the snow melted.

Clarice Bennett Burdick of Mayville wrote a poem:

THE STORM OF '41

All day a light snow fell to earth,
The March wind blew with playful mirth,
We each pursued our task that day
With thoughts that "Spring's not far away."
We did some good—perhaps some wrong,
But anyway, that's just life's song.
We little knew that e'er the morrow
To friends we loved could come dire sorrow.
The skies grew grey with evening's shade,
I thought—did you—that He who made
These beauteous plains where we abide
Should walk more closely by our side?
For life's just one up-hill-and-down,
That we should give, instead of borrow,
And help a fellow in sorrow,
That we should see these plains of ours
Could bloom with never-dying flowers
Of hope, and inspiration to those
Whose days are spent with books or plows;
If all of us could know, that we
As men, are naught, beside the eternity
Of nature, working slow and sure,
With gentleness, or havoc's fur
And so with roaring, sweeping stride
Case wind and snow, and countryside
Let Nature rule with awful hand
That night when Death held her command.
Oh Helpless ones, that stood the test
Of heroism—you did your best
To teach us all
Man's selfishness is out of place,
When man meets Nature face to face.[89]

134

A couple from Portland Junction, located approximately six miles north of Mayville, left Mayville a few minutes before the storm broke. Mr. and Mrs. Carl Enger stopped when they could not see the road any longer. It became very cold inside their car. Mrs. Enger wrapped pages from the Sunday edition of the Chicago Daily News around her legs. Mr. Enger started a fire on the floor of the car and he burned the grocery bags, the wrappings off many of the items, and school tablets. When the fire blazed too high, Mr. Enger put it out with snow that had sifted through the cracks, and then he started the process all over again.[90]

Taft, a small farm community, is located six miles north of Hillsboro. The Alfred Overmore farm near Taft became an important place for stranded motorists Saturday night because thirty people found their way there in the storm.

In Hillsboro, the Knights of Pythias hall was one of the facilities opened to rural folks seeking a place to wait out the storm. A man was rescued near Hillsboro on Highway 81 just as he had become unconscious. His will had been scribbled on a wrinkled brown sack.

Miss Frances Waters of Kelso, a Mayville college student, was home for the weekend. She went out on a date with Lowell Melsby of Hillsboro on Saturday night. They left Kelso, located six miles south of Hillsboro, and were heading for Hillsboro when the storm came up. Their car stalled three miles south of Hillsboro and the couple started walking to a nearby farm. The storm was too much for Waters and she became totally exhausted.

135

Melsby carried her until he became exhausted. Leaving her, he went to get

help. Melsby arrived in Kelso shortly after midnight. Search parties found

Waters lying across the railroad tracks Sunday morning.[91]

Fargo, Moorhead, Buffalo, Arthur, Wahpeton, and Breckenridge

Fargo, North Dakota's largest city, had 32,580 residents in 1940. On

the other side of the Red River is Moorhead, Minnesota with 9,491 people

living there in 1940.

On March 15, the Fargo Forum number one story told about the

landing of 100,000 British mechanized troops in Greece. Other front page

war news mentioned that Nazi warplanes bombed a half-dozen English cities

while the Royal Air Force blasted Gelsenkirchen, Duesseldorf, and

Rotterdam.

In Moorhead, on March 15, hundreds of farmers heard R. M. Evans,

national administrator for the Agricultural Adjustment administration, talk

about the unity of farmers under AAA programs, marketing quotas, and the

outlook for agriculture. Charles W. Stickney, chairman of Minnesota's

Conservation Committee, and Paul E. Miller, director of the extension

service at the University of Minnesota, were other speakers.

A band clinic was conducted in Fargo by Dr. Frank Simon, head of

the Band Department of Cincinnati Conservatory of Music. Musicians from

five Fargo-Moorhead schools played in the band clinic. The event attracted a large crowd and over 100 band directors and school officials on March 15.

Moorhead hosted Minnesota's District 23 basketball tournament. The championship game Saturday night featured Moorhead and Barnesville. The local team was favored, and a big crowd was expected.

There were eight theaters in Fargo and Moorhead in 1941. The biggest attraction was Gone With The Wind. Other movies being shown were: The Hurricane, Meet the Missus, Blondie Has Servant Trouble, No Time For Comedy, Junior G. Men with the Dead End Kids, White Flash, Dr. Cyclops, and Cecil B. DeMille's Land of Liberty with 139 stars.[92]

People enjoyed reading their favorite comics such as LI'L ABNER, ORPHAN ANNIE, BLONDIE, HENRY, DICK TRACY, THIMPLE THEATRE (POPEYE) and the GUMPS.

Radio programs had been very popular since the 1920's. Among the first was Amos 'n Andy. The first radio commentator in the United States was Hans von Kaltenborn, born in Milwaukee in 1878. His commentaries were impromptu, as he intermingled the latest wire service news. After Hitler invaded Poland, a poll revealed that more than half the radios in the United States were tuned to Kaltenborn. "Kaltenborn Edits the News" was heard on Tuesdays, Thursdays, and Saturdays and was sponsored by Pure Oil.

WDAY radio programs scheduled for Saturday night included:
6:00—Defense of America
6:30—Sports News
6:35—Latest News
6:45—Kaltenborn Edits the News

8:00—National Barn Dance, starring Eddie Peabody, a famous banjo
player and a huge cast of entertainers.
9:00—Uncle Ezra
9:30—NBC Orchestra
10:00—Hotel McAlpin Orchestra
11:00—News
11:05—Sports
11:15—NBC Orchestra
11:57—News
12:00—Sign Off

But President Roosevelt's speech interrupted regularly scheduled

programs. Basketball score updates were given throughout the night on

program breaks. Storm information had top priority after 9:30 p.m.[93]

Fargo's weather bureau received an urgent message from Pembina

around 7:40 p.m. It explained that winds in Pembina had jumped from 36

mph at 7:24 to 58 mph at 7:35. There were no radio warnings immediately

issued at Fargo. Why? The person left in charge at the weather bureau did

not have as much training as others had at that time. The information,

however, was noted and the situation monitored. Afterwards, E. J. Fox and

Ralph W. Shultz, meteorologist in charge of the weather bureaus for

Moorhead and Fargo, respectively, said that "even an experienced man

would have been fooled by the rapidity with which the wall of snow and dust

drove through the valley."[94]

There might have been no time to issue warnings if the decision had

been made right away. WDAY and KVOX, Moorhead's radio station, were

about ready to broadcast President Roosevelt's address at 8:30.

At 8:35 p.m. the wind in the Fargo-Moorhead area remained light

from the south and southeast at 15 mph. The winds veered to the west and northwest at 9:00 p.m. and increased in velocity. The storm had arrived.

The weather bureau at Hector Airport in Fargo customarily took hourly readings of wind speeds. When it became apparent that the storm might be a "record breaker," more frequent readings were taken. See Table 1

TABLE 1

WIND VELOCITIES OF THE MARCH 15, 1941, BLIZZARD AT HECTOR AIRPORT

Time	Velocity	Time	Velocity
8:35 p.m.	15 mph	11:35	55 mph
9:35	46	12:30 a.m.	55
9:55	72	1:30	48
10:08	74	2:35	45
10:20	70	3:30	44
10:35	56	4:35	42
10:50	60	5:35	41
11:05	65		

Source: The Fargo Forum, March 18, 1941

Hotels in Fargo-Moorhead filled up quickly as the strong winds battered the vicinity. Managers and employees worked throughout the night making sure the stranded folks were made as comfortable as possible. Mr. and Mrs. R. D. Carrol, managers of the Cole Hotel, broadcast an offer that out-of-town people could have rooms free of charge. Mr. and Mrs. Ed Powers were on their way home from visiting friends at St. Luke's Hospital, but they made it only as far as the Powers Hotel which, coincidentally, he managed. Powers went immediately to work. He helped place guests, rounded up blankets for the people in the lobby, and kept the cafe open. Powers advised everyone about the latest storm news. The wind blew out a window in the Graver Hotel, surprising those in the crowded lobby. The hotel carpenter happened to be working, so he boarded the window up quickly. At the Bison Hotel, an attendant was kept busy opening an inside door when the outside door was opened. The Metropole Hotel's big lobby and two waiting rooms had standing room only. Regular guests at the Comstock Hotel gave their rooms to women and children. Mr. and Mrs. George Moritz, proprietors of the Comstock, received special permission from the police to keep the bar open after legal operating hours as additional space for the large crowd. Lodging was free for many who sought shelter there, courtesy of the management. The Comstock coffee shop was jammed with people until three o'clock Sunday morning. In Moorhead, the New Columbia Hotel was out of room by midnight and its lobby was packed. Mr. and Mrs. A. W. Nelson, proprietors of the New Columbia, welcomed storm guests and after listening to their stories gave them rooms free of charge. Many local residents stayed in the lobbies of the hotels and returned home as soon as weather conditions permitted it.

There were 1200 people at the theater where <u>Gone With The Wind</u> was being shown. The theater manager interrupted the movie and announced, "There's a terrible blizzard raging outside." A woman became hysterical but was quieted before others panicked. About half of the capacity audience were from smaller communities near Fargo. The manager contacted WDAY and KVOX and the radio stations reported that patrons were safe at the theater. After the conclusion of the movie, radio sets were put up on stage and everyone listened to the storm reports. Various games were played and a number of skits were performed. Cafes nearby brought coffee, doughnuts, and hot dogs. Those from out of town stayed until about seven o'clock Sunday morning. What occurred there was typical of what happened in the other area theaters.

A large number of people stayed at the police stations in Fargo and Moorhead. The police took many children home in their squad cars. During the peak of the storm, one officer had to walk ahead of the car to guide it. When the storm broke, no extra policemen were on duty, but as conditions worsened all were called and put on alert. Moorhead police stationed at the outskirts of the city limits turned back a number of cars leaving town. Officers had ten cars towed off the highways and taken into Moorhead. Fargo police took similar actions to protect lives.

There were 2,000 screaming fans at the Moorhead junior high school building watching the Moorhead Spuds playing Barnesville when the terrific winds swept down from the northwest. The Spuds defeated Barnesville, 26 to 22. The wild victory celebration on the floor was cut short when Superintendent S. G. Reinertsen grabbed the microphone and declared, "Police have been stationed at all doors and no one will be allowed to leave because of the storm." Reinertsen assured the crowd it was no joke. He said, "A man has just come into the building. He lives only a block away. Yet he was near exhausted." After the trophies were presented, the crowd moved down to the gymnasium floor. School rooms were opened up and people settled in for the night. T. J. Boiger, an official of the Northwestern Bell Telephone Company, volunteered to operate the school's switchboard so people would have a chance to call their loved ones. He worked steadily until 3:00 Sunday morning. A bunch of coaches started a basketball game and more and more people wanted to play. Soon there were four teams playing and the pickup games lasted until 5:00 in the morning. KVOX's and WDAY's storm bulletins were broadcast over the school's public address system.

After the winds let up somewhat, the police allowed fans who lived nearby to leave the building. In one incident, a father left with his son holding on tight to the belt of his overcoat. He later remarked, "as soon as we turned the corner the wind literally took our breath away. We had to turn our heads into our coats to breathe. Blindly trudging down the middle of the street, we cut across back lots and reached our back door, out of breath, nearly frozen and a mass of snow. We knew that it was no joke."[95]

Early Sunday morning, volunteers went out and checked the roads. They discovered city roads blocked with snow but snowplows were seen clearing the highways. Between 9:00 and 10:00, more than 400 fans left the building. By 11:00, those from out of town were on their way home.

Martin A. Brandon of Fergus Falls wrote a letter praising the Moorhead police for keeping 400 people in the junior high school. He wrote: "As one of the parents of school children attending the basketball tournament at Moorhead, I want to compliment and commend your department's good judgment in keeping the school children in the building until they could be safely cared for when the unprecedented storm hit that area."[96]

On March 22, the Moorhead Spuds became the regional champions when they defeated Crosby-Ironton, 24 to 23 in Little Falls, Minnesota. They went to Minneapolis and played in Minnesota's High School Basketball Tournament. But they lost to Bemidji and Austin.

A farewell party for Mr. and Mrs. Walter Schroeder of Moorhead turned into an all-night event at the home of Mr. and Mrs. Albert Carlson in Moorhead. Between fifty and sixty people were at the party when the terrible storm descended upon the area. Of the out-of-towners, most came from the Barnesville and Fergus Falls area to attend the basketball tournament and the party afterwards. The home of Mrs. Brooks Brown, a daughter of Mr. and Mrs. Carlson who lived several blocks away, became the refuge of twenty-five party-goers. By three o'clock Sunday morning all but eighteen of the guests were able to return to their homes in Moorhead or found shelter with relatives. The remaining guests slept on any available beds, davenports, and floors in both houses. After the snowplows cleared the highways on Sunday, the Schroeders left with their children for St. Paul.

Fargo and Moorhead business establishments lost considerable merchandise after plate-glass windows were blown in by the storm. The damage estimate to the seventeen windows totaled $1,500, but there was no estimate for the damaged goods and merchandise in the store. These businesses included the O. J. DeLendrecie store and men's shop, the J. J. Newberry store, Wimmer's Jewelry, Romkey Vegetable Market, W. W. Wallwork Garage, the Graver Hotel, the Red Owl Super Market, the S & S Food Market, Jeff's Market, the Little Red Grocery, and the Houglum & Olson Furniture Store. A number of signs and doors were torn loose in the storm. At the Coca Cola Bottling works, two large doors were ripped from their hinges. Employees, summoned by the police, worked until three o'clock to repair the damage. A large flower box on a second-story window ledge at the New York Hairdressing Academy fell down to the street without injuring anyone. Four large billboards between Moorhead and Dilworth were blown down by the strong winds.

Three buildings at the North Dakota Agriculture College suffered substantial wind damage. Part of the roof of Francis Hall was blown off and had to be replaced. The Agriculture building had its roof supports badly wrenched and several tons of tile were torn from the roof. The Science Hall had numerous windows blown out and its roof was damaged.[97]

Georgia Maize, a student at North Dakota Agriculture College in 1941, remembers the storm well. She was residing at Ceres Hall on the NDAC campus. Ceres Hall was a combination women's dormitory, dining hall, and Home Economics Department. Earlier on Saturday evening some of the house residents had gone downtown with their dates. After the storm arrived, the housemother called the remaining women to come to the front door to see how bad the storm was. Those women who had left earlier were unable to return until Sunday.[98]

The Fargo public school buildings had many broken windows.

Something unusual happened at the Clay county highway shed Saturday night. A large door which opened on an overhead pulley track was swung outward, torn off, and finally rested on top of the roof.

An electric traffic signal at Eighth Street and Center Avenue was short-circuited, but was repaired on Sunday. H. A. Warner, superintendent of the Moorhead municipal power plant, reported electricity was out for several minutes for south-side residents. Poles were broken off and circuits in homes were blown during the storm. Everything was repaired on Sunday.

Garages and filling stations in the Fargo-Moorhead area had plenty of business after the storm. Wreckers pulled cars out of the ditches and brought them back into town. At least twenty-five cars were ditched in the Moorhead vicinity. Cars to be fixed were parked on the streets because the garages filled up quickly. It took several days before mechanics had completed all the repairs.

A man traveling on U.S. 10 was startled when the wind literally picked up his car and deposited it in the ditch. A tense moment passes He walked into Moorhead, about a mile away, after the wind let up somewhat. A newspaper reporter became aware of this incident through police reports, but the identity of the man who experienced the frightful ordeal remained unknown. Because of this and other episodes, a subheading in The Minneapolis Tribune for March 17 was "Wind Hurls Cars Off Highways."

Saturday evening, G. N. Nelson, a salesman for the Postage Meter Company of Minneapolis, and his wife left Breckenridge and were heading to Halstad, Minnesota, to visit some friends. The violent storm overtook the Nelsons. They crept along, straining to see the road. As the snow whirled about they sighted a car in the ditch. Stopping his car to investigate, Nelson found D. J. Sigdestad, his daughter Joyce, 14, and son Duane, 16, all of Webster, South Dakota, and Steward Sigdestad, a cousin from Pierport, South Dakota. They were on their way to visit relatives in Moorhead. Everyone piled into Nelson's car. Slowly working their way along the highway they noticed another car in the ditch. From it they rescued Leonard Brakke, a farmer who lived a mile off the highway. Walking outside in the bitter cold winds and swirling snow, Brakke led Nelson to the side road leading to his farm. Several times Nelson lost sight of Brakke, but by honking his horn Nelson was able to get Brakke's attention and he returned to continue guiding Nelson's car. The front wheels slipped over the bank of a high embankment, but the bottom of the car caught on the shoulder. It was 10:15 p.m. and they were literally hanging on the brink of death. Nelson kept the motor running and the heater on. The passengers dug out newspapers, correspondence sheets, clothing, towels, and gunny sacks. They stuffed the windows and door cracks to keep out the snow that was being driven in by the terrific winds. Taking a hatchet, Nelson chopped away at the back cushion of the front seat. This allowed all of them to lay down. They used the upholstery for stuffing cracks and as another layer of protection. Resting at its precarious angle, the motor was unable to get oil and stopped running about midnight. The seven huddled together, battled cold temperatures, and fought to stay awake. Because of the extreme cold they took off their shoes and warmed their feet by sticking them under their coats. About 2:30 a.m., Brakke decided to walk home because they were slowly freezing to death in the car. It seemed to be their only chance. Mrs. Brakke had paced the floor throughout the night. She hung a lantern first in one window, then another, in hopes that her husband could see the light. Brakke's retrurn made for a happy, although short lived reunion in the farmhouse. The passengers in the car were still in danger. About 40 minutes after he left, Brakke returned with his hired man carrying blankets, coats, and overalls for the women. Keeping their arms locked, they formed two groups with Brakke leading them safely to his place. Although nearly exhausted, they enjoyed plenty of hot coffee and food which Mrs. Brakke had waiting for them. Their ordeal took place eight miles south of Moorhead.

The group made their way into Moorhead later on Sunday.[99]

Returning from the Twin Cities on Saturday, Lincoln Nelson, a truck driver from Courtenay, North Dakota, noticed several cars between West Fargo and the Red Rooster filling station south of Mapleton on U.S. 10. At the filling station Nelson heard over his radio that the gale was blowing at approximately 76 mph. He cleaned the snow from under the hood of his truck and then headed back toward West Fargo. At midnight he rescued Mr. and Mrs. I. S. Walhood and their daughter. The motor of their car had filled with snow and stalled about a half-mile east of the Red Rooster filling station. Keeping his truck in low gear, Nelson continued on, going at the rate of three or four miles per hour through the deadly storm. He picked up two other stranded parties and searched other stalled cars for occupants. Nelson took everyone safely back to West Fargo but refused offers to be paid for his services. He said it was "his duty as a truck driver to help out his fellow men in distress," Mrs. Walhood, in a letter to The Fargo Forum, credited him with saving their lives. She wrote, "If there is such a thing as a medal for heroic deeds I think this young man should have it."[100]

Gardner, located twenty miles north of Fargo, had 103 residents in 1940. Bernice and Kenneth Larson, children of Mr. and Mrs. Frank Larson, were in Gardner on the evening of March 15. About nine o'clock, at the first sign of bad weather, they decided to go home. They were about halfway home when their car stalled. Abandoning their vehicle, they started walking home. The intense cold winds hammered their backs and the storm was getting worse. Within a short time, Miss Larson became exhausted and was

unable to walk any more. Kenneth tried carrying his sister for a ways but

was unable to make any progress. Reluctantly, he put her down. As the

snow whirled about them, he stood beside his sister. Time passed. The

situation reached the critical point. With much agony, Kenneth was forced

to continue without his sister. After eleven o'clock he made it home,

exhausted and badly frostbitten. The search for Miss Larson began at dawn,

and her body was found a short time later. Bernice Larson was twenty years

old when she met her death.[101]

In Cass County, several basketball tournaments concluded Saturday

night. North Dakota's Consolidated High School Girls Basketball

Tournament took place in Buffalo, a town with 245 residents in 1940. It was

an impressive group of teams entered in the tournament. Ayr, a small town

located in Cass County with 107 inhabitants in 1940, had won the state

championship the last three years and had a winning streak of 80 games

going into the tournament. Prior to the state tournament, Gilby had gone

10-0, Foxholm, 9-0, Halliday, 13-0, Greenland, 15-1, Norwich, 12-1, Regan,

17-2, and Wheatland, 10-4. All the games attracted big crowds. Ayr and

Norwich played in the championship game Saturday night. Ayr extended its

winning streak to 83 games.

The storm forced 500 basketball fans and players to spend the night

in the schoolhouse at Buffalo. The home economics students from Buffalo

high school and members of the local 4-H boys and girls clubs prepared a lunch. A small boy was reported missing but he was finally located in the building. Children slept on the floor of the basketball court, desks, and benches. Many adults played bridge and whist while others talked to their friends all night.

The other basketball tournament in Cass County that concluded Saturday night was in Arthur, a town of 335 people in 1940. Many folks turned out for the games for Arthur's Independent Invitational Basketball Tournament. There were teams from Hunter, Gardner, Hawley (Minnesota), Mayville, Mapleton, Casselton, and Fargo. Saturday morning the Hawley Hawks defeated Hunter and Mapleton beat the Fargo YMCA Ramblers to set up the title game. Hawley won the tournament. Spectators and players were stranded in Arthur overnight.

Richland County is located in the southeasternmost county in North Dakota and is at the southern end of the Red River Valley. Wahpeton, the county seat, had 3,747 residents in 1940.

Tournament fever gripped Wahpeton in March 1941. Wahpeton's high school basketball team had won twenty games in a row going into the state tournament. Saturday night the Wahpeton Wops faced the Grand Forks Central Maroons in the North Dakota Class A high school championship game. This was the first time Wahpeton played in the championship game, and the people were optimistic. The 1940-41 team had some outstanding players, including Louie Brewster, Glen Sturdevant, and Dorval Schmit. They were coached by Marty Engh, a star athlete at

Moorhead High School and Concordia College. The Wahpeton Commercial Club made arrangements with the Great Northern and Northern Pacific railroads for a special train to take its fans to Bismarck on Saturday. A pep band and 300 cheerful fans took the train to Bismarck. Blizzard winds roared into Bismarck before the start of the game, but the game went on as scheduled and Wahpeton won its first title.

As soon as the game ended, the celebrating began back in Wahpeton and Breckenridge. The Wahpeton fire siren started the celebration by blaring its siren for almost fifteen minutes. Adding to the noise were the railroad engines blowing their whistles in the Great Northern yards. Residents of both cities joined in the merriment.

The excitement continued through Sunday. Early that morning the fans and pep band who took the special train to Bismarck returned and the cheers started once again.

The storm did not put much of a damper on Wahpeton's celebration plans. The city had planned a triumphal parade down Wahpeton's main street after the "Empire Builder" let the players and fans off at Wahpeton Sunday afternoon. The "Empire Builder" usually stopped at Breckenridge, located just across the Red River, but a special agreement had been worked out. The parade, however, was canceled and the train made its regular stop in Breckenridge. They had a car caravan back to Wahpeton's high school and the team was honored there.[102]

In 1940, the Breckenridge high school boys won the 1940 Minnesota state basketball tournament. Afterwards the Breckenridge Rotarians invited the Wahpeton Rotarians to an Honor banquet for their state champions. At that banquet a Breckenridge speaker said, "Next year Wahpeton will win the championship in its state and Breckenridge fans must be counted in when it comes time to honor the Wops."[103] Amazingly, that is exactly what happened.

The Wahpeton area received about one-half an inch of precipitation during the storm. The temperature at Wahpeton fell from a high of 35 degrees Saturday to 6 degrees below zero Sunday morning. The local paper stated that, "The wind exceeded that of the November 11, 1940 blizzard."[104]

A remarkable but sad tale came from the Wahpeton-Breckenridge area. A Fargo man, Stanley W. Wachal, a sheep buyer for the Cudahy Packing Company, had been at a bowling tournament in Wahpeton Saturday night. Shortly after nine o'clock, Wachal and Gene Fender, the office manager for the Central Co-operative Association at West Fargo, started for home on U.S. Highway 75. They were about seven and a half miles north of Breckenridge when the storm engulfed them. Thinking that the car had gone off the road, Wachal stepped out of it. His hat went flying in the air. Wachal himself was blown a block down the highway by the wind. He dropped to the ground so he would not be pushed any further. After resting a bit he crawled into the ditch and tried to find the car. Wachal heard Fender calling him, but Fender could not hear his cries above the wind. He lost his hat and had no gloves. Wachal's face, hands, right leg, and the back of his neck became partially frozen. Four young people, a man and three women, came along in a car. "Please help me," Wachal pleaded. They said, "Hi," and took off. Finally, after almost two hours of yelling and moving about trying to stay warm in the bitter winds, Wachal was rescued by Henry Barth, a Doran, Minnesota, farmer and his son Ronald. They took him to Breckenridge for first aid. After failing to locate Wachal, Fender returned to Wahpeton to get some Fargo bowlers to help search for Wachal. Luckily, Fender met Henry Barth who told him that Wachal was at a motel in Breckenridge. Having moved from Omaha two years before, Wachal said he "never realized that such danger lurked on the prairie."[105]

Overall, forty people died in North Dakota. There were nine deaths recorded in the Red River Valley on the North Dakota side. Pembina County had five fatalities, while Walsh, Grand Forks, Traill, and Cass counties each had one death. Many tales of survival, courage, and strength came out of the storm. It was a blizzard that many people in North Dakota would never forget. See Figure 12.

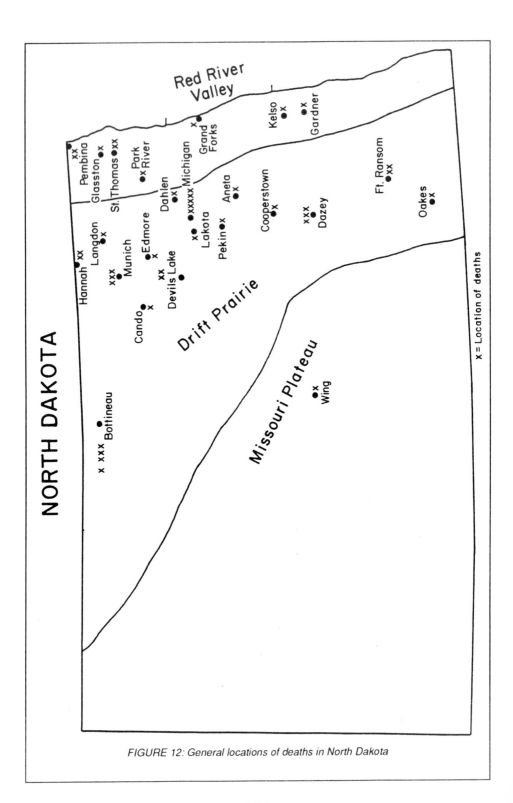

FIGURE 12: General locations of deaths in North Dakota

154

"Cranking the automobile in the field." Cavalier County, North Dakota October 1940. Photographer John Vachon, Library of Congress.

A sledge on main street of Starkweather, North Dakota, ca 1940. Photographic Archives, University of Louisville Standard Oil Collection. Photographer John Vachon.

Bottineau, North Dakota, Ca 1937. The Grand Forks Herald Photo Collection.
Elwyn B. Robinson, Department of Special Collections, Chester Fritz Library,
University of North Dakota. (Hereafter cited as E.B.R. SC, UND.

Cando, North Dakota, Ca 1939. Courtesy of E.B.R. SC, UND.

Langdon, North Dakota, Ca 1939. E.B.R. SC, UND.

Sarles, North Dakota, Ca 1939. E.B.R. SC, UND.

Devils Lake, North Dakota, Ca 1939. Courtesy of E.B.R. SC, UND.

Soo Line Depot of Devils Lake, North Dakota, Ca 1940. Photographer John Vachon, Photographic archives, University of Louisville, Standard Oil Collection.

Main street of Edmore, North Dakota, Ca 1940. Photographer John Vachon,
Photographic Archives, University of Louisville, Standard Oil Collection.

Brocket, North Dakota, Ca 1939. Courtesy of E.B.R. SC, UND.

Lakota, North Dakota, Ca 1939. Courtesy of E.B.R. SC, UND.

"Main Street in Michigan, North Dakota," October 1937. Photographer Russel Lee, Library of Congress.

Walhalla, North Dakota, Ca 1939. Courtesy of E.B.R. SC, UND.

Neche, North Dakota, Ca 1937. Courtesy of E.B.R. SC, UND.

161

Hamilton, North Dakota, Ca 1939. Courtesy of E.B.R. SC, UND.

Pembina, North Dakota, Ca 1939. Courtesy of E.B.R. SC, UND.

Cavalier, North Dakota, Ca 1939. Courtesy of E.B.R. SC, UND.

Drayton, North Dakota, Ca 1939. Courtesy of E.B.R. SC, UND.

Grafton, North Dakota, Ca 1939. Courtesy of E.B. R. SC, UND.

Park River, North Dakota, Ca 1939. Courtesy of E.B.R. SC, UND.

The storm kept local switchboard operators busy: Above picture taken by a Herald photographer shows the operators handling the many calls that came in during and after the storm. Picture courtesy of the Grand Forks Herald.

Storm scene Sunday morning in the 2700 block area of University Avenue. A snow plow was at work when this picture was snapped by a Herald photographer. Picture courtesy of the Grand Forks Herald.

Kempton, North Dakota, Ca 1939. Courtesy of E.B.R. SC, UND.

Northwood, North Dakota, Ca 1939. Courtesy of E.B.R. SC, UND.

166

Hatton, North Dakota, Ca 1939. Courtesy of E.B.R. SC, UND.

Mayville, North Dakota, Ca 1939. Courtesy E.B.R. SC, UND.

The front page of the *Grand Forks Herald* for March 18, 1941.
Courtesy of *The Grand Forks Herald.*

Vic and Rose Potulny of Fordville holding the March 18, 1941 issue of the *Grand Forks Herald*. The *Herald* interviewed the couple on the 5oth anniversary of the March 15, 1941 blizzard. Courtesy of *Grand Forks Herald*.

Boys with sleds along U.S. 10 at McKenzie, North Dakota, Ca 1940. Photographer John Vachon, Photographic Archives, University of Louisville, Standard Oil Collection.

Front page of the _Fargo Forum_ for March 18, 1941. Courtesy of _The Forum_.

CHAPTER III

THE STORM IN MINNESOTA

Minnesota's Weather Forecasts Prior to the Storm

The residents of Minnesota received their weather forecasts from

various sources. For those living in northern and northwestern Minnesota,

weather offices in Fargo, North Dakota; Moorhead, Minnesota; and

Winnipeg, Manitoba could provide them with the needed weather

information. The majority of the people received their forecasts from the

weather office in the Twin Cities. For March 14, 1941, the weather offices in

the Twin Cities and Fargo-Moorhead carried the same forecast for

Minnesota: "Partly cloudy Friday; followed by occasional light snow Friday

night or Saturday; no decided change in temperature." These weather offices

released identical forecasts for March 15, 1941, which were published in the

morning editions of the Grand Forks Herald, the Fargo Forum, and the

Minneapolis Tribune. The forecast for Minnesota called for: "Occasional

snow Saturday and Sunday; colder except extreme southeast Sunday." But

as the day unfolded, this forecast quickly became invalid. Using new information provided to them by the Chicago weather office, the Twin Cities and Fargo-Moorhead weather bureaus issued their own diverging forecasts for the remainder of the weekend. Because it was near Fargo, the Crookston Daily Times published the revised Fargo-Moorhead forecast for Saturday and Sunday in its Saturday evening edition of the paper. The new forecast called for: "Occasional light snow with a cold wave and strong northwesterly winds tonight and Sunday." It is fairly certain that other communities in the Fargo-Moorhead area received this revised forecast either through newspapers or by radio.

The majority of the residents of Minnesota received their weather information from the weather office in the Twin Cities. Its revised forecast for the March 15-16 weekend predicted: "Occasional light snow tonight and Sunday; cold wave with strong northwest winds Sunday and in northwest and west-central tonight." This would be the forecast published in Saturday evening newspapers in places such as Bemidji and Brainerd.

International Falls received a revised forecast that differed from the one issued from the Twin Cities. Carried in the Saturday evening edition of the International Falls Daily Journal, the forecast called for: "Cloudy with light snow flurries; a little colder tonight; Sunday northwest winds and colder; light snow." This forecast is quite similar to the one issued for Kenora and the Rainy River country by the Winnipeg weather office. As International Falls is located on the Rainy River and is closer to Winnipeg than the Twin Cities, it is quite possible the International Falls Daily

172

Journal published the Winnipeg forecast for the Rainy river area.

Hallock, St. Vincent, Northcote, Stephen, Argyle, and Warren

Northwestern Minnesota occupies the other half of the Red River

Valley. The size of the Valley is about the same in Minnesota as in North

Dakota. One major difference is that, unlike North Dakota, the Red River

Valley gives way to woods and lakes in Minnesota. See Figure 13. Kittson

County is the most northwestern county in Minnesota. Hallock, its county

seat, had 1,353 residents in 1940. The March 15, 1941, storm entered

Minnesota first in Kittson County. Around eight that evening the

temperature was above the freezing mark and a gentle snow was falling in

Hallock. The Kittson County Enterprise explained what happened next:

> All of a sudden the wind switched to the northwest and
> struck with such violent fury and within an instant's time the
> entire scene was transformed into a raging blizzard as the
> thermometer started to plunge downward as though it had
> been plunged into a cake of ice. The fury of the storm was
> such that persons driving were simply trapped and stopped
> in their tracks.[1]

Although no deaths due to the storm were reported in Kittson

County, there were numerous close calls, and there were some losses of

poultry and sheep. In one case, Mr. and Mrs. Martin Loken were headed for

Hallock from their place of residence on the Victor Johnson farm west of

Hallock when they were caught by the storm roughly two and a half miles

east of the Hall Moore farm. Faced with the prospect of freezing to death,

173

FIGURE 13: Cities and Towns of Minnesota.

Mr. Loken started out for the Moore farm, even though visibility was zero. Loken reached the Moore farm but collapsed from exhaustion and cold on the doorstep. Hearing his fall, the Moore family brought him inside. Other than a frostbitten face, Mr. Loken was okay. Hitching up a team of horses, Hall Moore's son and Stanley Carlson, a stranded visitor at the Moore farm, set out and brought Mrs. Loken back with them. She suffered frozen feet but her condition was not serious.

In Hallock itself, many people stranded in town took shelter in restaurants, the Grand Theatre, hotels, City Hall, the American Legion, and private residences. Some people did try to make it to their homes and succeeded in the effort. Fritcheof Anderson and the Walstead boys made it to their homes west of Hallock in spite of being badly frostbitten from their trek. Many basketball fans from Kittson County attended the district high school basketball tournament at Stephen on Saturday night. The sudden onslaught of the storm forced the fans to remain at the Stephen school through the night.

Other people caught in the blizzard were Dave Turner, a St. Vincent township farmer and his three children, ages 13, 11, and 6. Turner's wife had gone to Grand Forks earlier in the day and the children were in Humboldt. After going into town to pick them up, Turner was bringing them home when the blizzard stalled his car one-and-a-half miles from Humboldt (1940 population of 139). Without heat and adequate clothing, the Turners suffered considerably from the elements. Unwilling to see the children suffer

175

any more, Turner decided to seek help. After making the children promise not to leave the car, Turner set out for help. After reaching Humboldt, Turner returned with a rescue crew at three in the morning. Although suffering from exposure and minor frostbite, the children managed to survive the ordeal but it was a frightening experience for them. It was a double ordeal for Mr. Turner, as his wife was also stranded in the storm but came through unscathed.[2]

Another close call was experienced by Mr. and Mrs. Luke Younggren and their young children, 3 and 4 years old, and Mrs. Fink, who was the wife of the depot agent at Northcote. Leaving a neighbor's farm, they had only driven two miles when the storm was upon them. The car's engine quickly stalled, leaving them without heat. Becoming concerned about the situation, the Winters called to see if they had reached their destination safely. Finding out that they had not, the Winters called the sheriff, Elmer O. Pearson. With the assistance of County Engineer Jim Faherty, Pearson set out with one of the county snowplows to try to open the road where they believed the car had stalled. At the other end, Raymond and Glendon Winters and Edward Younggren set out to find the marooned party and reached them shortly before the sheriff did. The snowplow cleared the road back to the Winters farm, and the group stayed there the remainder of the night.

The village of Kennedy (with 338 residents in 1940) is located six miles south of Hallock on U.S. Highway 75. On Saturday night, Robert

Laude's father and his three brothers were on their way to Kennedy. Unfortunately, the storm stopped the engine in their car four miles from home. They remained in the vehicle a long time, but one of Robert's brothers was unable to stay awake. The Laudes decided to try to make it home. Getting a length of rope from the car, they tied one end to a front person and the other end to a back person. The two two individuals hung onto the middle portion of the rope. Many times en route home the force of the wind knocked them into the ditch. Their efforts to reach a neighbor's home in the storm failed. Bumping into their mailbox made the Laudes realized they were at the driveway to their home. The Laudes followed it and reached their house about two o'clock Sunday morning. Seeing her father and her brothers in clothes packed with snow led one of Robert Laude's sisters to exclaim that they looked like abominable snowmen. On Sunday the Laudes, seeing their own footprints only a few feet from their neighbor's house, realized that they had missed it by only a few feet in the storm.

A car that refused to start prevented Robert Laude's grandparents and aunt from experiencing the same fate. They were finally able to get the car started. But as Robert's grandmother and his aunt emerged from the house, the storm slammed into them, knocking Robert's aunt into the dinner bell post and his grandmother back into the house.[3]

Located twenty-four miles south of Hallock on U.S. 75 in Marshall County is Stephen. The 1940 census showed Stephen with a population of 673 people. In 1941, for the first time ever, Stephen hosted the District No.

32 high school basketball championship. See Figure 14. On Friday, March 14, Baudette shaded Argyle 16 to 14, and Roseau defeated Karlstad 29 to 14 to set up Saturday night's championship game.

Saturday evening there were 700 cheering fans in the auditorium as Argyle played Karlstad in the consolation game. At halftime Argyle's drumrettes did their routine, and Argyle beat Karlstad 33 to 23. As this was happening, the storm raced into Stephen about half-past eight. The Stephen Messenger described it as "a frightening blizzard, the savagery of which was probably never approached in the history of this section of Minnesota. The wind veered to the north with amazing suddenness, whipped the newly-fallen snow into swirling masses which blinded and terrified and left mere man helpless in his efforts to combat the fury of the elements apparently gone stark mad."[4] School officials made an announcement at half-time that due to the severity of the storm no child could leave the school unless accompanied by an adult. To enforce this decision, special police were used to watch the doors. Now and then, while the blizzard raged, a concerned father would come to the auditorium to take a child home.

When the Roseau basketball team did not show up for the championship game with Baudette, the coaches of the teams in the tournament formed opposing basketball teams and entertained the fans. Other activities that helped to pass the evening included volleyball and card playing. The auditorium stage was a busy place too. Superintendent Huseslid, Messrs. McCleary and Thorson, teachers, and Janitor Carlson

District No. 32

Basket Ball

TOURNAMENT

Stephen High School Gym
Friday and Saturday
March 14--15

Doors Open at 6:30 - Adm. 20c and 40c

Friday, March 14
8:00 P. M. - Baudette vs. Argyle
9:15 P. M. - Roseau vs. Karlstad

Saturday, March 15
8:00 P. M. - Consolation Game
9:15 P. M. Championship Game

Referees: Huber and Williams, International Falls

FIGURE 14: District No. 32 Basketball Tournament Ad. Source: The _Stephen Messenger_, March 13, 1941. Courtesy of the _Stephen Messenger_.

179

continued to work during the storm, helping fans be comfortable and keeping their spirits up. The school telephone was a popular place as stranded fans concerned about the fate of their loved ones elsewhere made many calls during the storm. This activity kept operators at the local telephone exchange busy. Patience was a requisite in dealing with congested phone lines, and calls were put through whenever the lines were open.

When midnight came and went with no let-up in the storm, school officials took steps to care for the large crowd for the remainder of the night. Improvised cots were set up for many of the women. The Stephen Commercial Club, under the leadership of its president, H. Ostbye, and past president, Dr. E. O. Nimlos, took the responsibility of feeding the group. Volunteers undertook several trips downtown for food and the Stephen High School home economics department provided hot coffee. After feeding the crowd at half-past one, the procedure was repeated again at five in the morning. By this time the storm was letting up a little and many people went home. With the arrival of dawn, tired fans streamed outside to enjoy a little more elbow room.

After defeating Karlstad on Friday night, the Roseau basketball team drove to Warren where they had sleeping accommodations. After seeing a movie in Grand Forks Saturday afternoon, the basketball team returned to Warren. About a quarter after eight, the eleven members of the basketball team, their coach, O. T. Lindberg, and Superintendent of Schools C. D. Hollister left Warren in two cars to go to Stephen twenty miles away.

After being on the road for fifteen minutes, they ran into the blizzard. Late

Sunday, Coach Lindberg called the Associated Press office in Minneapolis

and described what had happened to the Roseau team:

> Hello, this is Coach O. T. Lindberg of Roseau. I guess you
> missed our basketball score last night. I'm sorry I couldn't
> send it in but you see—we didn't play. We had some trouble.
>
> Just about four miles from Stephen, we were hit by this
> terrible storm. It must have been going all of 75 miles per
> hour. We couldn't see a thing. It came at us like a bullet.
> We couldn't see a foot, so we just had to stop on the highway.
>
> The squad was in two cars. There they sat until midnight,
> gasoline ran out and the heaters grew cold. Outside the
> storm roared as terribly as ever. In desperation, all 13 piled
> into one car. That way they kept each other warm.
>
> If the team could last through what we did last Saturday
> night it could win anything. I never spent such a terrible
> night.[5]

About eight o'clock Sunday morning, a search party led by T. J.

Bates, Dr. E. O. Nimlos, and Stub Pagnac found the basketball team and

brought them into Stephen. Most of them were in good condition except for

two boys who were suffering from chill (one had a frostbitten foot) and shock.

Taken to the Stephen Hotel, they were given medical attention. At the hotel

the basketball players were given a hot bath, a brisk rubdown, and then sent

to bed. After sleeping all day, the boys seemed fully recovered. Lindberg

believed the basketball team could have withstood the cold for no more than

a couple of hours after the time they were rescued.

The postponed game was held in Thief River Falls on March 19. Ray

Dahlquist's two free throws in the last 30 seconds gave Roseau a 23 to 21 victory over Baudette.

E. A. Anderson, a farmer who lived west of Stephen, left Stephen around eight o'clock Saturday evening. When he was about a half-mile west of the Avery farm, the storm was upon him and his car stalled. Anderson decided to try to reach the Avery farm on foot. Before setting out he fixed in his mind all possible landmarks. Following a barbed wire fence along the road, it took him over an hour to reach the Avery farm, the ordeal leaving him in a state of near exhaustion. The extent of his struggle was evidenced by the pair of shredded gloves he had. Contact with the barbed wire ripped his gloves to pieces. In one sense, Mr. Anderson was lucky. When he made his trek through the snow, temperatures had not yet dropped enough to do him serious harm. At eight o'clock Saturday evening it was 28 degrees in Stephen. By daybreak on Sunday it had slipped to 10 degrees below zero. Some Stephen area farmers were in Moorhead Saturday afternoon to hear agricultural specialists speak. In one incident, Nels Hvidster, Joe Urbaniak, and John Jacobson were on their way home when they ran into the storm. Their car stalled on the highway near Warren, Minnesota. They struggled through the storm for three-and-a-half miles before obtaining shelter in a farmhouse. From this experience Hvidster suffered a badly-frozen ear and Urbaniak had an injured leg.[6]

Argyle, with 857 people in 1940, is situated nine miles south of Stephen. Two Argyle residents, Mr. and Mrs. Erick Solvedt, lost their lives in the storm. After shopping in Oslo, Minnesota, they encountered the storm on the way home. Rather than remaining in their car, they decided to reach home on foot. They never made it and their bodies were found a couple of miles apart; when found, Mrs. Solvedt's body was found sitting upright with her hand clutching the wire on the fence.

Many of the experiences of being stranded in the storm dealt with running out of fuel after sitting in a stalled auto for a few hours. However, in one instance, the vehicle ran out of gas just as the storm was arriving. This happened to Ivan Riopelle and Adolph Michalski, residents of the Argyle area. This was unfortunate for the two men were lightly dressed and were unable to obtain warmth from the car's engine. After being in the car for nine-and-a-half hours, they walked to a nearby farm at five-thirty in the morning in 12 degree below zero temperatures. En route to the farm one of the men had to support the other, and both were exhausted when they finally reached the farm. Their ordeal left Riopelle with a frozen hand and Michalski with badly-frozen ears and feet.[7]

Ten miles southeast of Argyle on U.S. Highway 75 is Warren, the county seat for Marshall County with 1,639 people in 1940. The storm roared in from the north about nine o'clock, "churning the snow and dirt into a quick blizzard."[8] Wind speeds between 60 and 70 mph and measured gusts up to 80 mph were reported by the weather station in Warren. During much of the blizzard visibility was nil, and traffic came to a standstill. The storm lasted until late Sunday morning. Huge snowdrifts remained. Farmers and people from surrounding towns were stranded. Eating places in Warren remained open all night, and the businesses provided shelter for many people. Hotels were crowded with strandees. Folks at the Strand Theater stayed there a lot longer than originally expected. Continued poor weather Sunday morning forced the cancellation of church services and Sunday School classes. Few people attended church services later in the day.

On Sunday afternoon, snowplows departed from Warren to open highways in Marshall County. By Tuesday evening they had almost all of Marshall County's highways open.

O. W. Thomas, Lou Dietrich, and Frank Hamrick of Warren attended the agricultural meeting in Moorhead on Saturday. On their way home their car stalled south of Euclid. They remained in the car until morning, and then they made their way to a farmhouse. Adolph Bakke, who had spent the weekend in Bemidji, brought them back to Warren.[9]

One person employed the Eskimo method of burrowing in the snow to save his life. Waldemar Johnson, age 25, was a farmer who resided on a farm eight miles north of Warren. After his car stalled, Johnson left the vehicle and dug a hole in the snow in a deep drainage ditch. He remained in the hole covered by snow from about ten o'clock Saturday evening to ten o'clock the following morning. From this experience Johnson emerged with only a frostbitten ear.[10]

Several other people in the Warren area had narrow escapes. Robert Peterson suffered the calamity of a stalled vehicle south of Warren. Leaving his car, Peterson followed a fence to its end. Doubling back, he saw a light in the window of a farmhouse. Peterson managed to crawl into the house which turned out to be the Bernard Engelstad farm home. Peterson left when the storm abated in the morning. Sig Underdahl of Middle River was driving home from Warren when the storm overtook him. Then his pickup became stuck in the ditch. Underdahl set out on foot to find a place of refuge. Upon hearing a broadcast urging people to display any sort of light in their windows, a local Warren farmer, Art Vansickle, did so. It was fortunate For Sig Underdahl that Vansickle did so. Just after Vansickle put a bright light in his window, Underdahl, seeing it, staggered into Vansickle's house.[11]

Polk County: Crookston, Angus, Euclid, Fisher, Tilden Junction, and Fosston

Polk County had the highest death toll in Minnesota as the storm claimed ten lives there. A large county, it is located directly east of Grand Forks, North Dakota. Most of Polk county is in the Red River Valley. According to M. R. Hovde, federal meteorologist at Minneapolis, the center of the storm passed through Grand Forks. As a result, Polk county received the worst of the storm.

Crookston, the county seat for Polk county, is about twenty-five miles southeast of Grand Forks. Crookston had 7,161 residents in 1940.

Without television, going to the movies was a popular pastime in 1941, especially on the weekends. Shows playing at Crookston's two theaters

Saturday night were <u>Virginia City</u>, starring Errol Flynn, Miriam Hopkins, Randolph Scott, and Humphrey Bogart; <u>The Case of the Black Parrot</u>, with William Lundigan; and <u>Lone Star Raiders</u>, starring Robert Livingstone and Bob Steele. The Grand Theater had about 650 people in it, and there were roughly 250 people at the Gopher Theater when the storm descended upon Crookston. Moving quickly, the management stationed attendants at the exits to urge movie-goers to stay at the theaters. During the storm crisis, the manager of the two theaters, Ernotte Hiller, and his assistants handled more than a thousand phone calls from concerned parents and relatives. To help the movie-goers pass the time, amateur entertainers were asked to come up onto the theater stage and perform for the audience.

During the peak of the storm, high winds toppled the chimney from the Collins building next to the Gopher Theater onto the Gopher Theater with a crashing sound. Venturing out onto the roof to investigate for damage, Hiller and Kermit Halvorson had a narrow escape. While they were out there, parts of the stairway and back porch from the Collins building came crashing down around them. Finally, about four in the morning, as the storm started to let up, people began to leave the theaters via cab service or private cars. Two hours later 150 people remained at the Grand Theater with another 50 at the Gopher Theater. Concerned individuals were still calling the theaters as late as eight o'clock that morning. As a token of their appreciation, many theater-goers helped clean up their own mess before they left for home. Since many of the people were either children or from out of town, Hiller and his assistants made sure they were fed until they could arrange transportation home. A young Beltrami couple and their five-month-old baby were the last people to leave the Gopher Theater.

When the blizzard hit Crookston, there were six telephone operators on duty at the Northwestern Bell Telephone Company's local office in Crookston. Once the severity of the situation was realized, six more operators were recalled to work. They worked through the night, and those who were supposed to go off duty at nine o'clock that morning stayed on to help the others. The local office handled approximately 25,000 calls during the first 24 hours after the arrival of the storm. From midnight Saturday to midnight Sunday there were 750 long distance phone calls completed. The deluge of calls continued on into Monday.

At two o'clock Sunday morning, Al Hinckley and Gene Holt, members of the Crookston street department, braved the storm and used a city plow to pull cars out of snowbanks on West Sixth Street. In spite of the terrible weather, they were able to free several cars. Throughout Sunday, the street had only a narrow lane open.

Other people had the state highway patrol to thank. Carl Johnson, Arthur LeMassurier, Mr. Nelson, Mr. and Mrs. Arthur Vanseth and child of Grand Forks were among those the highway patrol rescued between Crookston and the Northwest School of Agriculture a half-mile northwest of Crookston on Saturday night. Storm conditions forced the highway patrol to give up their efforts.

The Minnesota Highway Patrol had a couple of its own stories to tell about its patrolmen stranded in the storm. Three miles north of Crookston, two highway patrolmen, T. K. Knutson and Arthur Lefgren, were stuck in a snowbank all night Saturday. Equipped with blankets and other emergency aids and keeping their motor running, they survived the night comfortably. Cal Cummings and Orland Ott, highway patrolmen stationed at Detroit Lakes, Minnesota, had to stay in Calloway, Minnesota, Saturday night.

Armand Loken of Crookston rescued two men from Thief River Falls, Mr. Boyle and Mr. Elliott, Sunday morning. The men were stranded five miles south of Crookston on U.S. Highway 75 by the storm. Boyle and Elliott had burned newspapers at intervals for six hours to keep from freezing to death.

The Chill Inn in Crookston was broken into by four people in order to escape the wrath of the storm. The owners of the inn were not there because the storm had trapped them downtown.

On Saturday night a birthday party was being held at the George Charboneau home in honor of his birthday. The party was in progress when the storm roared into Crookston. Mr. Charboneau's son was at the Gopher Theater with a friend, Earl Davis. Thinking that his ten-year-old son George had left the Gopher Theater during the storm with a friend, Earl Davis, George Charboneau, along with Fire Chief Ross Schmidt and Art Reber, walked through the streets of Crookston arm in arm for more than an hour looking for the boys. It was not until after ten o'clock that they learned the boys were safe at the theater. F. W. Spencer, a relative of Earl Davis, also spent many hours searching for the boys. Except for three members of the fire department, the guests at George Charboneau's birthday party spent the night at the Charboneau home. At ten o'clock the three firemen left the Charboneau party and answered a fire alarm. Spending the rest of the night at the fire hall, they were unable to get back to the party.

Very few guests showed up for the St. Patrick's dance party at the Masonic temple Saturday evening because the storm blew in before the band started playing. Instead of dancing, the couples passed the time visiting. The people were able to leave the Masonic temple after 1:30 a.m. Sunday, with the out-of-town guests being lodged for the remainder of the night in the homes of local members of the Eastern Star.

Another Crookston resident, Mrs. Harold Heldstab, experienced a night she would not soon forget. While shopping in downtown Crookston Saturday night, she became separated from her husband. Mrs. Heldstab took refuge in the home of her husband's mother. During the night she was informed that the police had found the abandoned Heldstab car stuck on Pine Street near Sixth Street before midnight. Her husband was nowhere to be seen. As the storm slowly abated early Sunday, Mrs. Heldstab departed for her own home. Seeking refuge in homes along the way, she found her husband in one of them at six in the morning. He had taken refuge there after the car stalled Saturday night.

The three garages in Crookston that operated wreckers were kept busy after the storm had passed. They pulled out over 500 cars stuck in snowdrifts during the storm. This did not include those vehicles marooned on the main highways which were pulled out by snowplows. Because of wind-driven snow packed under their hoods, many cars had to be repaired at local garages.

The high winds accompanying the storm did a strange thing, usually associated with tornadoes. A large window with 12 panes of glass in it was torn by the wind from a building owned by the Crookston Fibre Manufacturing Company, carried 50 feet, and then set down on the frozen ground without breaking a single pane of glass. Surprisingly, there was no other damage to any of the other buildings of the company. However, the company-owned flax straw piles did experience much dampness from wind-driven snow. Midnight Express, Inc., which leased a warehouse in Crookston, was not so lucky. Part of the roof over the freight dock was ripped off in the storm.

Gentilly is a small village located a few miles northeast of Crookston. Twenty-two guests at a surprise birthday party for Mrs. Louis Plante at Gentilly on Saturday night, received a surprise themselves when the storm came up, suddenly forcing them to spend the night at the Plante home. Some of the guests were unable to return home until Monday morning.

Mrs. Alphonse LaRochelle, age 33, lived in Kertsonville township east of Crookston. She was in Crookston Saturday evening with her husband. Upon hearing storm warnings over the radio she became concerned about the safety of her children. Unable to immediately locate her husband, she left for home between eight and nine o'clock Saturday evening. Mrs. LaRochelle was driving a light pickup truck, but it stalled on her a mile and a quarter from home. She tried to walk home but trudging through the storm left her exhausted. Mrs. LaRochelle then took shelter in a neighbor's car parked along the highway. Searchers found her body there Sunday evening.

One Crookston area farm family survived being outside in the storm in spite of leaving a stalled car three-fourths of a mile from their farm home. After the car stalled and the motor quit running, Mr. Tilman Wermager and his son Truman, age 16, left Mrs. Wermager and three other sons in the car and set out on foot for their farm to pick up horses and a sleigh. Following a high grade and a fence, they reached the barn. After harnessing the horses and hitching them to the sleigh, Mr. Wermager and Truman set out for the car. In the meantime, Mrs. Wermager and son Duane were lying on the two younger Wermager boys to keep them warm. After much trouble, Mr. Wermager and Truman reached the car. On the way back to the farmhouse the horses became lost in the storm. Using the furrows of a plowed field as a guide, Mr. Wermager led the horses to safety. They reached the farm at one in the morning. The next morning the horses' tails were still frozen. The only injuries the Wermagers suffered from the storm were frostbite on Mr. Wermager's face and wrists and on Truman's face and toes.

Mrs. Eric Norrie of rural Crookston was a breeder of purebred

Naragansett turkeys. She had kept most of the birds through the winter for breeding purposes. But the storm put a severe crimp on her efforts. It hit with such suddenness that many of the birds were unable to reach shelter only a few yards from where they were standing. On Sunday, Mrs. Norrie and others surveyed the farmyard to see how the flock had withstood the storm. They found dead fowl in nearby treetops. Gobblers were discovered frozen in the strutting pose. Overall, Mrs. Norrie lost 140 turkeys.

The Northwest School of Agriculture was situated on the windward side of Crookston with few trees for protection. On the night of the storm, Stanley Osborne gave a lecture on Australia and New Zealand. About twenty guests took refuge in the school's dormitories during the storm, including Mr. and Mrs. Stanley Osborne. Some visitors had attended the lyceum but they never made it home that evening. Instead, they had an extended chat with the Osbornes. A few stranded motorists from U.S. Highway 2 groped their way to the school. A short circuit in power lines cut off power to the school for twelve hours during the storm.

Miss Marian Frykman and Miss Martha Merle Manning, members of the school's faculty, were returning to the campus but their car stalled near the Great Northern tracks. They stayed there all night and were rescued Sunday morning. The ladies returned to work Monday and showed no ill effects from their ordeal.

After hearing reports of stalled cars and missing people near the school, students organized a search party Sunday morning to look for stranded motorists. While exploring the area, one of the students, Dale Walter, collapsed from the cold and exhaustion. It became necessary to administer first aid to revive him.

On Monday, snow removal crews were able to open the main entrance to the school. People could drive their cars only as far as the Kiehle building, as large snowdrifts blocked the other roads around campus.

On Saturday night, Mr. and Mrs. Elmer Green drove into Crookston to buy their five-year-old son William Henry a birthday gift. Leaving Crookston around nine o'clock, they were returning to their farm home five miles northeast of Crookston when their pickup stalled less than a mile from home. When Mr. Green opened the door on the pickup, high winds broke the windows on the truck. Without protection from the window, the Greens believed they would have a better chance of survival if they walked to shelter. Noticing a fence alongside the pickup, Mr. and Mrs. Green, holding hands, decided to follow it. After reaching the end of it, Mr. Green noticed the light from a neighboring farm. After battling deep snowdrifts, Mrs. Green was too exhausted to go on and Mr. Green could not carry her. Bundling his wife's clothing about her, Mr. Green left her by a large tree and walked to the Harry Herberg farm. Returning with Mr. Herberg, the two men tried to carry Mrs. Green with them. Because of her inability to stand up, in addition to the high winds and deep snow, the men could not carry her. Green and Herberg returned to the Herberg farm and came back with the elder Herberg sons. This time they were able to carry Mrs. Green back to the Herberg house, but she was dead by the time they reached there. The next morning Mr. Green returned to his own home. His three small children and the older Herberg children had spent the night alone in the Green home. Later in the day he walked to Crookston to get the mortician to come to the Herberg farm and pick up his wife's body.

On Saturday, Mr. and Mrs. Elmer T. Ellington and Miss Harriet Coger left Grand Forks for Crookston without telling anyone of their destination. On Sunday they were reported missing. Since they did not tell anyone of their destination, searchers did not know where to look for them. On Monday morning, Miss Kathryn Salo, Polk County Red Cross nurse, drove out toward Fisher, Minnesota, where searchers were combing the countryside for another person lost in the storm, Mrs. Orland Bailey. Shortly before noon, on her way back to Crookston, Miss Salo noticed some bodies in a field less than a quarter of a mile from the Northwest School of Agriculture. She immediately went to the Sheriff's office to report her discovery. The bodies were those of Mr. and Mrs. Ellington and Miss Coger. After their car stalled, they had evidently tried to seek shelter.

W. G. Mattson, Ed R. Christenson, and Harry Bearles found a unique way to tell how cold it was inside their vehicle. While en route from Red Lake Falls to Crookston, their car stalled six and one-half miles east of Marcoux Corner. Although supplied with ample gas, their engine became wet, preventing them from using their heater. By wrapping themselves in extra clothing they had brought along, they kept warm. They used part of an

194

apple as a thermometer to determine how cold it was. If the apple froze, they figured they would freeze. They were rescued before that happened.

Another town on U.S. Highway 75 is Angus, nine miles southeast of Warren. A farmer from there, George Goodwin, was a very fortunate survivor of the storm. Goodwin usually left his car parked near the highway and then walked to his farm whenever he went somewhere. He repeated this routine Saturday night, but the storm engulfed him before he could make it to his farm. Becoming lost, Goodwin wandered around in the storm for seven hours. Then he found a telephone pole and leaned on it. Dozing off, Goodwin dropped to the ground but recovered in time and got up. A pause in the storm allowed him to see his farmhouse. He crawled home and into bed. Goodwin's family was away, unable to get home in the storm. When they did get home and saw his condition, they rushed him to the hospital in Warren. Although the storm left Goodwin with a badly-frozen face and toe, the doctors' prognosis for his recovery was good.

High winds blew in all the windows on the north side of the barn on the Lawrence Anderson farm near Angus. Coming out to the barn on Sunday morning, all Mr. Anderson could see of his cattle was their hind ends. They were standing in snowdrifts piled against the south wall of the barn. Fortunately, he did not lose any cattle.

The storm kept Mr. and Mrs. Harold Swain and Mr. and Mrs. Andy Volland stranded in Crookston Saturday night. When able to return to their respective farms on Sunday, both couples discovered the outside doors on their homes blown open. Their residences were filled with snow that caused much damage to the rooms and furnishings.

The railroads did their bit in rescuing people stranded in the blizzard. Gust Johnson of Hallock, Alfred Berg and John Vagle of Lake Bronson, and Melvin Kullberg were rescued by a Great Northern train a few miles outside of Euclid, Minnesota. The men had spent ten hours in their stalled car and it was 12 degrees below zero and falling. Gale winds made it very miserable. Gust Johnson happened to see the bright headlight of an oncoming train, the Winnipeg Limited. Leaping from the car, Johnson stumbled his way towards the tracks. Conductor Joseph Nelson, St. Paul, and Engineer H. A. Nelson, Crookston, stopped the train when they caught sight of a man frantically waving his arms. Once aboard the train, the men admitted they could not have withstood the bitter cold much longer. All of them were suffering from exposure when rescued. Conductor Nelson roused the dining car crew from their sleep and the cooks served them drinks of hot brandy. Nelson refused to accept any money from the men to pay for their transportation. The Winnipeg Limited continued on its run but stopped again after traveling a couple of miles. This time the train picked up two men who had been walking down the highway in the storm. Further south, a man and a woman were carried aboard. In three unscheduled stops, the train saved eight people from freezing to death.[12]

After leaving Crookston at a quarter to nine Saturday evening, the Peterson family from Shirley, a Great Northern station seven miles north of

Crookston, drove north on U.S. Highway 75 until they came to the turnoff that led to their home. They had driven about a half mile west when they were inundated by the storm. After remaining in the car for a short period of time, they decided to walk to the Van Dahlen home a quarter mile away. The Petersons walked for some time in the storm, keeping a tight grip on their son between them, and were unable to find the Van Dahlen home. The Petersons then tried to return to their vehicle but were unable to locate which road it was on. All this walking left Mrs. Peterson exhausted and she fell. She asked her husband if they could rest a while. In an effort to warm up his son, Mr. Peterson held the boy inside his coat. But even as Mr. Peterson made this effort, he felt the boy becoming cold in his arms. Mr. Peterson decided to make one more attempt to reach help. After wandering for more than four hours, Mr. Peterson reached the Joseph Veenstra home at Shirley station about two o'clock Sunday morning. Unfortunately, there was no means of transportation at the Veenstra home. Not until late Sunday afternoon, after Highway 75 had been reopened, was Mr. Peterson able to catch a ride and return to Crookston to report that his wife and child were missing. A search party was organized, headed by local deputies, that began looking for Mrs. Peterson and her son. About six o'clock Sunday evening they located their bodies a mile south of the Northern Pacific tracks about two miles west of Highway 75 and ten miles north of Crookston. Taken to a Crookston hospital, Mr. Peterson survived the ordeal but suffered from shock and frozen cheeks and shoulders.

Fisher, a town eleven miles west of Crookston along the Red Lake River, was notorious for a sharp curve in U.S. Highway 2. During storms, motorists often missed the curve there and ended in the ditch.

The Fisher Independent basketball team, along with 100 fans, were marooned in Manvel, North Dakota for the night. On Sunday morning they followed a snowplow home, reaching their destination at noon.

Mr. and Mrs. Rudolph Michael from Fisher were counting their blessings on Sunday morning. Just as they were leaving Crookston Saturday night, the storm swept into the city. Taking shelter at the Fairmont cream station, they remained in Crookston until Monday morning.

The storm caught Mr. and Mrs. Henry Sturger, who lived near Fisher, on the road and their car stalled. Realizing they were less than a half-mile from home, they decided to walk the remaining distance. They could not make it, however, and found shelter in an abandoned granary. In the effort to reach the granary, Mrs. Sturger's legs were frozen. To keep his wife and himself warm, Mr. Sturger ripped wood from the granary wall and made a fire. After spending the night in the granary, they were able to leave the next day. Mr. Sturger immediately took Mrs. Sturger to St. Vincent's Hospital in Crookston where physicians saved her legs.

Mr. and Mrs. Orland Bailey of Hibbing, Minnesota and their three small children became stranded when their car stalled on U.S. Highway 2, a mile from Fisher. To stay warm during the night, everyone huddled in the back seat with the parents on the outside to keep the children warm. Mrs.

Bailey's feet became cold and her husband gave her an extra pair of stockings he had been wearing to put on. Some time between eight and nine o'clock Sunday morning, Mrs. Bailey, age 22, decided to go get help as her husband was sick. Despite her family's protest, she set out on foot. Snowplows began opening Highway 2 at eleven o'clock that morning. Soon afterwards, a Fisher resident came upon the Bailey's car and took the Bailey children to Fisher where they were put aboard a train and sent to Grand Forks to visit Mr. Bailey's parents, Mr. and Mrs. John Bailey, the original destination of the Baileys. The same resident then took Mr. Bailey to Crookston where he reported his wife missing to the sheriff's department. On the same day, Fisher residents organized a search party to try to find Mrs. Bailey, but the severity of the storm forced them to call off their efforts. A search party, under the direction of the sheriff, was organized Monday morning. It consisted of sheriffs' posses, game wardens, highway patrolmen, the county engineer's staff, and volunteers. After combing the Fisher area on Monday, the searchers found her body that afternoon on the Minnie Ross farm six miles west of Crookston. Mrs. Bailey's frozen body was only a few yards from the Ross home between two small buildings used by sugar beet workers during the summer. Her body lay close to the buildings which would have provided her shelter from the storm. Mrs. Bailey was the last fatality to be accounted for in Polk County.[13]

On Saturday night prior to the arrival of the storm, Mr. and Mrs. Sid Bonaime and their two-year-old child had become stuck in the ditch on

Highway 32, a mile and a half south of Marcoux Corner, located sixteen miles east of Crookston on U.S. Highway 2. Mr. Bonaime, age 27, was the Great Northern depot agent at Tilden Junction. A truck came along driven by Louis Maygra and he attempted to pull Bonaime's car from the ditch but failed. Bonaime went to the Harvey Bombardier home a quarter mile from the car to get help in pulling his car out of the ditch. Bonaime, Mr. Bombardier, and Louis Maygra tried to extricate the car from the ditch with a team of horses but were unable to do so. Mr. Bombardier then returned to his home with his team, leaving extra blankets to keep the Bonaimes warm. About midnight, after the car ran out of gas and the heater could no longer keep them warm, Bonaime became fearful of the cold; he decided once again to go to the Bombardier home for help. Before leaving, he wrapped his wife and child in the blankets. Soon after his departure, Harvey Bombardier and Louis Maygra brought more blankets to keep Mrs. Bonaime and her child warm. After the storm had let up a little, they were taken to safety. Efforts were then made to find Sid Bonaime. On Monday noon his body was located along the railroad tracks a mile east of Dugdale, next to a place known as Dead Man's Grove. Instead of reaching the Bombardier farm the wind had blown Bonaime in the opposite direction, and he had walked over seven miles from the car.[14]

Fosston (1940 population of 1,271) is about forty-five miles southeast of Crookston on U.S. Highway 2. The body of Ervin Engebretson, age 40, a bachelor farmer from Fosston, was found on the roadway to his farm halfway between the main highway and his home, about a quarter mile away. He had left his stalled car and tried to walk the remaining distance to his farm.

Norman County: Ada, Lockhart, Halstad, and Syre

Norman County, located directly south of Polk County, is in the Red River Valley with the Red River as its western boundary. Ada, the county seat, recorded a population of 1,938 in 1940. The storm reached Ada at ten o'clock Saturday evening. Roads were quickly blocked by snow driven by winds up to 85 mph. In one hour the temperature at Ada dropped from 33 above to 6 above zero.[15]

There were many stories of survival in Norman County. Mr. and Mrs. Myron Benbo of rural Fosston and his brother and sister-in-law Mr. and Mrs. Albert Benbo of rural Lockhart, were traveling to the Albert Benbo farm east of Lockhart when the car became stalled in the storm. They were stranded a mile and a half from the Benbo farm and were five miles east of Lockhart. Abandoning their stalled car, the couples wandered in the storm for four hours before reaching a grove of trees on the Leslie Davidson farm, not far from the Benbo farm. Mrs. Myron Benbo collapsed from the ordeal they had been through, but the other three carried and dragged her to the Davidson barn. After waiting there for an hour and a half, Mr. and Mrs. Albert Benbo left the barn and were able to reach the Davidson farmhouse. Mr. Davidson returned with them to the barn and carried Mrs. Myron Benbo

201

back to the house. Although all the Benbos were suffering from some frostbite, Mrs. Myron Benbo was in the worst shape. Blocked roads prevented them from being taken immediately to the hospital. Finally, a snowplow followed by an ambulance reached the Davidson farm about a quarter after six Sunday evening and took the Benbos to the Ada hospital. In the hospital, Mrs. Benbo could not recall making it to the Davidson barn or house.

Another woman was in the hospital in Ada suffering from frostbite. Mrs. Harold Ruch and her husband left their stalled car on the highway southwest of Ada and walked to their farm a short distance away. In the exertion to reach her home, Mrs. Ruch suffered frostbitten legs.

Eight people lost their lives to the storm in Norman County. Mrs. Oscar Sandy and her nine-month-old son Harlan Duane of Moorhead were visiting Mrs. Sandy's sister Mrs. John Bergman and her mother at their home two miles west of Ada on Saturday. The Bergman home was two miles west of Ada. When the storm was at its worst, a chimney fire broke out at the Bergman home. Seeking refuge from the fire, Mrs. Sandy took her baby and made for the Lloyd Ness home across U.S. Highway 75 from the Bergman home. Losing her bearings in the storm, she started to wander. On Sunday, Mrs. Sandy and her baby were found frozen to death in the highway ditch.

After going to Ada on Saturday, Mr. and Mrs. Herman Treichel and their four sons, Orville, 16, Willard, 6, Howard, 3, and Stanley, three months, left for their farm around ten Saturday morning. A little while later they were engulfed by the storm and their car stalled only a half-mile from home. With Orville's help, Mr. Treichel carried Howard and Stanley to the Treichel farmhouse. With Orville, Howard, and Stanley safe at home, Mr. Treichel returned to the car to pick up his wife and son. On the way back to the farm they became lost in the storm and wandered for an hour before reaching their house. While the strenuous effort put Mr. Treichel in the Ada Hospital on Sunday suffering from exposure and exhaustion, it was too much for Willard, who died Sunday from exposure.

Mr. and Mrs. Ludwig Foss and their daughter Roselyn, about 18, lived near Beltrami, a town fifteen miles south of Crookston that had 213 residents in 1940. After being in Ada on Saturday, they started for the Theodore Stromstead farm seven miles southwest of Beltrami where they were employed. On their way there they encountered the storm and their car stalled three and a half miles west of Lockhart, a small town located about ten miles north of Ada. Deciding to walk to safety, they headed south with the wind along a county road. They did not get far before they collapsed. Early in the morning, Mr. Stromstead and his son found their bodies several hundred feet from the Driscoll and Sullivan farms.

Elmer Maland, a 42-year-old Halstad farmer, was in Halstad (1940 population of 570) Saturday evening. Around nine o'clock, he left for his home a little over two miles northeast of Halstad. Maland's frozen body was found by Martin Jensen, a neighbor, about two o'clock Monday afternoon in a field about a quarter mile from his home. The body was not discovered sooner since none of Maland's family were at home Saturday night. His wife and daughter were visiting in Shelley, Minnesota, and his son was away from home Saturday, not returning until Sunday night.

Joe Sear, age 63, who had been employed at the Franz Silverton farm near Detroit Lakes since the fall of 1940, left that place on Tuesday, March 11, saying he was going to Detroit Lakes. His body was found at five o'clock Monday afternoon, March 17, in a meadow a little more than two miles southwest of Syre, Minnesota. Syre is located more than fourteen miles southeast of Ada, Minnesota. Sear's suitcase was found three-quarters of a mile from his body.[16]

Ottertail County: Fergus Falls

Directly south of Norman County is Clay County, with Moorhead as its county seat. Immediately south of Clay County and hugging the Red River is Wilkin County. Breckenridge is its county seat. East of Wilkin County is Ottertail County. While most of Ottertail County is located in Minnesota's famous lake country, part of the county is in the Red River Valley. Situated fifty miles southeast of Moorhead and twenty-five miles directly east of Breckenridge on the edge of the Red River Valley is Fergus Falls, the seat of Ottertail County; 10,848 people resided in Fergus Falls in 1940.

As elsewhere, residents of Fergus Falls were enjoying spring-like weather on March 15, 1941. During the day the temperature climbed to 34 above in Fergus Falls. Farmers came to town to shop and enjoy themselves. Many residents, especially high school students, had traveled to Moorhead to take in the district basketball tournament. Around ten o'clock, accompanied by a roar of thunder and several flashes of lightning, the storm engulfed Fergus Falls. Light snow and high winds had been forecast for the Fergus Falls area, but no one expected a storm that would be as severe as the Armistice Day storm of the previous November. Old-timers considered that one to be the worst one in their memories. But here came another one—4 months, 4 days, and 4 hours after the arrival of the Armistice Day storm. One major difference between the two storms was the time of their arrival in Fergus Falls. When the Armistice Day storm had arrived, it was still daylight in Fergus Falls. People who were out and about could see the bad state of weather conditions. The arrival at ten o'clock of the March 15 storm prevented many people from seeing the terrible state of the weather. The Armistice Day blizzard had been accompanied by much more snow than the March 15 storm. The addition of blowing dirt mixed with the snow ("snirt") made visibility even worse than it would ordinarily have been—even at night. It made breathing more difficult for those out in the storm. When people talked of almost being suffocated by the wind, blowing dirt was a contributing factor. The Fergus Falls Daily Journal did not call it the "Black Blizzard" for nothing. During the night the wind began to let up, and the temperature continued to fall. By Sunday evening it was 9 below in Fergus Falls.

At least 500 farmers and their wives were caught in Fergus Falls by the storm. Some of them started for their homes in their cars but were forced to return to Fergus Falls due to the severity of the storm. Others saw their cars become stalled in the storm as wind-driven snow made the distributor caps on their engines wet. They walked back into Fergus Falls and returned with other motorists who helped them bring their families to safety. Along with other stranded motorists, the farmers filled the cafes and hotels of Fergus Falls. When some of the cafes closed at two in the morning, motorists took refuge in restaurants and hotels that remained open all that night. Some filling stations stayed open all night and were kept busy dealing with snow-packed engines and cars low on anti-freeze. Believing that spring was just around the corner, some motorists had failed to put in sufficient amounts of anti-freeze. Conditions were so poor in Fergus Falls that twenty-five city residents remained overnight at the Elks Lodge rather than risk stalling their cars in an attempt to reach homes some distance from the lodge.

Fergus Falls telephone switchboards were deluged with calls from people concerned about the safety of their loved ones, especially the high school students at the basketball tournament in Moorhead. Between midnight Saturday and midnight Sunday, 708 long-distance phone calls were placed through Fergus Falls switchboards. There were so many local telephone calls made that at times it was impossible to handle them all.

The storm left most highways in Ottertail County impassable. The wind-driven snow packed the drifts so hard that V-shaped snowplows bounded over four- and five-foot drifts. Only with the use of a rotary snowplow could they be opened. Once a rotary plow opened a drift, a V-plow could keep it open for a while. However, since a V-plow could not throw snow as far as a rotary plow, it had its limitations. Several passes through a drift by a V-plow left no room for more snow. The March 15 storm left drifts as high as twelve to fifteen feet on some Ottertail County roads and four-to-five-foot drifts in stretches up to five miles on other roads. The county engineer believed it would take more than a week to completely open the roads in Ottertail County. In spite of the high winds, there was little storm damage in Fergus Falls.

Although no storm-related deaths were reported in Ottertail County, there were many near misses. None had a more harrowing story to tell than Mr. and Mrs. Herbert Nickel and Miss Pearl Dunham, all residents of Fergus Falls. After spending part of Saturday evening at Underwood, a village nine miles east of Fergus Falls, they headed for home about half past eleven that evening. After traveling a while on the highway, they realized they could not go any farther. In their attempt to return to Underwood their car went into the ditch several times. The storm made for such poor visibility as to prevent them from seeing the side of the road. Unable to extricate their car from the ditch the second time, the Nickels and Miss Dunham decided to attempt to reach Underwood on foot. As a precaution, before they left the vehicle, however, Mrs. Nickel turned on the headlights so they might be able to see them if they had to return to the car. Believing they could reach Underwood by a shortcut, they set out across a field. Unfortunately, deep snowdrifts made headway difficult. In their struggle through the snow, Miss Dunham lost her shoes and was forced to walk in her stocking feet. Badly exhausted, their faces and hair covered with ice, they decided to return to the car. Mrs. Nickel's precaution paid off as they were able to locate the car lights in the storm and return to the automobile.

With Mrs. Nickel suffering badly frostbitten legs and Miss Dunham with frozen hands, they kept the motor running and the heater on. Despite these efforts, the frozen limbs would not thaw out. Around six in the morning the car ran out of gas. Fortunately, by this time the wind was abating and it was getting daylight. Seeing a windmill in the distance they knew a farm was nearby. As he was the most warmly dressed, Mr. Nickel set out for the farm. After his departure, a Mr. Haukebo came by in his car. The women flagged him down. After picking them up, Mr. Haukebo picked up Mr. Nickel who was returning to the car. They drove into Underwood from where a call was made to Fergus Falls to summon a physician to attend to the ladies. They were then sent immediately to St. Luke's Hospital in Fergus Falls. Returning over the highway, Mr. Nickel noticed their tracks during the night did not lead to Underwood but away from town. If they had not returned to the car they could have easily wandered about in the storm until exhaustion overcame them, and they would have frozen to death.[17]

Many heroes emerged from the March 15, 1941, storm, and Lewis Tysdal who lived near Fergus Falls was one of them. Out driving in his truck in the storm, Tysdal rescued an elderly farmer from a car and put him in the cab of his truck. Then coming upon a stalled car, Tysdal rescued three Fergus Falls boys near Foxhomme, a village about eleven miles west of Fergus Falls. The boys climbed into Tysdal's truck box which contained a friendly bull. Near French, Tysdal picked up a young farmer whose car had stopped. Around two in the morning, he picked up two more stranded motorists near French. They also hopped into the truck box. Tysdal now had seven stranded motorists aboard his truck. He continued to search cars along the highway and drove with his door open so he could see the road. Eventually they reached the Anton Lill farm. After an hour in the house, someone noticed a light near the highway. Once more Tysdal trudged out into the elements and located a car in the ditch. In it was a man and two women—all without overshoes. They were brought into the Lill house. The guests passed the rest of the night drinking coffee and playing checkers. After breakfast, the guests made their departure. Through his efforts, Lewis Tysdal had rescued ten people in the storm.[18]

Traverse County: Wheaton

One of the origins of the Red River Valley begins near Browns Valley,

Minnesota. A continental divide separates the drainage of the Red River from the Minnesota River at Browns Valley. Lake Traverse and Mud Lake below it straddle the Minnesota-South Dakota border. From Mud Lake the Bois de Sioux flows north to join the Ottertail River coming from the east at Breckenridge, Minnesota, to form the Red River. Traverse County borders these two lakes and extreme northeastern South Dakota and southeastern North Dakota. Wheaton is in Traverse County and lies about twenty-five miles southeast of Breckenridge. In 1940, Wheaton had 1,700 residents.

Wheaton escaped the brunt of the storm which dashed into town shortly after ten o'clock Saturday evening. People in Wheaton immediately left for their homes, and there were no reports of people being injured because of the storm in the Wheaton vicinity.[19]

Of the seventy-one victims of the storm in North Dakota and Minnesota, twenty-eight perished in the Red River Valley, nine in North Dakota and nineteen in Minnesota. Many of the victims were in areas that were close to the valley but not actually in it. As the most familiar geographic feature in eastern North Dakota and western Minnesota with Grand Forks and Fargo located in it, the name of the Red River Valley became synonymous with the storm. With many of the reports on the storm coming from these two cities, it was for good reason the storm was known as the "Red River Flash Storm."

Morris, Willmar, Benson, Granite Falls.

Located out of the Red River Valley about forty miles southeast of Wheaton is Morris, the seat of Stevens County. Morris enjoyed a population of 3,214 in 1940. On March 15, 1941, people residing in and around Morris were savoring the victory of the Morris high school basketball team in the district basketball championship the previous evening. Morris had defeated Benson to capture the local crown, and now everyone was looking forward to the regional tournament.

Just as the 1940 Armistice Day storm had caught the residents of Morris off-guard, so did the March 15, 1941, blizzard. After whistling through Wheaton, the storm engulfed Morris full force by eleven o'clock Saturday evening.

Professor R. O. Bridgeford was the local weather observer in Morris. He made his weather observations at the weather station at West Central School in Morris. At a quarter past midnight he recorded a wind speed of 66 mph. The gale kept up this velocity for over two hours before dropping. Bridgeford noted that it was the highest wind speed recorded in Morris in the last fifty-four years. It was a greater wind speed than even those winds accompanying a wind storm which swept through Morris in May 1934. The temperature in Morris skidded from 31 above Saturday evening to 8 below Sunday morning.

Despite such high winds, Morris came through the storm in fairly good shape. Once the storm had arrived, people who were downtown quickly

211

left for home either on foot or by car. Train service was disrupted but mostly from problems arising elsewhere. High winds and low visibility kept Great Northern night trains tied up at Willmar and Fargo. They did not arrive in Willmar until late Sunday morning. Deep snowdrifts at Sauk Centre prevented Northern Pacific trains from reaching Morris until Wednesday morning. Telegraph wires into Morris came through the storm unharmed. Otter Tail Power Company only had a few power interruptions. These were caused by some service wires being blown down. Northwestern Bell Telephone Company had a similar experience. Trees crashing onto telephone wires disrupted telephone service for seven local telephones. Some utility wires also were broken when a scaffold being used to build an addition onto the local armory was blown down.[20]

Benson, the seat of Swift County, lies twenty-five miles southeast of Morris. Its residents (2,729 in 1940) has been listening to storm warnings from Fargo radio stations prior to the arrival of the storm around eleven o'clock Saturday evening, but the ferocity of the storm still took them by surprise. Although no snow accompanied the storm as it engulfed Benson, high winds blew dirt and existing snow around enough to block roads. This made for disrupted train and mail service, and slowed people from reaching their destinations.[21]

Thirty-three miles southeast of Morris is Willmar, the seat of Kandiyohi County. In 1940, Willmar had a population of 7,623 residents. The storm reached Willmar shortly before midnight Saturday. The wind accompanying the storm blew at speeds from 38 to 45 mph throughout

Sunday. Squalls of light snow mixed with considerable dirt made for zero

visibility and left drifts on many of the highways, which made driving

hazardous. The path of the storm extended north from Highway 12 from

Delano, then west through Litchfield, Willmar, Benson, and Morris. The

towns west of Morris, such as Ortonville and Montevideo, showed little or no

evidence of the storm.[22]

By midnight the cold front had reached Sioux Falls, South Dakota,

and the high winds filled the air with dirt.

Granite Falls (2,388 residents in 1940) is located forty miles

southwest of Willmar along the Minnesota River in Yellow Medicine County.

As with most of the rest of southern Minnesota, Granite Falls experienced

mostly blowing snow and dirt with little or no accompanying precipitation.

The storm seemed to be concentrated north of U.S. Highway 12. It whipped

through Granite Falls around eleven o'clock Saturday evening but did little

damage. But late travelers, especially basketball fans in Dawson with the

Granite Falls team, had trouble keeping their cars on the road due to the

high winds.[23]

About thirty miles southeast of Granite Falls, just off the Minnesota

River and along the Redwood River, lies Redwood Falls, the seat of Redwood

County. Redwood Falls recorded a population of 3,270 in 1940. The storm

left some wind damage in Redwood Falls. Four carloads of travelers were

forced to take shelter in the City Hall and Legion Clubhouse in Redwood

Falls early Sunday.[24]

Twenty-seven miles east of Willmar, along U.S. Highway 12, is Litchfield (3,920 residents in 1940), the seat of Meeker County. Litchfield received the brunt of the storm. It began snowing lightly early Saturday evening in Litchfield. When it arrived the storm used the combination of light snow, dirt from neighboring fields, and 75 mph winds to reduce visibility in the Litchfield vicinity to zero. Many travelers were stranded in Litchfield and Eden Valley. Rock-hard drifts kept many parishioners away from church on Sunday. The storm sent ten people to the local hospital for treatment of frostbite.[25]

Hutchinson, in McLeod County (3,887 residents in 1940), lies about twenty miles southeast of Litchfield. The temperature soared to 40 above in Hutchinson on Saturday afternoon. It started to snow lightly that evening. Once the storm made its appearance in Hutchinson, the temperature began to fall rapidly. It slipped to 4 below on Sunday and to 7.5 degrees below zero on Monday before rebounding. Hutchinson received 0.08 inch of precipitation before and during the storm.

One of the unfortunate casualties of the blizzard was the loss of wildlife. "Peep" Nelson, a rural Hutchinson mail carrier, counted seventy-four dead pheasants on Otter Lake on Wednesday, March 19. Most of them were females. The Hutchinson area had experienced a similar loss from the Armistice Day storm.[26]

Pipestone, Worthington, and Fairmont

Seventy-two miles southwest of Granite Falls, next to the South
Dakota border, is Pipestone, the seat of Pipestone County. Pipestone was
home to 4,682 people in 1940. The city was enjoying mild weather on
Saturday, March 15. Temperatures were in the 30s Saturday afternoon and
evening. They reached a high of 38 early Sunday morning before the storm
forced them downwards. Accompanied by high winds, it arrived in Pipestone
late Saturday, stranding quite a few motorists in Pipestone cafes. By eight
o'clock Sunday morning the temperature had slipped to 1 above in Pipestone,
on its way to 2 below both Sunday and Monday. Pipestone recorded 0.17 of
an inch of precipitation on Saturday and Sunday.[27]

Worthington, Minnesota, is located in Noble County about sixty
miles east of Sioux Falls, South Dakota. The 1940 census gave Worthington
a population of 5,918 people. The storm reached Worthington about a
quarter after midnight Saturday. Worthington had received some snow
Friday night and about another half-inch Saturday night. The winds peaked
at 50 mph in Worthington between three and four Sunday morning. The
temperature did not slide below zero in Worthington until Monday morning,
when it fell to 2 below zero.

For the velocity of the winds, Worthington suffered little storm
damage. But the quick drop in temperatures on Sunday froze up many
engine blocks on cars, causing much damage in some instances. Many
motorists had not anticipated the rapid drop in temperature. They failed to

take steps to protect their engines and left their cars outside Saturday night. Car problems kept local service stations busy on Sunday. Despite the high winds, the fact that the temperature did not get as cold in Worthington as other areas helped substantially. Local physicians and hospitals reported no cases of exposure. The Worthington area reported no disruption of telephone, telegraph, or power during the storm.

One person who experienced storm problems in the Worthington area was Chester Hill of Ewington township. He was driving on U.S. 16, and was near the Sioux Valley Corner, sixteen miles east of Worthington. Emerging from the protection of a grove of trees, his car was hit so hard by the force of the wind that he lost control of it and went into the ditch, sustaining about $50.00 damage. Locating shelter in a barn, Hill spent the remainder of the night there. In the morning he flagged down some westbound motorists and was able to get home. His car was taken into a Worthington garage for repairs.[28]

Fairmont, the seat of Martin County, is fifty-eight miles east of Worthington on Interstate 90. It had 6,988 residents in 1940. On Saturday, March 15, the Fairmont Daily Sentinel carried the same Minnesota forecast as most of the rest of the state for Saturday and Sunday.[29] After a mild Saturday, the temperature stood at 33 above in Fairmont at midnight. It then rose to 36 above but began to fall rapidly after the storm entered the Fairmont vicinity about half past one Sunday morning. After hovering near zero most of Sunday, it rose to 5 above during the night before falling to 2 below at half past eight Monday. Unlike some other parts of Minnesota, Fairmont received little or no snow. What it experienced was a dirt storm with winds so strong that houses were jarred from the blasts. People encountered difficulty in trying to control their cars on roads. The dirt storm created fog-like conditions in southwestern Minnesota. The lack of snow prevented drifts from building on highways and blocking traffic. Southwestern Minnesota escaped the death and destruction that other areas encountered. An exception was one Fairmont business, the Fairmont Railway Motors, where the storm tore a large section of roofing off the main building. Ironically, the same roof had been replaced after being blown off in the Armistice Day storm. After the passage of the storm, dozens of Fairmont businessmen were out cleaning the four inches of dirt from around their property.

Minneapolis-St. Paul, Mankato, Fairbault, Red Wing, Albert Lea, Austin, Rochester, Winona, and Caledonia

In 1940, 492,370 people resided in Minneapolis, with another 287,786 in St. Paul. The Twin Cities area escaped the worst effects of the blizzard. On Saturday, March 15, the temperature climbed to 36 above in Minneapolis. At 6:30 p.m. CST Saturday, it was clear in Minneapolis, although 0.18 of an inch of precipitation had been received within the previous 24 hours. The storm brought 53 mph winds to Minneapolis. The weather readings at 6:30 p.m. Sunday reflected the passage of the cold front. The skies were still clear, but the temperature hovered near zero for most of Sunday. The barometer had soared to 30.24 inches. On Monday morning the temperature dropped to 8 below zero. At 6:30 that evening skies remained clear, and the barometer continued to rise to 30.49 inches. The Twin Cities received no precipitation from the storm.

The large headlines in the March 17, 1941, <u>Minneapolis Tribune</u> read: "47 Die, 10 Missing, Scores Hurt in Red River Valley Flash Storm; Wind Hurls Cars Off Highways, Bodies Litter Fields; Thousands Marooned." The strong wind and cold temperatures of the storm forced the Minneapolis fire department to make nine special runs to answer emergency situations.

Minneapolis did suffer one casualty from the storm. Burton Bjork, age 26, a laborer for the Great Northern Railroad, was called to work at three o'clock Sunday morning to clean switches that had become filled with snow from the storm. Unable to hear the engine because of the storm's high wind, Bjork failed to get out of the way of a switch engine and was run over. The engineer on the switch engine told Dr. G. W. Callerstrom, Hennepin County Deputy Coroner, that he did not see Bjork and only knew he was there when the impact of hitting him jarred the engine.

St. Paul also suffered one fatality when Mrs. Anita Petruchek, age 43, of Dayton Bluff was found frozen to death in the road one block from her home.[30]

Mankato, in Blue Earth County, sits astride the Minnesota River about sixty miles southwest of the Twin Cities. In 1940, 15,654 people resided in Mankato. Riding on the back of a high northwest wind, the storm slammed into Mankato shortly after midnight Saturday night. Wind gusts reached 50 mph at the Mankato Airport. The wind roared all day Sunday, while it "wrecked signboards, blew off storm windows, put out rural telephone lines and interrupted power service in this area."[31] Travel was extremely hazardous Saturday night as snow flurries and sleet accompanied the wind. Some cars were forced into ditches near Mankato, but there were no reports of serious accidents. The temperature skidded from 38 above Saturday to 3 degrees below zero Sunday morning and to 6 degrees below zero that night. It was the coldest March temperature recorded in Mankato in five years.

In spite of the storm conditions, Northern State Power Company reported no serious power outages. However, tree limbs blowing across wires did cause some power outages on a couple of lines. Telephone service was interrupted for some farms and the village of St. Clair. Roads in the Mankato area came through the storm in good shape, although the thawing before the storm on gravel roads had made them virtually impassable from mud. After the storm the ruts froze, making for rough driving.[32]

Fairbault, the seat of Rice County, is located along today's Interstate 35 about forty miles northeast of Mankato. The storm reached Fairbault after midnight Saturday sending temperatures, which had reached 34 above on Saturday, plunging to 2 below on Sunday morning. After crawling back up to 4 above, the temperature slipped to 6 below on Monday morning. Fairbault escaped the death and destruction that other areas had experienced. The storm delayed some buses a half hour Sunday morning.

A local sheriff, Frank Weir, showed quite a presence of mind during the storm. About 150 people were at the Gingham Nite Club when the storm arrived in Fairbault. Weir immediately called the night club and ordered it to remain open and for the people to stay there until the storm was over. The night club kept its floodlight on all night; the manager hoped the bright light would aid people who were lost in the storm. And it did. During the night, stranded motorists made it to the night club. Other Rice County night clubs adopted a similar procedure to help those caught in the storm.[33]

Red Wing (9,962 residents in 1940) is in Goodhue County and sits along the banks of the Mississippi River about thirty-five miles southeast of the Twin Cities. The temperature soared to 41 above in Red Wing at noon Saturday. Once the storm hit Red Wing, the temperature dropped rapidly. By Monday morning it was 6 below zero in Red Wing. By noon Monday, Red Wing's main roads were open, but motorists were asked not to drive on secondary roads as they were still partially blocked.[34]

About fifty miles south of Fairbault, just off Interstate 35, is Albert Lea, the seat of Freeborn County (1940 population of 12,200). Six young people, five from Albert Lea and one from Hollandale, spent Saturday evening visiting in Austin. On their return they ran into the storm. They turned north on Highway No. 16 to take Geraldine Christensen home to her residence in Hollendale. The wind was so strong and visibility so poor that several times the car was almost blown into the ditch. They finally reached the Christensen residence in Hollandale and remained there for the rest of the night.

The next morning the five Albert Lea residents started for home. Upon reaching Clarks Grove west of Hollandale, they stopped and went into a restaurant to warm up. At the restaurant they learned that five people from Geneva (a town about six miles northeast of Clarks Grove) had experienced a fate similar to theirs during the night. The Geneva residents were in Albert Lea Saturday evening. On their way home, storm conditions prevented them from going any farther than Clarks Grove. Unfortunately for them, nothing was open in Clarks Grove. They were forced to spend the remainder of the night in their car on one of Clarks Grove's streets keeping the car heater running to keep them warm.[35]

Approximately twenty miles east of Albert Lea on today's Interstate 90 lies Austin (18,307 residents in 1940), seat of Mower County. As with the Fairmont Daily Sentinel, the Austin Daily Herald carried the Minnesota forecast. The cold wave accompanied by strong northwest winds was expected to reach Austin Sunday or Sunday night. The temperature readings certainly bore this out as they dropped from 38 above on noon Saturday to 3 below at six o'clock Monday morning.[36]

Located about seventy miles southeast of the Twin Cities along the

Zumbro River is Rochester, home of the world famous Mayo Clinic. According to the 1940 census, 26,312 people lived in Rochester. The storm arrived in Rochester early Sunday morning. The wind started to rise and blew steadily at 45 mph with gusts reaching 75 mph. Some snow fell with the storm, and blowing with what snow lay on the ground reduced visibility and caused drifting. The temperature fell in Rochester from 28 above a half hour past midnight Saturday to 1 below only five and a half hours later. By early Monday the temperature had fallen to 8 degrees below zero. It was the coldest St. Patrick's Day temperature ever recorded in Rochester.

The storm on March 16 forced all plane flights except one to be canceled in and out of the Rochester Airport. Buses were able to run in and out of Rochester although those headed for the Twin Cities found it tougher going north than those coming south. All of the main highways in the Rochester area were open on Monday, though drifts did block some county and secondary roads in the area. Train service was delayed somewhat by the storm, but the trains were getting through. By Monday airplane schedules were back to normal. There were only two cases of frostbite reported in the Rochester vicinity. The storm forced some schools to remain closed Monday.[37]

Like Red Wing, Winona sits next to the Mississippi River. Located about forty miles east of Rochester, Winona is the seat of Winona County. The 1940 census recorded 22,940 residents. In March 1941, residents were looking forward to spring which would be signalled by the breakup of ice on the Mississippi River. As elsewhere, balmy temperatures were the rule on Saturday, March 15. By noon the thermometer recorded 38 above in Winona, but the storm dropped the temperature to 3 above Sunday morning before it climbed back up to 7 above at noon. A half inch of precipitation was received in the twenty-four hours from noon Saturday to noon Sunday, and the cold wave brought 45 mph winds Sunday.

Despite the inclement weather, the Winona Republican-Herald referred to the storm as the "Red River Valley Blizzard." The Saturday evening edition of the Winona Republican-Herald carried the same forecast for Minnesota as most other newspapers in the state for Saturday evening and Sunday. It read: "Minnesota; Occasional light snow tonight and Sunday; Cold wave with strong northwest winds Sunday and northwest and west-central tonight." For the Twin Cities the forecast stated: "Light snow Saturday night and Sunday; Cold wave with strong northwest winds Sunday." For Winona and vicinity: "Occasional light snow tonight and Sunday; much colder Sunday with cold wave. Strong northwest winds Sunday and Sunday night." The cold wave was not supposed to reach southeastern Minnesota until Sunday, and it did not. Once again the Weather Bureau was on target with its forecast.

In spite of the bad weather, the Minnesota Field Trial Association held its retriever trials at the Izaak Walton League cabin, near Winona, on Sunday. A special dog train was engaged to bring 125 people and 35 dogs from the Twin Cities to Winona. Mayor Floyd R. Simon and a large crowd with cars took them to the Izaak Walton cabin. The cabin provided the warmth for the dog handlers and fans alike. The handlers would dash outside and put their dogs through their paces before retreating to the warmth of the cabin. Winona dogs fared well in the competition, winning all three stakes—the derby stake, the non-winner stake, and the open-all-age stake. The event was covered extensively by the news media with cameramen from Paramount News and photographers from Twin City newspapers as well as from Sports Afield, Country Life, Life, and Sportsman and Golfer. Their solution to keep their hands from becoming numb was to alternate working inside and outside. KSTP radio station and the local American Legion Band provided entertainment In the cabin. There was a large crowd on hand to watch the trials, including an individual from Vancouver, British Columbia. After the evening banquet the special train departed for the Twin cities at a quarter after nine that evening.

The inclement weather delayed the 1941 spring fashion showing in Winona by one week. The special section of the Winona Republican-Herald covering this event also was delayed a week.[38]

The accuracy of the forecast for Austin as to the time of arrival of the cold wave is born out in a tragic fatality of the storm at Caledonia, about seventy-five miles east of Austin. Late Sunday evening, Albert Horn, 77, a Caledonia resident, left his home despite the poor weather and his wife's pleas to remain at home. He was wearing a dark hat, a light brown coat, dark blue trousers, and mittens. He did not have any overshoes on. Poor weather on Monday frustrated attempts to locate him. Bloodhounds were brought in from La Crosse, Wisconsin, on Monday to try to locate Horn. They trailed his scent for a half mile from his home but lost the trail after that. The sheriff's office and enrollees from the local CCC camp could not find him. Horn's body was finally located Wednesday evening in a ravine about a mile from his place of residence. Both his cap and mittens were not on him. From marks in the snow it was evident that Horn had stamped in the snow in an effort to keep warm.

Roseau, Warroad, Baudette, Thief River Falls, Goodridge, St. Hilaire, and Red Lake Falls

Once out of the Red River Valley, the storm swept into the wooded country of Minnesota, an area of not only woods but rolling hills and lakes also. The woods tended to slow the winds of the storm down somewhat but not in all cases. One exception was in Roseau County. A large part of Roseau County is open country suitable for farming. The county seat of Roseau County is the city of Roseau, which had a population of 1,775 in 1940.

Saturday was a beautiful day in Roseau. Temperatures climbed to near the melting mark. It was a typical busy Saturday in town with shoppers out and about. As evening approached many people left for Stephen to attend the basketball tournament.

Roseau had a strong basketball team that won twenty games during the 1940-41 season without a loss and were the favorite to win the annual district basketball tournament to be held in Stephen, Minnesota, March 14 and 15, 1941. On Friday night Roseau beat Karlstad in the semifinal round, setting up the championship match with Baudette Saturday. Everyone in the community was excited and many planned on attending the game in Stephen.

Later a disastrous storm blew in. The temperature at Roseau fell rapidly Saturday night to 12 degrees below zero Sunday morning. According to M. J. Hegland, the Weather Bureau observer at Roseau, the wind gusts from the storm exceeded 60 mph at Roseau. By Monday morning the temperature had slipped to 19 degrees below zero.[40]

Twenty miles northeast of Roseau on Lake of the Woods is the city of Warroad, which had a population of 1,309 in 1940. The sudden onslaught of the storm at nine o'clock Saturday evening changed people's plans. It would be the worst blizzard to hit Warroad all winter as temperatures slipped to 14 degrees below zero Sunday morning. Although no deaths were reported in the Warroad vicinity, many area residents spent the night at friends' homes while out-of-town visitors stayed overnight at the lodging facilities. A St. Patrick's Day dance was scheduled at the Lodge Hall in Warroad for Saturday night. The storm kept the large crowd at the hall for the night. However, the weather did not put a damper on the celebration. The dancers took up several extra collections, and Clarence Meyer's Band played almost until dawn. Although worn out by the affair, the band did quite well financially.

The high wind broke one power line in Warroad. Early Sunday morning a Warroad Light and Power crew repaired the line, restoring service.[41]

Baudette is about forty miles southeast of Warroad along the Rainy River. As the seat of Lake of the Woods County, it enjoyed a population of 1,017 in 1940. On March 14, Baudette defeated Argyle and thus would meet Roseau in the championship game in Stephen. But activity in Baudette ground to a halt when the storm engulfed the city a little after nine Saturday evening. It stranded about thirty-five young people for the night at a dance in the Spooner township community hall.

Triangle Bus Company operated a bus line between Thief River Falls and Baudette. On Saturday night the bus left Greenbush headed for Baudette with six passengers. After proceeding only a mile, Neumel Rippy, the driver, stopped the bus. When he stepped outside to adjust a radiator hose, the storm almost suffocated him. Unable to see the highway, Rippy decided not to proceed any further. After much difficulty he was able to turn the bus around and return to Greenbush. After spending the night there, the bus made it to Baudette on Sunday.

As with others, Baudette's fans and cagers were surprised when the Roseau team did not show for the title game. On Sunday morning they learned what had happened to the Roseau team. On March 19 the postponed game was played in Thief River Falls, and Baudette lost in the last 30 seconds to Roseau on a couple of free throws.

Because snow-blocked roads prevented buses from bringing students to school, there was no school in Baudette on Monday.[42]

Southeast of Roseau in Pennington County is Thief River Falls which had 6,019 residents in 1940. The city was enjoying a pleasant, spring-like day on March 15, 1941. It was the first Saturday night of 1941 that stores in Thief River Falls stayed open until nine o'clock. A dance was being held at the Sons of Norway Hall with music being provided by Jolly Aaseby and his orchestra.

The mild weather continued into the evening with light snow and a slight breeze from the south. Then, shortly after nine o'clock, the wind switched around to the north and blew with terrific force. In just a matter of a few minutes the temperature dropped 20 degrees and continued to slide downwards until it was well below zero Sunday morning.

Because stores were open, most shoppers had not departed for their homes when the storm hit. They stayed in town for the night at hotels, cafes, the Soo depot, or at friends' homes. Quickly realizing the severity of the blizzard, Thief River Falls police visited the local movie theaters and told the youngsters they were not to leave for home unless taken by police or their parents.

On Highway 32 south of Thief River Falls, a large snowdrift almost ten feet high and a half a block long extending along the highway west from the Oakland Park sanatorium kept thirty-five cars from getting through. By late Sunday, two snowplows, one belonging to Pennington County and one to the Minnesota Highway Department, had the road open.

A local couple, Mr. and Mrs. Erickson, was stranded overnight at Goodridge, located twenty miles east of Thief River Falls, and it took them seven hours to reach their home on Sunday.

Carl Brahs, manager of the local Land O'Lakes plant, was returning from Minneapolis and he had just driven into his yard when the storm hit. V. C. Noper lived less than a mile west of Thief River Falls. Starting for home in the storm, Noper traveled only a short distance before abandoning the effort. He stayed the rest of the night in a nearby cabin. After visiting at the Oakland Park sanatorium in Thief River Falls, five Warren ladies left for home at a quarter to nine Saturday evening. Traveling 12 of the 30 miles to Warren, they encountered the storm. Staying in their car, they had enough gas to keep the car running and the heater going until five o'clock Sunday morning. They were rescued by a snowplow several hours later.

Pennington County experienced one fatality from the storm. Francis J. Weckwerth, age 22, lived on a farm southeast of Thief River Falls. He became concerned about the safety of his brother Harold, age 16, who was visiting at the nearby Andrew Arne home. Despite his family's pleas, Weckwerth set out on horseback to find out what had happened to his brother. Becoming lost in the storm, Weckwerth failed to reach the Arne home. His horse returned to the Weckwerth's barn without him. At dawn, Weckwerth's frozen body was found about 50 feet from the barn, sitting in an upright position along a fence.

In 1940, Goodridge, which is located about twenty miles east of Thief River Falls, had a population of 122. On Saturday night, Rod's Cafe prepared quite a few lunches for the crowd gathered at the Goodridge Community Hall. They were holding a farewell party for the Goodridge and Highland volunteers. Unfortunately, the storm descended on Goodridge before their catered meal could be served, so the lunches remained at Rod's Cafe, while the crowd stayed at the Community Hall for the night.

Mavie Verle Ingberg went into town Saturday. While returning to his farm, the storm caught up with him. Concerned about Verle's safety, his brother Harold traveled to the nearby Oski home to look for him. The rescuers turned car lights in all directions until Verle saw them. Although exhausted, Verle made it to the Oski home.[43]

St. Hilaire, with a population of 288 in 1940, lies eight miles south of Thief River Falls. A dance was being held in St. Hilaire Saturday evening with Sax Aaseby and his orchestra providing the music. Those who made it to the dance had little time to enjoy it as the storm was upon them shortly after nine o'clock.

With the storm occupying their thoughts, St. Hilaire residents did not expect another catastrophe to hit them that night. With the blizzard raging outside, a fire broke out. It was a fireman's worst nightmare come true. Starting in a soft drink parlor on main street, the fire quickly swept through two frame buildings and one brick building before extinguishing itself against the wall of another brick structure. Firemen could do little in the 65 to 75 mph winds to stop the blaze except try to keep their balance. Mr. and Mrs. Grovum and their two small children lived in one of the buildings that burned. The flames spread so rapidly that the Grovums had to flee out into the blizzard winds clad only in their night clothes.[44]

Red Lake Falls, located eighteen miles southwest of Thief River Falls in Red Lake County, had 1,530 people living there in 1940. Five miles northwest of Red Lake Falls is the village of Wylie. Berg Moren, age 56, a bachelor farmer, lived on a farm a half mile south of Wylie. After spending Saturday evening in Wylie, Berg started walking home in the storm around eleven that evening. His frozen body was found along the highway.

<u>Bemidji, Mahnomen, Detroit Lakes,</u>

<u>Park Rapids, Wadena, Wrightstown, Brainerd,</u>

<u>Little Falls, Alexandria, St. Cloud, and Mora</u>

One hundred miles southeast of Grand Forks, North Dakota, on U.S. Highway 2, is Bemidji, Minnesota. Bemidji, the seat of Beltrami County, had a population of 9,427 residents in 1940.

On March 15, 1941, Bemidji was enjoying balmy weather. The thermometer climbed to 31 above that afternoon under blue skies. There was little hint of the storm that was about to hit them, though the evening edition of the <u>Bemidji Daily Pioneer</u> had a forecast that gave an indication of what was about to happen. It read: "Occasional light snow tonight and Sunday; cold wave with strong northwest winds Sunday and in northwest and west-central tonight." As with forecasts for other cities in the storm area, this forecast was more accurate than it was given credit for. The storm arrived in Bemidji about the time it was forecast to. Winds piled about two inches of new snow into huge drifts, which made travel difficult. The winds peaked at 30 mph in Bemidji about midnight Saturday before slowly tapering off by Sunday morning. The woods at Bemidji kept the wind speed down.[45] The temperature there dropped to 10 degrees below zero Sunday morning. It warmed up to only 4 degrees below zero on Sunday before slipping to 22 below zero by Monday morning. It was Bemidji's coldest temperature in a month.[46]

A Grand Rapids couple had a close call near Bemidji. Ed Loney was a pharmacist in Grand Rapids. After his drug store closed around ten o'clock Saturday evening, Mr. Loney and his wife left to visit friends in Bemidji. They were about seven or eight miles from Bemidji when the storm engulfed them. In their attempt to drive through it, the Loney's car went off the highway into a ditch. They were rescued a short time later by a passing school bus and taken to Bemidji. On Sunday, the Loneys had their car pulled out of the ditch, and they returned to Grand Rapids that evening, once the storm had let up.[47]

Mahnomen, seat of Mahnomen County, is located sixty miles south of Thief River Falls on U.S. Highway 59. After a mild day, it started to snow lightly in Mahnomen Saturday evening with temperatures well above the zero mark. The Mahnomen Pioneer reported that "shortly after 10:00 p.m. the mercury began to drop one degree a minute and at about 10:20 p.m. the wind struck with the ferocity of a flame from a blast furnace."[48]

Mahnomen County suffered two fatalities from the storm. They were Mrs. Jacob Bjerken, age about 45, and her son Palmer, age 8. Mr. and Mrs. Bjerken and their two sons, Arnold, age 13, Palmer, and a daughter Violet, had been visiting one of their neighbors only a short distance from home. They started home in the storm, but their car stalled a short way from their home and the Bjerkens decided to walk the remaining distance. They walked huddled together with Mr. Bjerken carrying Palmer in his arms. But Palmer and Mrs. Bjerken apparently were choked to death by the wind and blinding snow within a short time of each other. Mr. Bjerken and Arnold continued on through the storm. Mr. Bjerken became exhausted and fell unconscious into the snow. Arnold revived his father by slapping and shaking him, and eventually they reached the house.[49]

It was half past ten Saturday evening when the onslaught of the storm hit Detroit Lakes, a city in Minnesota's lake country forty miles due east of Fargo, North Dakota. As the seat of Becker County, Detroit Lakes had 5,015 residents in 1940. In just a few minutes the temperature fell from 26 degrees to 0 and then to 10 degrees below zero by early morning. Wind speeds at Detroit Lakes were estimated to be seventy miles per hour.

In Detroit Lakes, a couple of restaurants stayed open until five o'clock Sunday morning, providing shelter for stranded people. Ten cars made a dangerous journey during the height of the blizzard from the Savard Club to Detroit Lakes. The cars stayed close to each other so each one could see the tail lights of the car in front of it. On Sunday garages and wreckers were kept busy bringing in stalled cars and getting them to run again. As elsewhere, motorists found shelter in farm homes or city residences. Detroit Lakes did not experience much storm damage, although a couple of farmers lost some turkeys. Their loss was not as bad as that of the Armistice Day storm which had raged for fifty hours in Detroit Lakes.[50]

One anxious parent from Detroit Lakes was attending the district basketball tournament in Moorhead when the storm hit there. He broadcast an appeal over the radio asking that someone back in Detroit Lakes go to his home and see if the babysitter he had hired, a young girl, and his children were safe.[51]

Becker County recorded two deaths resulting from the storm. The victims were John Lennox, age 37, and his wife Donna, age 28, from Fargo. They had gone to Detroit Lakes with their seven-year-old son Charles Raymond to visit Mr. Lennox's stepfather, Frank Vanderwarka. After spending part of Saturday evening visiting at a neighbor of Mr. Vanderwarka, Clyde Stull, who lived a half mile away, they started to walk back to the Vandewarkas. According to Becker County Sheriff Max Olson, they made it half way back when they decided to turn and walk with the wind. Mr. and Mrs. Lennox stumbled into a swamp that had snow several feet deep in it. Threshing about in the snow led to exhaustion and then collapse, first Mrs. Lennox and then Mr. Lennox. Mr. Lennox tramped out a path about 100 feet long in the snow in an effort to keep from freezing. But it was not enough. After looking for the bodies most of Sunday, searchers found them in a swamp five miles northeast of Detroit Lakes about half past four that afternoon.[52]

Afterwards, the Detroit Lakes Tribune claimed the only warning people in and around Detroit Lakes had of the storm came from a radio broadcast originating at Moorhead, Minnesota, that talked about a blizzard raging there. The newspaper said the storm caught hundreds of Detroit Lakes residents by surprise.[53]

Although not in the Red River Valley, Detroit Lakes was close enough to it so that it did not have the protection of deep woods as did places farther east in Minnesota. A considerable amount of farmland around Detroit Lakes meant quite a bit of open country. This situation also existed with other Minnesota cities close to the Valley. These included Roseau, Thief River Falls, and Mahnomen.

Park Rapids, located forty miles east of Detroit Lakes in Hubbard County, had a population of 2,643 in 1940. Roaring into Park Rapids just before midnight, the storm packed winds estimated to be 50 mph. It tore many storm windows loose from their fastenings. Other damage included a broken window in Dr. D. M. Houston's office and a large sign torn from Butler's store. Two hundred people were forced to spend the night at the

Park Theater, and many more stayed at the Royal Theater. The conversation during the night centered on the Armistice Day blizzard of the previous November and now in the spring another blizzard surprised them. A group of Native Americans from Ponsford waited out the storm in the armory. Local farmers also housed stranded motorists. Saturday night, twenty people stayed at the Frank Nel farm on the south edge of Park Rapids. Blocked roads were another common occurrence. South of Park Rapids, twenty cars were stalled in snowdrifts along a four-mile stretch of U.S. 71. Another twenty-two cars were stalled on Highway 34 between Park Rapids and Long Lake. Considerable trouble was encountered in trying to open Highway 87 through Hubbard County, so many people were stranded in Park Rapids until Wednesday.

After visiting in Park Rapids, Mr. and Mrs. Henry Mack, daughter Esther, 16, son Sammy, age 7, and son Joe, age 4, of Ponsford were returning home when caught in the storm about two miles from Osage. After their car went into the ditch, they abandoned it and headed for the Webster farm a mile away. They made it, but Mrs. Mack's arms and legs below the knee and her arms were frozen. Esther's legs above the knees were frozen. First aid was quickly administered. After the roads were opened on Sunday, they were taken to park Rapids for medical treatment. They both recovered.[54]

Forty-six miles southeast of Detroit Lakes in Wadena County lies Wadena, which had a population of 2,916 in 1940. It had been snowing there for about an hour when the blizzard struck Wadena shortly before eleven o'clock Saturday evening. Within a few minutes the wind whipped the snow around so much that visibility was reduced to a few feet. The temperature skidded from 28 above early Sunday morning to 20 degrees below zero by Monday morning. The precipitation from the snow amounted to 0.21 of an inch. The storm did not cause any fatalities in Wadena county although many people suffered from exposure. The <u>Wadena Pioneer Journal</u> considered it to be the worst blizzard in the history of the northwest.

The wind accompanying the storm was so strong that it ripped the sign off the Engh bakery and part of the metal sign in front of the Gamble store. A metal-covered roof on a nearby farm suffered a similar fate. After tearing it loose, the wind twisted the metal and forced it to hang over the side of the building. As the wind dashed down Jefferson Street, it smashed the plate glass window in the Krause drug store. It blew a door open in the building where the Davis Clinic, Skei drug store, and Jung and Yetter, lawyers, were located. Cold temperatures froze water pipes on the second floor of the building, causing them to break.

Many cars became stalled due to blocked roads forcing their occupants to abandon them. More than 200 people faced a dangerous situation along highways heading into Wadena. Some of them walked to nearby shelters while others huddled in their stalled cars. One motorist who was able to get from Aldrich to Wadena counted twenty-six stalled autos in the fourteen-mile stretch of highway between the two cities. Cafes and taverns stayed open all night, jammed with people unable to get home. The lobbies of the two hotels in Wadena were crowded with people. The wind accompanying the storm did much damage to windows and signs in Wadena. The storm caused the telephone system to be swamped with calls. Additional operators had to be called back to duty to handle the volume. The storm kept wreckers from local garages busy. They were on the go for almost twenty-four hours, either to move stalled cars on streets and roads or to pull other ones out of ditches.

At Wrightstown, thirteen miles south of Wadena, Mr. and Mrs. Arvid Tenney and daughter Carol and Mr. and Mrs. Charles Franklin and their children were visiting at the Bert McQuay farm. On the way home their car went in the ditch about a mile from home. Forced to abandon the car, they walked to safety with Mr. Tenney carrying Carol wrapped in a blanket. Neither Mrs. Tenney nor Mrs. Franklin wore overshoes, mittens, or any type of head protection as they walked through the storm.

Another narrow escape from the storm was experienced by Mr. and Mrs. Peter Gedde of Wadena, their son and his wife, and their nine-year-old grandson. Their car slid into the ditch two miles west of Wadena on Highway 29. After more than two hours in the car, they were taken to Deer Creek by an unidentified man and spent the rest of the night at a cafe there.

A party of six people made up of Mr. and Mrs. Maynard Castle, Mr. and Mrs. Marvin Castle, and Mrs. August Ludwig and daughter were coming home late Saturday evening when they were forced to abandon their car a little ways out of Wadena. They then were able to reach the Gust Plepkorn farm about a half mile away. Mrs. Maynard Castle, who was only lightly dressed, was numbed quickly by the cold and strong wind, but with the help of the others, she was able to keep going. Maynard and Marvin Castle lost their hats in the storm and looked so rumpled that when a young Plepkorn girl answered the door she fainted at their appearance. She had been home alone with her elderly grandfather. Within a short time her parents arrived from Wadena, having been forced to walk the last half mile home. Five more carloads of people sought shelter in the Plepkorn home before the storm subsided. Mrs. Maynard Castle was forced to spend two days in the Wesley Hospital for treatment for her frozen hands and feet.[55]

Brainerd is located forty-six miles east of Wadena. As the seat of Crow Wing County, it is nestled alongside the Mississippi River. In 1940, 12,071 people made Brainerd their home. In the twenty-four hours up to 8:00 a.m. on Saturday, March 15, Brainerd received 0.07 inch of precipitation (snow). This caused slippery roads in the Brainerd area. The temperature reached 36 degrees at noon Saturday in Brainerd, causing the snow to melt. As with the Bemidji Daily Pioneer, the evening edition of the Brainerd Daily Dispatch carried the same revised forecast from the Twin Cities weather office that warned of an approaching cold front for northwest and west central Minnesota Saturday night. But falling temperatures Saturday night made the roads slippery again. The storm reduced visibility to zero, making travel hazardous. The temperature fell to 16 degrees below zero on Sunday morning.

With the falling temperatures and high winds, travel on highways in the Brainerd area became treacherous once the storm arrived. The main highways leading from Brainerd all were blocked until late Sunday morning and on and off again for the rest of the day as drifting snow plugged cuts made by the snowplows. In spite of the twenty-four hour schedule maintained by the thirty-two snowplows of the local Minnesota Highway Department district, roads still were hard to keep open. Stalled vehicles created higher drifts on roads than normally would be the case, and that made things more difficult. Some of the worst stretches of highways with stalled vehicles included Brainerd to Fort Ripley and Highway 210 west to Staples and Wadena. Blocked roads prevented the first bus from Minneapolis from reaching Brainerd until three o'clock Sunday afternoon. Farm homes near Highway 371 between Little Falls and Brainerd became havens for twenty motorists who had abandoned their vehicles. By Monday all the highways in the Brainerd area were open, although motorists were advised to drive carefully because the huge drifts along the highways obstructed the view of motorists. The Brainerd area made it through the storm without a single fatality or injuries due to exposure, frostbite, or car accident.[56]

Located on the banks of the Mississippi River thirty miles south of Brainerd in Morrison County is Little Falls, which had 6,047 residents in 1940. Around midnight Saturday, it started to snow in Little Falls. With full blast, the storm descended upon Little Falls about 15 minutes after

240

midnight Saturday. While the snowfall ended quickly, the same could not be said for the wind.

Storm damage in Little Falls was mostly to windows and signs. By the time the blizzard reached Little Falls, most people who had been out and about had gone home. The storm did prevent the Minnesota Power and Light bowling team, their wives, guests, and the Long Prairie team and their wives from getting home Saturday night. After participating in a bowling tournament in Long Prairie, they went to a night club near Sauk Centre. When the storm arrived, they decided to make the attempt to go home, but the lead car stalled in the storm. Early in the morning they tried again and succeeded in reaching Sauk Centre between six and seven in the morning. They then tried to reach Little Falls via St. Cloud but found that route blocked. Not until three o'clock Sunday afternoon did the Little Falls bowlers reach home, after following a snowplow into Long Prairie.

Severe storm conditions are times of great concern for people who deal with emergency situations, for example, doctors and firemen. During the middle of the night on March 16, a Little Falls physician received a telephone call concerning an expectant mother. Leaving Little Falls about three in the morning, he headed for his destination, which was a farm home on Highway 28 southwest of Little Falls near Flensburg. After waiting in the car for about 10 minutes, he thought he should try to get to a farmhouse. He was able to reach a deserted farm building. Locating a lamp, the physician lit it and warmed his hands and feet. Then taking the lamp, the physician put it in the window as a signal. In the meantime, a motorist from Long Prairie had reached the farmhouse of the expectant mother. The motorist and another man then set out to find the physician. They shoveled through drifts and found the physician's car. They also found an overshoe the physician had lost. Then they saw the light in the window. They found the physician and took him to the farm before the baby was born.

There were 430 students absent from Little Falls High School Monday morning. Several buses came to school that day (one of them at noon) with very few students aboard. Two teachers could not make it to school Monday, while another one was brought to school via bobsled from her home southeast of Little Falls.

On Monday afternoon most of the highways in Morrison County were still blocked and drifts were deep. In spots the thickness of the snow crust forced snow-removal equipment weighing up to five tons to ride on top of the snow instead of plowing through it. Then, all of a sudden, the crust would break, and the equipment would become stuck. Because of the incredible drifts, the county crew expected to have a long row to hoe from then until the spring breakup.[57]

Alexandria, seat of Douglas County, is three miles off Interstate 94 and is about forty-five miles southeast of Fergus Falls, Minnesota. Alexandria recorded a population of 5,051 in 1940. People stranded in Alexandria because of the storm gave the Alexandria Telephone Company one of its busiest nights in history. Calling home to reassure relatives of their safety, they made 371 long distance phone calls on Sunday, a record for the Alexandria Telephone company. Between midnight Saturday and six o'clock Sunday morning, 206 calls were made. The Armistice Day blizzard of the previous November enticed 10,200 calls, while there were 7,800 calls made during and after the March 1941 storm. Until late Sunday, a full shift of operators had to be kept on duty to handle all the calls.

One of the most terrifying stories of narrow escapes in Douglas County was experienced by L. S. Norden of Brandon. He was driving home Saturday night from Alexandria when his car became stuck in a snowdrift three miles southeast of Garfield. Struggling through the storm, he managed to reach Garfield but collapsed near the Coop Oil Co. service station. Norden's weak call for help was heard by Julius Linser, but Linser was unable to locate him. After Linser went to bed, he again heard a weak call for help. Investigating the situation once more, Linser located Norden, who by this time had become delirious from cold and shock and suffered badly from frostbite. Linser did what he could to keep Norden alive for the rest of the night. As soon as roads were opened on Sunday, Norden was taken to St. Luke's Hospital in Alexandria. There Dr. Clifford treated him for his injuries which included a badly frozen left hand and serious frost bites on the ears and heels.[58]

St. Cloud, seat of Stearns County, is located fifty miles northwest of the Twin Cities on the Mississippi River. The 1940 census showed St. Cloud to have a population of 24,173. Soon after the storm roared into St. Cloud, the wind rose to 41 mph. Abating slightly at times on Sunday, it increased in velocity to 39 mph late Sunday afternoon before veering to the north at 18 mph at 9:00 p.m. Sunday. The storm dropped temperatures in St. Cloud from 29 degrees Saturday evening to 8 degrees below zero at 8:30 a.m. Sunday. After climbing to the zero mark Sunday afternoon, the temperature sank to 14 degrees below zero Monday morning.

Stearns County repeated the familiar litany of stalled cars, stranded motorists, and blocked highways of other areas in the storm's path. Highways would be clear of snow for a mile, then a huge drift would block the road. No accidents or deaths due to the storm were reported in the St. Cloud area. After battling drifts all day Sunday, Minnesota highway department snowplows were called in long after dark. The drifting snow and poor visibility made it very hard to keep roads open, as drifting snow filled in the cuts made by snowplows. The Minnesota Highway Department officially closed all highways in central Minnesota Sunday night, but highway department crews had them all open again Sunday. Snowdrifts from the storm varied tremendously in size. On the highway to Kimball, they were large enough to cover hen houses, garages, and front porches of houses. While St. Cloud streets remained mostly clear of drifts, in rural areas virtually all the roads were blocked.[59]

Forty-six miles northeast of St. Cloud along the Snake Rive is Mora, the seat of Kanabec County. In 1940, Mora had 1,494 residents. It had its share of stranded motorists, blocked highways and closed schools. Hard snowdrifts made things difficult for snow removal operations, especially in the Snake River flats north of Mora. In that vicinity the highway department was unable to open the highway until late Monday, but they were able to have the highway from the Twin Cities open by noon Sunday, which allowed the afternoon buses to run.[60]

International Falls

International Falls, seat of Koochiching County, lies next to the Rainy River which runs between it and Fort Francis, Ontario. In 1940, 5,626 people called International Falls home.

On March 15, 1941, the residents of International Falls certainly were not expecting a major snowstorm. The forecast for International Falls, released by the evening edition of the International Falls Daily Journal, influenced their thinking. It said: "Cloudy with light snow flurries; a little colder tonight; Sunday northwest winds and colder; light snow."[61]

After light snow fell Saturday evening, the storm arrived in International Falls during the night. Storm winds peaked at 26 mph at 6:30 a.m. Sunday. The low wind speed was caused partially by the deep woods around International Falls. Another reason was that International Falls was near the edge of the storm system where wind speeds would be less. The cold front quickly lowered temperatures in International Falls. The thermometer sank to 19 degrees below zero by Monday morning. International Falls and the rest of Koochiching County did not suffer any storm damage, and all main highways remained open.[62]

Grand Rapids, Aitkin, Hibbing, Virginia, Chisholm, and Ely

Seventy-five miles southeast of Bemidji on U.S. Highway 2 next to the Mississippi River in Itasca County is Grand Rapids. In 1940, Grand Rapids was home to 4,815 people. The storm did little local damage in and around Grand Rapids, but two or three inches of snow that had fallen recently blew around and filled roads and piled up drifts higher than those of the Armistice Day blizzard. The temperature dropped from 30 degrees early Sunday morning to 11 degrees below zero later that morning. By Tuesday morning the temperature had fallen to 27 degrees below zero. The intense cold accompanying the storm made it dangerous to be out in it for even a short period of time. It was the fourth bad storm in the span of one year to hit Grand Rapids. The other storms included the sleet storm of April 6, 1940, the tornado on July 24, 1940, and the Armistice Day blizzard of the previous November.

A Grand Rapids couple, Mr. and Mrs. Ted Reynolds, drove to the Twin Cities Sunday to visit their son who was enrolled in a barber school. They encountered little difficulty getting to the Twin Cities but passed many stalled cars on their way down there. It was not until they read Twin Cities newspapers that the Reynolds realized how bad the storm was.[63]

Fifty-two miles south of Grand Rapids on the Mississippi River is Aitkin (2,063 residents in 1940), seat of Aitkin County. The storm had a major impact on Aitkin. Many people were stranded. Two extra operators had to be brought in to the Aitkin telephone office to handle the deluge of calls over the weekend and on Monday. School was closed in Aitkin on Monday and Tuesday as all available snow removal equipment tried to reopen the roads. Some rural schools were closed longer. The lack of sleet accompanying the storm kept poultry losses down in comparison to the Armistice Day storm of the previous November.[64]

Located sixty miles northeast of Grand Rapids is Hibbing in St. Louis County. Hibbing had 16,385 residents in 1940. On Saturday night, March 15, Buhl defeated Coleraine for the district 28 basketball championship held in Hibbing. The storm entered the Hibbing area around two o'clock Sunday morning. Virginia (1940 population of 12,264) is about twenty-five miles northeast of Hibbing. The storm arrived there at half-past two Sunday morning. Temperatures which reached 30 above in Hibbing on Saturday night dropped quickly after the storm arrived, falling to 6 degrees below zero by daybreak Sunday. The temperature kept falling Sunday and slid to 17 degrees below zero by Monday morning. High northwest winds piled the snow into large drifts, clogging the roads and highways in open areas and blowing them clear in other places. They blew at 40 mph during the daylight hours on Sunday before dying down at sunset.

Although somewhat delayed on Sunday, buses and trains kept to their schedules. Most roads were partially open by noon Monday with the snow removal crews busily working to open the remaining roads. This storm was comparable to the Armistice Day blizzard which tied up all the traffic in the Hibbing area.[65]

Chisholm is located about six miles northeast of Hibbing. It had 7,487 residents in 1940. Al Luzaich, age 62, a Chisholm-area farmer, tried to make it to his home during the peak of the storm but was overcome by exhaustion and collapsed. On Monday, a miner on his way to work found Luzaich's frozen body.

Ely, on the edge of Superior National Forest, is about fifty miles northeast of Virginia, Minnesota, and 5,970 people resided there in 1940. Ely felt the full effects of the blizzard. The wind pounded the snow into deep drifts, and the temperature slipped to 14 below zero by Sunday evening. High winds on Sunday forced the cancellation of the Ely Ski Club Tournament. The high wind ripped the top off of one Ely resident's car. Two Ely school teachers and another couple were visiting at Basswood Beach on Saturday. They attempted to return to Ely on a snow sled Sunday morning. It broke down, and they were forced to walk the last six miles back to Ely.[66]

Cloquet and Duluth

Situated about twenty miles southwest of Duluth, Cloquet had 7,034 residents in 1940. The center of the storm went through the Cloquet area and it experienced 70 mph winds, zero visibility, blocked roads, and

248

considerable property damage. Arriving in Cloquet early Sunday, the storm lasted all day, and temperatures quickly fell from 25 above to below zero.

One storm fatality was recorded in the Cloquet vicinity. When the storm arrived, Paul Lyytinen, age 50, was at Esko with some friends. He worked at his uncle's farm outside of Esko. When the storm broke his plans to return there had to be changed. Realizing the severity of the storm, Lyytinen remained at the Esko creamery until seven o'clock Sunday morning when he started for home. Unfortunately, Lyytinen lacked an overcoat, and after walking a mile in the storm, he was forced to take shelter underneath a township hall. His frozen body was found there early Thursday morning.[67]

Located at the western end of Lake Superior, Duluth had 101,065 residents in 1940. On Saturday, temperatures in Duluth ranged from 26 to 32 degrees. At 6:30 p.m. it was cloudy in Duluth and the barometer stood at 29.55 inches. Strong northerly winds, frigid temperatures, and occasional snow flurries were expected to arrive in Duluth on Sunday. The weather was fine on Saturday evening, and business was normal. Local residents were happy with the final results of the district 26 Basketball Championship Tournament, held in Duluth on March 14 and 15. Duluth Central won the title on Saturday night by defeating Two Harbors.

The weather forecast for Duluth printed in the March 16, 1941, edition of the Duluth News Tribune stated: "Cold Wave Due in Duluth Today." Most residents were sleeping when the storm roared into Duluth just before six o'clock Sunday morning. Ironically, the worst conditions were experienced at the beginning of the storm. The initial gusts, lasting about six minutes, were recorded at 70 mph, which established a new wind-velocity record at Duluth.[68] Throughout the day the wind slowly abated. When the front did hit Duluth, it dropped temperatures quickly. From a reading of 25 degrees at 3:30 a.m. Sunday, the thermometer plunged to 2 below at 5:30 a.m. of the same day. Duluth received 1.2 inches of snow during the storm. Unlike the mixture of snow and dirt that blew in the Red River Valley, the snow that fell in Duluth was pure white because the Minnesota woods kept the soil from blowing with the snow.

At 6:30 p.m. Sunday it was still cloudy in Duluth, but the barometer had risen to 30.07 inches. The thermometer fell to 15 degrees below zero Monday morning. By 6:30 Monday evening the barometer had climbed to 30.30 inches.

There was considerable wind damage in Duluth because of the storm. Hundreds of houses were damaged, and a fire early Sunday caused $14,000 damage to the Midway Hotel there. Other wind damage in Duluth included ripping off half the roof of the Consolidated Elevator Company, leaving more than one million bushels of wheat exposed. At one school in Duluth a metal desk, 30 feet wide and 90 feet long, was torn from the building. All around Duluth, windows, doors, and chimneys were damaged and telephone lines put out of commission by the wind.

Superior, Wisconsin, experienced a similar fate.[69]

As far as Minnesotans are concerned, they faced the blizzard of the century on November 11, 1940. It came as a surprise. Hunters were found frozen to death in their shirt-sleeves because temperatures were recorded in the sixties early in the day. The death toll for the Armistice Day blizzard was fifty-six people. Most of the deaths occurred in southern Minnesota. Storm conditions lasted for two days. The Twin Cities received 16.2 inches of snow and glazed ice crushed trees and power lines. Many roads remained closed until the end of the month. The sharp decline in temperatures during the storm burst engines that had not been protected with antifreeze.[70]

Four months later, another storm came as a surprise. It also was a killer. The March 15, 1941, blizzard caused the death of thirty-one Minnesotans. Most of the deaths occurred in the Red River Valley because the storm arrived in the valley when people were still out traveling. People in other areas in Minnesota were more fortunate because the Alberta Clipper roared in when they were home and in bed sleeping. There was not much difference in the velocity of the winds between the two storms, and the mild temperatures earlier in the day created a false sense of security in both cases. While the Armistice Day blizzard lasted for two days, the March 15, 1941, storm lasted only about seven hours. Only a small amount of snow fell during this storm. Ironically, the Armistice Day blizzard affected mainly southern Minnesota, while the March 15, 1941, storm affected mainly northern Minnesota. See Figure 15.

Oslo
xx

Wylie Hazel
●x ●x

Crookston
Fisher x xxx ● Tildon Jct.
xxxx x Fosston
Lockhart ●x
●xxx Mahnomen
Halstad ● Ada ●xx
x xxx ●x
Syre
Detroit Lakes
●xx

Chisholm
●
x

Cloquet
●x

MINNESOTA

xx
■
Minneapolis - St. Paul

Caldonia
●x

x = Location of deaths

FIGURE 15: General location of deaths in Minnesota.

252

CHAPTER IV

THE GREAT LAKES REGION: AND NORTHEASTERN UNITED STATES:

THE DEADLY BLIZZARD SUBSIDES;

RECORD BREAKING COLD TEMPERATURES

After rushing through North Dakota and Minnesota, the low system moved through the Great Lakes region.

The storm swept at least thirty-four fishermen, including the wives of two Baraga men, offshore onto an ice floe in Lake Superior near Marquette, Michigan. Winds of 50 mph hit the fishermen as they fished for lake trout five to ten miles off Michigan's Upper Peninsula. The strong winds broke the ice up and cast groups adrift on ice floes and pushed them further from shore. Captain Fred Sollman of the Portage Lake Coast Guard Station said that, "unless the drifters could reach the shelter of the Huron Islands, eight miles off the Northern Michigan mainland, there is little hope they can survive the storm." The sheriff of Baraga County stated there was "virtually no hope."[1]

Ten fishermen were able to reach safety that day. Four of them made their escape before noon Sunday by jumping onto a large ice floe when it broke loose from the ice field off Keweenaw Point, close to Skanee, Michigan. The other six reached shore after dark on two smaller ice floes.

The fishermen who were out of danger reported that "the ice was disintegrating rapidly under waves of 25 feet high waves."[2] Aware of deteriorating conditions on Lake Superior, Captain Sollman could not send search-and-rescue teams out with power surfboats because of the 50 mph wind. The Coast Guard fired off flares and patrolled the shoreline. Steadily falling temperatures forced shore patrols to work in relays. Later, deteriorating conditions southeast of Skanee forced the cancellation of a patrol on the beach there.

Late Sunday evening the winds switched slightly from the northwest to the north. It was hoped that a north wind would blow any survivors back to the mainland. If the weather conditions improved, the Coast Guard planned to launch a surfboat from Skanee on Monday morning to look for survivors in and around the Huron Islands and the uninhabited coast southeast of Skanee.[3]

The marooned fishermen survived the bitter cold and long hours of the night with courage and savvy. The first evidence of their fate came Monday afternoon when several men were spotted coming towards shore on an ice floe at L'Anse, Michigan. Although thoroughly chilled, they were able to broadcast their experiences on a radio hookup of the National Broadcasting Company from a nearby garage. This interview was heard nationwide. Braving waves about 10 feet high and temperatures near zero on the ice floe, they had about lost hope of being rescued when the wind

shifted and sent their ice floe back towards shore. Soon most of the other

fishermen returned to shore. Other fishermen were able to reach islands in

Lake Superior and remained on them overnight. They protected themselves

by constructing shelters of driftwood and ice. On Monday, Coast Guard

boats picked them up. Although several men suffered from frostbite, their

condition was not believed to be serious.[4]

Michigan had two storm fatalities.

As the storm moved through Wisconsin, three fatalities were

recorded. One of them, George A. Clark, age 32, of Seymour, Wisconsin, met

his death as he tried to put chains on a truck stuck in a snowdrift.

Struggling to put them on, he was hit by a car.

During the morning hours of March 16, Chicago experienced pleasant

temperatures. The thermometer registered a high of 36 degrees at 9:00 a.m.,

but cold, blustery conditions quickly became the order of the day, and the

temperature skidded downward to 10 above later in the day.

The brisk cold wave caught many motorists by surprise, especially

when they tried to start their cars. The Chicago Motor Club said 1,200 calls

for emergency service were made in Chicago and its suburbs between

midnight Saturday and eleven o'clock Sunday evening.

On March 17, the stark headline of the Chicago Daily Tribune

declared "46 DEAD, 20 MISSING IN GALE." Chicagoans read how people

from North Dakota and Minnesota died in the blizzard and what some folks did to survive the storm.

It was the coldest St. Patrick's Day in Chicago since 1900. Chicago was greeted with 46 mph winds and a temperature of 1 above at 7:00 a.m. By midafternoon the temperature stood at only 10 above.[5] The combination of high winds and cold temperatures made it miserable for people watching the annual St. Patrick's Day parade in Chicago. Snow forced the cancellation of a similar parade in Cleveland, but in spite of bad weather, New York City held its regularly scheduled parade.[6]

Tragedy struck Plymouth, Indiana, where three children burned to death Sunday night when the abandoned school bus they were in burned on a farm near Plymouth during the height of the cold windstorm. Luckily three other children and some goats made their escape as Plymouth firemen fought to put out the blaze.

By 6:30 p.m. CST Sunday, the low pressure system was located north of the Great Lakes. At that time the lowest barometric reading associated with the low was 993 millibars (29.31 inches) at Sault Ste. Marie, Michigan. At the same time, the top reading for the high trailing the low came from Williston, North Dakota, which reported in with a reading of 1034 millibars (30.54 inches). Because of World War II, Canada had discontinued making most of its weather data available to the United States. As a result, these barometric readings were the extremes at 6:30 p.m. CST Sunday for the low and high in the United States.

By Sunday night the low was centered in the middle of Ontario.

Because of this, Ontario received the brunt of the storm. Over 20 towns in Ontario were isolated more than 48 hours, from Sunday through Tuesday, by the storm. Trains were either delayed or did not make it to their destination. Highway No. 11, the main road into northern Ontario, was blocked by huge snowdrifts. One of Canada's largest military training reservations, Camp Borden, was almost isolated by the storm.[7]

Because of the fast-moving cold wave, on Sunday night the Weather Bureau directed northwest storm warnings to be displayed up and down the Eastern Seaboard from Eastport, Maine, to Cape Hatteras, North Carolina. The Weather Bureau stated that a "severe disturbance" centered over the upper Great Lakes would move eastward, "causing increasing southwest winds shifting to strong northwest Monday morning and reaching gale force."[8]

A blustery sleet storm hampered rescue operations of a sabotaged eastbound passenger train in Pennsylvania Sunday night. The Buckeye Limited, bound from Cleveland to Pittsburgh, derailed near Balden, Pennsylvania, located twenty-one miles northwest of Pittsburgh. After a preliminary investigation, E. W. Smith, railroad Vice President, said, "All the spikes were removed from the outer rails and one rail was moved in on the ties," and "Splice bars which connect the rails were found at the river's edge and along the bank where they were apparently thrown by saboteurs."[9] Four passenger cars plunged into the Ohio River but the locomotive and two cars remained on the tracks. There were about 100 passengers aboard the

Flyer and 70 were injured, 20 seriously. They were rushed to hospitals in

Rochester and Pittsburgh. Many suffered from immersion in near-freezing

water. Four people died in the wreck, including the engineer who was

crushed to death when coal poured into his cab. Rescue crews worked in cold

and slippery conditions. Emergency personnel could barely see because the

sleet dimmed the searchlights. Furthermore, the storm interrupted lines of

communication and delayed reporting of the accident to nearby cities.[10]

One storm-related death was recorded in Pennsylvania.

The cold front spread in a southeasterly direction from the Ohio

River Valley to the Texas Panhandle. On Monday morning, March 17, some

of the low temperatures recorded included 12 in Cincinnati, 6 in Cleveland, 8

in Indianapolis, and 14 in Louisville, Kentucky.

Northeastern United States

In New York wind speeds from the storm reached 45 mph at Buffalo.

By Tuesday evening, Albany had received 6 inches of snow. Fast-rising

snowdrifts in Chautauqua County, New York, buried two snowplows.

Blocked highways in some western and central New York counties prompted

New York state police to warn against travel in those areas. Stalled autos

stranded hundreds of motorists. Bus service was canceled and many schools

were closed. High winds and snow-blocked roads forced the Weather Bureau

personnel at Syracuse to spend the night at Syracuse's Municipal Airport

Weather Bureau. The storm caused four deaths in New York.[11]

On Sunday, March 16, in New York City the thermometer climbed to 51 above. The overnight low only slipped to 35 above. At 4:00 a.m. Monday it was still 42 above in the city. But as the cold front passed through the city, temperatures started to fall, until it was only 15 above at 3:00 a.m., Tuesday, March 18. Wind speeds peaked at 40 mph on Monday but averaged 32 mph all day before diminishing after midnight Monday. It was the worst cold wave to hit New York City during the 1940-41 winter. In spite of the blustery weather conditions, the city held its annual St. Patrick's Day parade. A gust of wind knocked a ninety-year-old woman watching the parade to the ground just as she turned a corner on her way home. She suffered a fractured skull and was taken to a hospital.[12]

The wind picked up in the northeast again on Tuesday, March 18. This reoccurrence of high winds in the northeast may have been caused by the low pressure system turning in a circle in Canada before heading out to sea. Winds that day reached speeds of 60 mph among the tall buildings of lower Manhatten in New York City. Despite the high winds, little wind damage was reported, and a regular schedule was kept at La Guardia Field. Only 33 flights between New York, Buffalo, Boston, and Washington, D.C. were canceled. There were many complaints of air sickness. The high winds did affect shorter flights, as they were unable to attain an elevation high enough to get above the strong wind levels.[13]

On March 18, the intense low pressure system continued to move in a northeasterly direction. By 7:30 p.m. EST Tuesday the center of the low was

north of Maine in Quebec. The lowest American reading near it was 993

millibars (29.33 inches) near Caribou, Maine. Gale force winds hit New

York, southeastern Pennsylvania, Delaware, New Jersey, and southern New

England.[14]

That same day the cold wave continued to spread southeastwardly

across the eastern United States. Low temperatures recorded that morning

included 3 above in Chicago and Milwaukee, 6 in Indianapolis, 9 in

Cleveland, 10 in Cincinnati, 12 in Louisville, 15 in Newark, 22 in

Chattanooga, 26 in Birmingham, and 22 in Atlanta. The New England

states also recorded cold temperatures on Tuesday. These included 20 below

on top of Mount Washington in New Hampshire, 10 below in northern

Vermont, and 12 above in Boston. Wind speeds in New England on Tuesday,

March 18, varied from 20 mph at lower elevations to 99 mph atop Mount

Washington.[15]

The low pressure system was slow to leave eastern Canada. On

March 19, strong westerly winds continued in the Northeast along the New

England and North Atlantic state coastlines. The highest wind speed

recorded that day was 56 mph along New York's shores. On the same day,

Caribou, Maine, recorded a barometric reading of 995 millibars (29.39

inches). On March 20, the low pressure system finally moved east of Maine.

The barometer rebounded at Eastport, Maine to 1008 millibars (29.76) that

day. Clear skies reigned over the northeast. However, because of the slow withdrawal of the low pressure system from the area, it would be March 23

before the barometric pressure finally topped 30 inches in eastern Maine.[16]

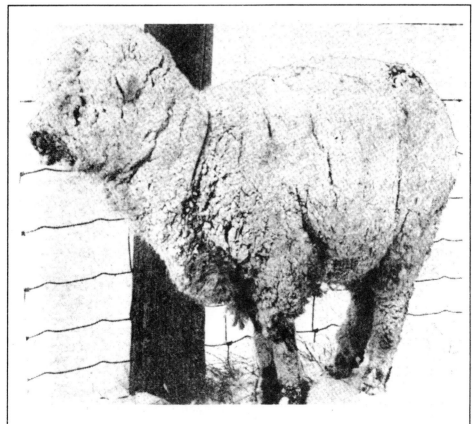

A survivor of the storm, this ram was hugging a fence line four miles north of Grand Forks when photographed by a Herald photographer. Picture courtesy of the Grand Forks Herald.

CHAPTER V

AFTERMATH AND CONCLUSIONS

Aftermath

With the arrival of daylight on Sunday, people in the storm area

started to regroup. Missing loved ones were discovered either unharmed or,

in tragic instances, found to have perished in the storm. The daylight

allowed stranded motorists to make it to safety. Roads were plowed out,

electrical and telephone service was restored. Cars stalled on roads and in

ditches were dug out and towed to nearby filling stations where the vehicles

were thawed out and put in running order. Hourly radio reports began to

reveal the mounting death toll.

When the storm roared through the Upper Midwest, local

newspapers were unaware of the unfolding tragedy. Even on Sunday

morning the extent of the devastation was still unclear to them. But by early

that afternoon, the dimensions of the tragedy were becoming clear.

Reporters began making phone calls throughout the storm area to learn

what happened to people in various communities. They worked continuously

262

from Sunday afternoon until Monday evening, gathering and rechecking information in an effort to determine the size and scope of the tragedy. The news media from other areas of the country kept calling local news outlets for information on the blizzard. By Monday evening journalists had a record of what had happened to many of the victims of the storm.[1]

There was much reader interest in the storm, as could be inferred from the demand for newspapers in the days following the blizzard. The Fargo Forum reported a record number of newspapers run from its presses in a 24-hour period—18,322 papers for Monday evening's edition and 20,052 for the Tuesday morning edition, for a total of 38,374 papers.[2]

In 1941, many people from the Upper Midwest had gone south for the winter. They were interested in happenings that occurred back home while they were gone. So friends and relatives back in North Dakota bought extra copies of local papers to send to them. An East Grand Forks resident, Angus McDonald, was shown in Hot Springs, Arkansas, holding a Grand Forks Herald with news of the storm on the front page. The picture was taken by a Hot Springs photographer. McDonald wrote to the Herald and reported that the blizzard was the main topic of conversation at Hot Springs for several days.[3]

The storm raised people's concerns about the safety of friends and relatives. On Monday, the Northwestern Bell Telephone Company reported a record number of long distance telephone calls in Fargo between midnight Saturday and midnight Sunday. During that 24-hour period, 2,500 long distance phone calls were attempted and most of them were completed.[4]

Although the United States was not officially at war, it was mobilizing its forces. Draftees were being inducted into the military, and existing army and national guard units were conducting training exercises. The March 15 blizzard disrupted much of this activity. The cold wave following the storm dropped temperatures to near freezing in Mississippi. There at Camp Shelby (located fifty miles from the Gulf Coast), 30,000 troops of Ohio's 37th National Guard division shivered in the damp cold.[5] At the Indiantown Gap draft camp near Harrisburg, Pennsylvania, cold weather stopped nearly all activity for the 13,500 troops of Pennsylvania's 28th division quartered there. They had to deal with temperatures between 13 and 22 degrees and winds of 30 mph. On Tuesday, March 19, temperatures below the freezing mark forced draftees at Camp Upton, New York, to bundle up. Military police, sentries, and others who had to be outdoors were issued fur caps and gloves. On the same day Camp Edwards, Massachusetts, experienced gale force winds that swept across the Cape Cod military reservation. The winds stirred sand and gravel up so much that at times buildings in the camp disappeared from view. The temperature fell to 17 degrees causing the cancellation of all outdoor training and some indoor classes.[6]

The storm also delayed the entry of young men into the army closer to home. Blocked roads and late trains kept 25 men from Clay County from going to Moorhead until Sunday to report to their local draft board. On

264

Monday morning they went to Fort Snelling, Minnesota, to enter the army.

American Legion posts had planned a dinner and farewell program for the

men at Memorial Hall in Moorhead, but bad weather prevented out-of-town

Legionnaires from attending the dinner and program, so it was canceled.[7]

Because of the storm, St. Patrick's Day observance in Grand Forks on

Monday, March 17, 1941, was a somber occasion in comparison to previous

years. A number of shamrocks and sprigs of green could be seen in the city.

In honor of Ireland's patron saint, many women wore green dresses. But the

Irish in Grand Forks talked more about the March 15 storm than they did of

memories of Ireland.[8]

On Tuesday, March 18, 1941, at the request of Governor Stassen,

state agencies in Minnesota began to canvass the storm area in Minnesota to

determine whether relief measures would be necessary. According to Walter

W. Finke, director of social welfare, field workers of his division conferred

with county welfare officials to appraise the situation.[9]

The cost of human life from the storm was high. In Canada eight

people died, two in Saskatchewan and six in Manitoba. Further south, in

North Dakota, forty individuals perished, while Minnesota recorded thirty-

one deaths. Wisconsin had three fatalities, and Michigan two. Pennsylvania

suffered one storm fatality, and New York had four storm victims. All

together, eighty-nine people died as a result of an intense Alberta Clipper.

During the week following the blizzard, people started to come to

terms with the loss of their loved ones. Funerals were arranged and held throughout the storm area although blocked roads delayed arrangements in some cases. On Wednesday, March 19, 1941, John Moses, Governor of North Dakota, was urged to issue a proclamation calling for memorial services for the victims of the storm on the next Sunday, March 23, 1941. Governor Moses agreed and issued the following proclamation:

> North Dakota has suffered an irreparable loss in the death of its citizens as a result of the disastrous storm which recently swept across the eastern portion of our state and into our neighbor states of Minnesota and Wisconsin. The deaths, suffering and bereavement left in the wake of this disaster has moved all our people to the deepest feeling of sympathy for those who lost their lives and for those who are left to mourn; the many heroic acts of courage and fortitude which shine in this hour of tragedy call forth our highest admiration and respect. It is only proper that we who have been spared give appropriate expression to our feeling of sympathy and respect. Therefore, I, John Moses, as governor of the state of North Dakota, do hereby set aside and dedicate Sunday, March 23, 1941, as Memorial Sunday. And I urge all our people, as they assemble in their places of worship, to pay fitting tribute to those whose lives have been taken, to extend sympathy and comfort to those who have suffered the loss of a loved one, and to honor those by whose courage and bravery lives were saved and suffering alleviated.[10]

According to North Dakota Game Commissioner William J. Lowe, the few reports he had received from game wardens and farmers indicated not as much loss of upland game as first believed.

One after-effect of the blizzard was the spring flooding in the Red River Valley, which was considerable in the northern Red River Valley in the spring of 1941. Part of the problem of spring flooding is frozen ground and hardened snowdrifts. The hardened snowdrifts are caused by the alternating freezing and thawing of snow during the winter. The drifting of snow all

266

winter fills road ditches and by spring they are quite hard. This is what happened with the storm of March 15, 1941. It drove snow into the ditches, and the freezing and thawing that followed it turned the snow to ice. Both this and frozen ground prevents spring runoff water from seeping into the ground. In the spring, hardened snowdrifts also block ditches and other waterways. In 1941, these conditions blocked the runoff of water and led to flooding.[11]

Conclusions

One question however remained in the back of many people's minds. Why was there so little warning of such an intense storm? The answer to that question is a complicated one. It involves different factors, some that are weather-related and some that are not.

One weather-related factor is the jet stream. Alberta Clippers occur when upper-level jet stream winds sweep from northwestern Canada to the southeast at a rapid speed. In 1941, the Weather Bureau had never heard of the jet stream. Their occurrence would not be discovered until the latter stages of World War II by American bomber pilots flying bombing missions to Japan. High-speed jet stream winds interfered greatly with their efforts to reach their targets. The importance of the jet stream in relation to weather would not be discovered until later.

According to Ralph W. Schultz, meteorologist in charge of the

Weather Bureau station at Hector Airport in Fargo, the wind was spotted at Edmonton, Alberta, 840 miles northwest of Fargo, 15 hours before it reached Fargo. The cold front moved at an average speed of 56 mph, a remarkable speed.[12] Ordinarily, weather conditions in Regina, Saskatchewan, which is half way between Fargo and Edmonton, do not affect the Red River Valley until 24 hours later. Although Alberta Clippers are known to be fast-moving storm systems, the Weather Bureau did not expect the storm to travel that fast.[13]

The first indication the Chicago Weather Bureau, the regional office for the north central states, had of a sharp change in the weather came from information gathered at points in northwest Canada. Though readings of high winds and snow were put on a weather chart at 1:00 a.m. March 15, the regional center believed the data at that time was not conclusive enough to warrant drawing up revised forecasts for North Dakota and Minnesota.

Six hours later the weather chart showed continued strong winds in southern Alberta. Such changing conditions dictated a revised forecast. At 6:30 a.m. the Chicago Weather Bureau issued a new forecast for North Dakota. It read as follows, "Light local snows tonight and Sunday with cold wave and strong northerly winds." The information was passed on to the Fargo-Moorhead offices at that time.

A meteorologist stationed in Chicago, H. A. Downs, predicted on Saturday, March 15, that a massive cold wave from Canada would arrive in the Dakotas Saturday night, spread to Minnesota, Iowa, Nebraska, and

Wisconsin on Sunday, and on to Illinois, Indiana, and Michigan on Sunday night and Monday morning. For the most part, his forecast was accurate except that the high arrived a little sooner in some places.

C. A. Donnel of Chicago, supervisor for the north central states, thought the weather bureau "had done a truly remarkable piece of forecasting."[14] The regional office gave notice of the oncoming storm 12 hours in advance.

The first forecast of March 15, 1941, for North Dakota that many of its residents and citizens from northwestern Minnesota read or heard was: Considerable cloudiness with light local snow Saturday and Sunday; colder Sunday. This forecast was carried by the morning editions of local newspapers. On Saturday morning this was the first weather forecast mentioned by area radio stations. It was the first and only forecast that many people would use, and they made their plans accordingly.

The weather bureau at Hector Airport in Fargo customarily issued a separate forecast for Fargo-Moorhead and vicinity based on the state forecast "with such variations as was felt necessary to meet local conditions." This local forecast was issued at 9:45 a.m. Saturday. It was published in newspapers and broadcast on radio stations. How widely it was broadcast became the center of some controversy. The forecast read: "Occasional light snow with a cold wave and strong northwesterly winds tonight and Sunday."

Fargo-Moorhead had one weather flag site, atop the Moorhead City Hall, and a "cold wave" flag was flown there all day Saturday. E. J. Fox, the federal meteorologist in charge of the Moorhead Weather Bureau, made a series of phone calls to Fargo-Moorhead business firms that shipped perishable goods. Fox mentioned the "cold wave" warnings, and he advised the shippers to take precautionary measures. For many years the meteorologists in the Fargo-Moorhead area gave special warnings to those who needed it the most.[15]

On the morning of March 15 the forecast for Minnesota that most of its residents read or heard called for: "Occasional snow Saturday and Sunday; colder except extreme southeast Sunday." After receiving the new forecast from Chicago, the Minneapolis Weather Bureau issued its own revised forecast Saturday. It called for: "Occasional light snow tonight and Sunday; cold wave with strong northwest winds Sunday and in northwest and west central tonight."[16] Except for newspapers in outlying areas such as the Crookston Daily Times and the International Falls Daily Journal, most Minnesota newspapers carried this revised forecast in the Saturday evening edition of their daily newspaper.

The first notice the Fargo Weather Bureau had of the violent wind in the Red River Valley came from Pembina where the wind increased in speed from 36 mph at 7:24 p.m. to 58 mph at 7:35 p.m. Even with that information, the Weather Bureau at Fargo did not issue an immediate warning. One reason for this was that the Fargo-Moorhead weather bureau did not have an experienced man on duty at that time of the evening. Fox and Schultz believed, "even an experienced man would have been fooled by the rapidity with which the wall of snow and dust drove through the valley."[17] The storm moved from Pembina to Fargo in little more than two hours.

With an inexperienced man on duty and President Roosevelt scheduled to speak at 8:30 p.m., it simply was not possible to issue an emergency warning in time.

People wanted to know why Florida hurricanes could be spotted many hours in advance, but storms in North Dakota and Minnesota come as a surprise. Fox and Schultz pointed out that Florida was surrounded for hundreds of miles by a network of report stations. With all these stations, a hurricane could be spotted many miles away. Since a hurricane usually traveled slowly, its course could be carefully checked. In northwestern Canada in contrast, the weather stations were much farther apart, in some cases hundreds of miles. This distance led to slow transmission of information.[18]

F. W. Reichelderfer, head of the United States Weather Bureau, thought the forecasts of the storm were "very efficient." He noted that the Weather Bureau had experienced some difficulties in preparing forecasts for the Upper Midwest, difficulties caused by many Canadian weather stations ceasing to issue weather reports because of wartime restrictions.[19]

Officially, because of World War II, Canada did not provide the United States with any weather information. But unofficially, as in this instance, they did provide the United States Weather Bureau with vital weather data.[20]

Mr. Schultz prepared a special report for the Weather Bureau in Washington, D. C. In it he recommended that one experienced meteorologist remain "on the job whenever an extremely cold wave or high wind condition is spotted and follow through." He emphasized, however, that the Fargo-Moorhead Weather Bureau did not have sufficient trained and experienced personnel to maintain 7-day, 24-hour service.[21]

Both Fox and Schultz maintained that the forecast for North Dakota which called for "light local snow tonight and Sunday with cold wave and strong northerly winds" should have indicated to weatherwise people in North Dakota that a sizable storm was very likely.[22]

It could have been that many people did not understand Weather Bureau terminology. To the Weather Bureau, the word "strong" as used in United States weather reports, meant something of much greater volume than was in the popular conception. Listed in Table 2 on the next page are the official wind velocity classifications used by the Weather Bureau in 1941.

TABLE 2

OFFICIAL WIND VELOCITY CLASSIFICATIONS

Wind Velocity Classification	Miles Per Hour
Fresh	19 to 24
Fresh to Strong	25 to 31
Strong	32 to 38
Strong to Gale	39 to 46
Gale Winds	47 to 54
Gale to Whole Gale	55 to 63
Whole Gale	64 to 75

Source: The Fargo Forum, March 19, 1941.

Fox and Schultz pointed out that while the Fargo weather station did record a reading of 74 mph at one particular moment, "the Moorhead maximum reading based on five minutes duration was 41 mph or only three points above the 'strong wind' maximum." As Mr. Schultz noted, a "strong wind" forecast was not that common. It was made less than once a month, or on the average, even less than once every three months.[23] To people living in the Upper Midwest, "strong" winds were quite common, but not of the velocity that the word "strong" meant in the Weather Bureau classification.

273

To the residents of the area, winds of 25 mph seemed like "strong" winds and were common.

Fox and Schultz believed that the mild weather on Saturday morning, March 15, 1941, made people skeptical of the Weather Bureau's forecast of probable storm conditions. They attributed it to "wishful thinking" on the part of many people, since Saturday was a day rural people customarily went to town for shopping and recreation.[24]

In regards to the activities of the Weather Bureau at Moorhead during the storm, E. J. Fox sent the following report to the chief of the U.S. Weather Bureau in Washington, D.C.:

> In addition to Saturday's cold wave and strong wind warnings and warning to stockmen broadcast from the 5,000 watt station WDAY at Fargo and broadcast over the 10:00 a.m. popular scheduled weather and travel information weather roundup network comprising four North Dakota stations and KVOX at Moorhead, the warning was broadcast three times from the 1,000 watt station KFJM at Grand Forks. This latter station also broadcast special warnings of approaching 40 to 50 mph winds and low to zero visibility at 5:15 p.m. and at 15 minute intervals thereafter until the storm struck. Jamestown broadcast the warning eight times and Minot 12 times during the day.[25]

In the aftermath of the storm, William Langer, United States Senator for North Dakota, received many complaints from its citizens about the number of warnings issued by the weather bureau. Many people thought there was only one warning—given at 9:45 a.m. Langer sent a telegram to F. J. Bavendick, the associate meteorologist in charge of the Bismarck weather station. He wanted to know if the morning forecast issued at 9:45 a.m. was the only notice given to the public.

Reacting strongly to this charge, Bavendick tried to set the record straight. Bavendick said he called KFYR in Bismarck at 3:00 p.m. and told them that the storm reported on their morning bulletin was moving towards North Dakota. He told them it was increasing in intensity and the chance of it affecting North Dakota was more probable than had been indicated by the morning weather map. Bavendick mentioned that KFYR broadcast a warning at the first break in programs and he thought KFYR repeated it several times during the afternoon.

At 6:20 p.m., a special airway weather report from Bismarck was put on the CAA teletype and sent to all interested stations. The report indicated zero ceiling, one-eighth mile visibility, and a 30 mph wind. Other messages were filed later when the wind increased.

About 6:30 p.m. the weather bureau notified KFYR that the storm was moving into Bismarck. Additional warnings were requested at the studio. A special weather bulletin was sent over to the Bismarck Auditorium where the Class A state basketball tournament was in progress. The tournament director made the announcement.[26]

Bavendick said it was unfortunate that so many lives were lost. But as he noted, with so many farmers out Saturday it would have been a miracle that some lives had not been lost. Bavendick defended the activities of the weather bureau, and he reported it was making fine improvements. Bavendick did admit that it was impossible for the weather bureau to forecast the exact time a storm would arrive or to indicate the exact severity of it. He believed the March 15, 1941, storm had given meteorologists something to think about.[27]

Bavendick noted that very few cars were run during the winter months twenty years ago. Motorists used to have to drain the engine block after running their errands. Antifreeze eliminated this practice and over the years vehicles became more powerful and dependable. Bavendick suggested that people had become less cautious as travel became easier. He was impressed with North Dakota farmers who had stretched wires from their homes to their barns in case of a sudden blizzard. But this practice had declined in recent years.[28]

M. R. Hovde, the federal meteorologist in Minneapolis, also backed up Fox and Schultz. Hovde said the March 15, 1941, forecast could have been issued from Miami, Florida, as long as it was based on the various weather readings supplied by the weather stations in the forecast area. He said the position of the weather office issuing the forecasts was not of great importance. Hovde believed the establishment of a regional weather bureau office in Minneapolis would be a 'fine thing' as it would give the Dakotas and Minnesota 24-hour weather service. However, Hovde concluded that the establishment of such a regional weather office would not greatly change forecasts such as the one that hit the storm area on March 15, 1941. Hovde emphasized the forecast from his bureau on Saturday calling for a "cold wave and northwest winds" gave a proper warning of what was to come since it was impossible to tie a prediction down to a specific temperature or wind velocity.[29]

Hovde thought he might have "to figure out a new and stronger wording for such forecasts in an effort to drive home the warning they contain." He said the Weather Bureau could not force people to comply with such warnings. He noted that "many people read a forecast of a large temperature drop and a strong wind and do not seem to realize that a 50 mph wind, plus snow and temperatures 5 to 10 degrees below zero forms a killing combination."[30]

Senator Langer discussed the controversy with the Weather Bureau's chief meteorologist, Charles Mitchell. Mitchell told Langer that the Chicago weather office had received a warning from Edmonton, Alberta at 11:00 a.m. Saturday about the storm. In turn, the Chicago weather office immediately notified its Minnesota and North Dakota stations about a storm and cold wave that required livestock be protected.

Langer believed that reports from North Dakota and Minnesota indicated that the weather bureaus there might not have given adequate warnings of the blizzard after the Chicago weather office had sent the storm information.[31]

After talking to Mitchell, Langer wanted a congressional investigation to determine the reason for "the lack of notice being given by the Weather Bureau." He introduced a resolution (SR 89) in the United States Senate "calling upon the senate commerce committee to investigate and recommend action to prevent future loss of lives and property." His resolution stated seventy lives were lost and that an investigation was "essential for the purpose of obtaining adequate information to enable the people, especially the farmers, to adopt such safeguards as to prevent the occasion of a similar disaster."[32]

There is no evidence that the Senate Committee on Commerce which handled the resolution ever did anything about it. It is possible that the Committee was distracted by the events of World War II, as was the rest of the country, and saw the war as of greater importance than the investigation of a blizzard.

As hard as North Dakota was hit by the blizzard, it was even worse for Minnesotans. Coming on the heels of the 1940 Armistice Day storm that killed fifty-six people, a second killer blizzard was hard to take.

Harold Stassen, the governor of Minnesota, telegraphed Secretary of Commerce Jesse Jones (the Weather Bureau was under the jurisdiction of the Commerce Department) to protest against "inadequate weather warnings" which the governor believed had contributed to the casualties. Stassen noted that the Weather Bureau on the East Coast could forecast within 48 hours when a hurricane would hit the East Coast. Stassen said, "There must have been some way to have warned those people in North Dakota and Minnesota."[33]

On Wednesday, March 18, 1941, Jesse Jones, Secretary of Commerce, replied to Stassen's telegram. Jones stated that the Weather Bureau was not at fault and that adequate storm warnings had been issued Saturday morning. He said the forecast issued at 9:35 a.m. Saturday morning for

Minnesota called for "occasional light snow tonight and Sunday, cold wave

with strong northwest winds Sunday beginning in the northwest and west

central portions tonight." Jones stated that at 10:42 a.m. this forecast was

broadcast, with an added warning that "stockmen are advised to protect

their herds by driving stock to shelter and housing young stock."[34]

Stassen was dissatisfied with Jones's reply. On the very next day,

Thursday, March 19, 1941, he renewed his demand that Jones investigate

what Stassen termed the failure of the Minneapolis weather bureau to give

sufficient warning of the March 15 blizzard. As to the weather forecast

broadcast at 10:42 a.m., Stassen declared it "was made over only one small

radio station and was not released for general publication or radio

announcement by the radio stations that reach throughout this territory."

Stassen noted that the 9:35 a.m. announcement referred to a cold wave with

strong northwest winds for Sunday, but in fact the cold wave with a gale hit

on Saturday evening. Stassen thought that the weather office at Fargo had

advance information of the storm but were prohibited from giving warnings

to the newspapers or the radio. Furthermore, Stassen asked Jones for an

investigation of the weather announcements preceding the 1940 Armistice

Day blizzard.[35]

One after-effect of the March 15 blizzard was the demand for a

regional weather office at Minneapolis. Actually steps had been taken in

that direction prior to the March blizzard. The 1940 Armistice Day blizzard probably accelerated the process. On January 29, 1941, Congressman

Buckler of Minnesota introduced a bill (H.R. 2792) authorizing an

appropriation for a weather station at Minneapolis. The bill was referred to

the Committee on Agriculture.[36] Nothing came of it.

The March 15 storm renewed interest in such a bill. On March 25,

1941, Congressman Bolles of Minnesota introduced H.R. 4156 which called

for the establishment of a regional weather office at Minneapolis. This bill

was also referred to the Committee on Agriculture.[37]

Soon after this, on April 14, 1941, Senator Ball introduced a similar

bill (#1317) in the United States Senate. This bill was referred to the

Committee on Commerce.[38]

Instead of authorizing a regional weather office at Minneapolis, an

amendment was offered in the Senate that called for a restoration of funds,

$37,000, that were to be used for enlarging weather stations at Billings,

Montana and Seattle, Washington. The argument used for restoring the

funds was that the districts in the West were "too large for the district

forecaster to give adequate attention to weather conditions in all individual

localities, and to prepare specific forecasts."[39] The Billings office was to

serve North Dakota and South Dakota. The funds for the Seattle office were

later deleted from the bill that President Roosevelt signed into law on June

28, 1941.

Additional pressure for a regional weather office in Minneapolis came

from Minnesota. Still, state representatives Hagen from Crookston and

Hanson from Erskine introduced a resolution in the Minnesota state legislature that urged Congress to authorize appropriations for a full-time, modernized weather station in the Twin Cities. Mr. Hagen stressed the fact that the geographical location of the Upper Midwest made the people living there subject to the full force of weather extremes. He said the 1940 Armistice Day blizzard and the March 15, 1941, storm typified these extremes. Hagen stated there was a great need for more adequate weather reporting service in the Upper Midwest.[40]

There is no basis for the complaints that the Weather Bureau did not send out adequate warnings of the blizzard. The Weather Bureau did give notice of the approaching cold front with light snow and strong northwest winds many hours before the storm hit. It must be remembered that in 1941 the Weather Bureau did not have sophisticated equipment to detect sudden storms. Weather satellites were unknown, weather stations were far apart, and the Weather Bureau did not have the use of radar and computers. The existence of the jet stream and its effect on weather was unknown to the Weather Bureau in 1941. It relied on ground observations that were called or radioed into a central office where the data was recorded on weather charts. It was virtually impossible for the Weather Bureau to predict the exact speed, intensity, and direction an Alberta Clipper would take, especially with Canadian weather stations not reporting because of World War II.

Even with sophisticated equipment, the National Weather Service recently was surprised by an Alberta Clipper on February 4, 1984.

Temperatures were mild throughout North Dakota and Minnesota and snow

fell lightly that Saturday afternoon. But all of a sudden high winds blew in,

catching many people by surprise. This storm resulted in twenty-two deaths

in North Dakota and Minnesota.

It is hard to fault the Weather Bureau for the suddenness of the

storm of March 15, 1941. Even if people had heard the warnings, that might

not have deterred them. It was difficult to believe a dangerous storm was

coming on such a beautiful day.

As C. V. Freis of Englevale, North Dakota noted in a letter to the

Fargo Forum:

> Uncle Sam's Weather Bureau could put warnings every ten
> seconds, they would go unheeded. Several parties advised us
> that the radios were sending out warnings of an approaching
> storm Saturday afternoon. In spite of these warnings and
> after the snow began to fall around 7:00 p.m., people were
> getting into their cars to go places. It is easy for the general
> public to get out and go, and with the present day cars they
> do not wear the clothing they should for cold weather,
> consequently, when they are caught, death lurks around the
> corner.[41]

The March 15 storm and the 1940 Armistice Day blizzard were

similar. First, there was the large loss of life, 56 Minnesotans in the

Armistice Day blizzard, 71 deaths were recorded in North Dakota and

Minnesota from the 1941 blizzard. Second, both storms occurred when

unusually large numbers of people were out and about. On November 11,

1940, many hunters were out taking advantage of the fact that it was a

holiday and the weather was mild. March 15, 1941, was a Saturday. For people of the Upper Midwest this meant going to town for shopping and recreation. Another event that exacerbated the situation for the March blizzard were the annual basketball tournaments in North Dakota and Minnesota. Folks in the small towns of the Midwest rallied around their local schools and basketball teams. They tended to turn out in force to support their teams, especially at tournament time. The mild weather of November 11, 1940, and March 15, 1941, gave people a false sense of security. In the case of the March 15 storm, people tended to want to get out of their houses after being inside all winter.

One cannot overemphasize the importance of radio in 1941. The only radio stations in North Dakota at that time included WDAY in Fargo, KSJB in Jamestown, KFYR in Bismarck, KGCU at Mandan, KLPM at Minot, KDLR in Devils Lake, and KFJM in Grand Forks. Major radio stations had not yet been established in northwestern Minnesota in 1941. They were forced to listen to WDAY in Fargo and KFJM in Grand Forks for local news and weather reports. However, there was KVOX in Moorhead, Minnesota. Two major radio stations that people in the storm area listened to regularly were WLS in Chicago and WHO in Des Moines. Radio stations remained on the air past normal operating hours to relay emergency messages.

Vehicles in 1941 did not have radios as standard equipment but they could be installed upon request. Because of the shortage of radio stations in the storm area, auto travelers often encountered "dead spots" where they lost radio reception. People in cars received better reception from distant radio stations than they did in their homes.

Radio stations had regularly scheduled times for weather information. Announcers read the forecast of approaching cold wave and strong northerly winds. As far as we know, the word "blizzard" was not used. This word attracts attention on the northern prairie. Since it was a mild day and spring was just around the corner, a violent blizzard seemed remote. People were out and about and enjoying themselves. Many folks misinterpreted the warnings or they never heard them.

Another thing that made the blizzard so unexpected was that never had such an intense blizzard come in March. As the Grand Forks Herald noted about the storm:

> In its suddenness and fury [the storm] was a sensational one. Only warnings as sensational in form as the storm itself would have kept any considerable number of persons off the roads. If the Weather Bureau had issued such sensational warnings of a storm which had not yet developed in force, and the storm had then failed to meet specifications, the Bureau would then have been charged with unreliability and reckless sensationalism. Probably a better organized system of public warning would have helped, but it would have prevented only a few of the tragedies which actually occurred.[42]

The timing of the arrival of the March 15, 1941, storm in different areas helped determine whether that area suffered few or many casualties in the storm. It hit the Canadian prairies either early in the morning or during the daylight hours. People were either still in bed or were just getting up when the storm roared through Edmonton and Calgary. Further south and east on the Canadian prairies the daylight hours enabled people to see what

284

they were up against and take appropriate measures. It was not until the storm hit southern Manitoba that things became worse. In Manitoba, six deaths resulted from the storm.

In the northern end of the Red River Valley the storm arrived at dusk or shortly thereafter. Within two hours it reached the southern end of the Valley. Throughout the Valley and counties adjacent to it, people were out and about, engaged in shopping or other activities.

By the time the storm arrived in eastern and southern Minnesota it was late enough that a majority of the people were at home. Partially as a result of the timing factor, only five fatalities were reported in Minnesota outside of the Red River Valley, which received the brunt of the strong winds. For good reason the Minneapolis Tribune called it the "Red River Valley Flash Storm."

Some other factors help explain why there were more deaths in eastern North Dakota and western Minnesota. The lack of available tree cover in eastern North Dakota and western Minnesota, plus the relatively flat terrain (especially the Red River Valley), provided little protection for stranded travelers. Although some shelterbelts had been planted before 1941, under the Soil Conservation Service Program of the 1930s, the trees were not mature enough in 1941 to make a significant difference in protecting people from the storm. Wind speeds in the wooded areas of Minnesota were not as high as they were in open country.

There was a different scenario in the blizzard of March 1966, when there were complaints that shelterbelts near roads caused drifts that tended to block the roads.

Actually, the number of people killed by the blizzard could have been much higher than it was. Fatalities remained as low as they did because (1) of the presence of mind of hundreds to stay in their cars rather than venture out in the blizzard, (2) the storm did not last long, and (3) heroism by unknown hundreds, risking death to save others.[43]

The vast majority of the fatalities in the March 15, 1941, storm resulted from people leaving stalled vehicles and trying to go for help or reach safety, or simply walking from one destination to another. In either case the results were often fatal. Only a handful of people died from carbon monoxide poisoning in the storm. Old timers concluded that a storm of equal strength in the days of horse and buggy would have resulted in fewer deaths. Before automobiles became the chief means of transportation, people dressed for outdoor travel since they would be exposed to the elements in their buggies, sleighs, wagons or on horseback. Even if they were caught in a storm, many times their horses would take them to safety. A horse could travel across country either by itself or pulling a sleigh. A car could not.

Cars and trucks had heaters, but the heating system consisted of only one heat duct, usually on the passenger side. Drivers had problems with visibility, even under normal winter conditions. Without defrosters, some owners rigged up a fan and directed the heat to their windshield. By today's standards the heating system was quite primitive.

People traveling in autos in many cases did not dress warmly enough for handling an emergency, and probably were without a survival kit. These problems are still common. But the vast majority of people who stayed in their vehicles survived the ordeal. The bodies of the cars offered protection from the elements.

How long after the storm had passed and people talked about it depended on the impact it had on a particular area. The Canadian newspapers rarely mentioned the blizzard after they first reported it. Papers in towns of North Dakota and Minnesota on the edge of the storm wrote about the effects of the blizzard but did not feature it. The major newspapers of the Red River Valley thoroughly covered the subject and carried stories about the blizzard for several weeks. The Fargo Forum and the Grand Forks Heald printed special storm editions. Big-city newspapers in other parts of the United States had sensational headlines with their initial coverage, but there was little follow-up reporting.

People living in northeastern North Dakota and northwestern Minnesota would remember the March 15 blizzard for the rest of their lives. The violent background sounds of war and the pace of the world events pushed the storm tragedy aside.

The pioneer customs faded away. The wire from the barn to the house came down and candles and kerosene lamps were used only in emergencies. Soon, putting candles and kerosene lamps in the windows during storms would be just a memory.

Grand Forks Herald

SUNDAY EDITION

NAZIS MARCH AGAINST YUGOSLAVIA, GREECE

U. S. Steel Strike Set Tuesday

British Set To Hit Back

Slavs, Russia In Pact

Long Expected Push Launched in Balkans; Hitler Berates Foes

Say Attack 'Not on People of Greece'

Nazis Give Reasons For War

The Weather

2 Killed In Mill City Plane Crash

Chinese Send Japs Into Full Rout

Mother Kills Daughter, Self on N. D. Farm

To the Public

Forx Motor Sales, Inc.

Front page of the Grand Forks Herald on April 6, 1941. Eight months later the United States would be drawn into World War II. Courtesy of the Grand Forks Herald.

Notes

Preface

[1] Laurence Ramsey to Douglas Ramsey, n.d.

[2] Mrs. Laurence Ramsey to Douglas Ramsey, n.d.

[3] "Speaking of Pictures . . . These are Defense Posters," Life (March 24, 1941), pp. 12, 13, 15.

[4] The Fargo Forum, 18 March 1941, p. 1.

[5] Minneapolis Morning Tribune,17 March 1941, p. 1.

[6] Bernard Grun, The Timetables of History: A Horizontal Linkage of People and Events, English Language Edition, with a Forward by Daniel J. Boorstein (New York: Simon & Schuster, Inc., 1982), p. 516-18.

[7] Ibid.

[8] Traill County Tribune (Mayville, North Dakota), 20 March 1941, p. 3.

Introduction

[1] The Fargo Forum, 19 March 1941, p. 1.

[2] The Forum (Fargo, North Dakota-Moorhead, Minnesota), 8 January 1989, pp. 1, A14.

[3] U.S. Department of Agriculture, 1941 Yearbook of Agriculture: Climate and Man, "The How and Why of Weather Knowledge," by F. W. Reichelderfer (Washington: Government Printing Office, 1941), p. 129.

[4] The Fargo Forum, 19 March 1941, p. 1.

[5] U.S. Department of Agriculture, 1941 Yearbook of Agriculture: Climate and Man, "How the Daily Forecast is Made," by C. L. Mitchell and H. Wexler (Washington: Government Printing Office, 1941), pp. 579-98.

[6] Ibid.

[7] Charles C. Bates and John F. Fuller, America's Weather Warriors, 1814-1985 (College Station, TX: Texas A & M University Press, 1986), pp. 49-50.

[8] Ibid.

[9] Mitchell and Wexler, "Daily Forecast," pp. 585-86.

[10] The Fargo Forum, 21 March 1941, p. 1.

Chapter I: The Canadian Experience: A Daylight Storm

1 The Dawson News, 15 March 1941, p. 1.
2 Ibid.
3 Lethbridge Herald, 14 March 1941, p. 6.
4 Edmonton Bulletin, 15 March 1941, p. 2.
5 Ibid.
6 Calgary Herald, 15 March 1941, p. 1.
7 Medicine Hat News, 15 March 1941, p. 1.
8 The Leader-Post (Regina, Saskatchewan), 17 March 1941, p. 1.
9 Swift Current Sun, 15 March 1941, p. 3.
10 The Leader-Post, 17 March 1941, pp. 1-3.
11 Weyburn Review, 20 March 1941, p. 1.
12 Ibid.
13 Ibid.
14 Calgary Herald, 17 March 1941, pp, 1, 5.
15 Winnipeg Tribune, 15 March 1941, p. 19.
16 Ibid, 17 March 1941, p. 5.
17 Winnipeg Tribune, 18 March 1941, p. 9.
18 Brandon Daily Sun, 17 March 1941, p. 1.
19 The Boissevain Recorder, 20 March 1941, p. 1.
20 The Carberry News Express, 19 March 1941, p. 1.
21 The Daily Graphic (Portage La Prairie, Manitoba), 17 March 1941, p. 1.
22 Winnipeg Tribune, 18 March 1941, p. 5.
23 Ibid., 15 March 1941, p. 19.
24 Ibid., 18 March 1941, pp. 1, 5.
25 Ibid.
26 The Morden Times, 20 March 1941, p. 1.
27 Winnipeg Tribune, 18 March 1941, p. 1.
28 Morris Herald, 20 March 1941, p. 1.
29 Winnipeg Tribune, 17 March 1941, p. 5.
30 Ibid.

Chapter II: The American Experience: A Night of Terror For North Dakotans

1 Plentywood Herald, 20 March 1941, p. 1.

[2] Grand Forks Herald, 14 March 1941, p. 1.

[3] Fargo Forum, 19 March 1941, p. 1.

[4] Ibid.

[5] Williston Daily Herald, 17 March 1941, p. 3.

[6] Ibid., p. 1.

[7] The Dickinson Press and Dickinson Recorder Past, Richardton Times, and Belfield Review, 20 March 1941, p. 1.

[8] Ibid.

[9] Bismarck Tribune, 15 March 1941, p. 1.

[10] Ibid., 17 March 1941, p. 1.

[11] Ibid.

[12] Minot Daily News, 17 March 1941, p. 1.

[13] Fargo Forum, 22 March 1941, p. 2.

[14] Elwyn B. Robinson, History of North Dakota (Lincoln: University of Nebraska Press, 1966), p. 7.

[15] Bottineau Courant, 19 March 1941, pp. 1, 8.

[16] Ibid,

[17] Ibid.

[18] Turtle Mountain Star (Rolla, North Dakota), 20 March 1941, p. 1.

[19] Ibid.

[20] Pierce County Tribune (Rugby, North Dakota), 20 March 1941, pp. 1, 8.

[21] S. Res. 89, 77th Cong., 1st sess. (1941).

[22] Cavalier County Republican (Langdon, North Dakota), 20 March 1941, p. 1.

[23] Ibid., pp. 1, 6.

[24] Ibid.

[25] Grand Forks Herald, 1 April 1941, p. 10.

[26] Cavalier County Republican, 20 March 1941, pp. 1, 6.

[27] Ibid.

[28] Ibid.

[29] Odin Bremseth to Larry Skroch, 22 March 1990.

[30] Devils Lake Daily Journal, 17 March 1941, p. 6.

[31] Odin Bremseth to Larry Skroch, 22 March 1990.

[32] Edmore Herald News, 20 March 1941, p. 1.

[33] Ibid.

[34] Grand Forks Herald, 21 March 1941, p. 3.

[35] Ibid., 25 March 1941, p. 2.

[36] Ibid.

[37] The Lakota American, 20 March 1941, p. 1.

[38] Ibid., p. 4.

[39] Ibid., p. 1.

[40] Grand Forks Herald, 27 March 1941, p. 1.

[41] New Rockford Transcript, 21 March 1941, p. 1.

[42] S. Res. 89, 77th Cong., 1st sess. (1941).

[43] Griggs County Sentinel (Cooperstown, North Dakota), 20 March 1941, pp. 1, 6.

[44] Ibid.

[45] Valley City Times Record, 18 March 1941, p. 1.

[46] Fargo Forum, 18 March 1941, p. 1.

[47] Ibid., 23 March 1941, p. 1.

[48] R. D. Larsen to Larry Skroch, 5 August 1990.

[49] Jamestown Sun, 17 March 1941, p. 1.

[50] S. Res. 89, 77th Cong., 1st sess. (1941).

[51] Valley City Times Record, 18 March 1941, p. 1.

[52] S. Res. 89, 77th Cong., 1st sess. (1941).

[53] R. D. Larsen to Larry Skroch, 5 August 1990.

[54] Fargo Forum, 18 March 1941, p. 8.

[55] Mrs. H. J. Gronbeck to Larry Skroch, 2 January 1991.

[56] Dickey County Leader (Ellendale, North Dakota), 20 March 1941, p. 1.

[57] Sargent County News (Forman, North Dakota), 20 March 1941, p. 1.

[58] Cavalier Chronicle (Cavalier, North Dakota), 19 January 1940, p. 1.

[59] Jerry Cooper with Glen Smith, Citizens as Soldiers: A History of the North Dakota National Guard (Fargo: North Dakota Institute for Regional Studies, 1986), pp. 265, 270

[60] Walhalla Mountaineer, 20 March 1941, p. 1.

[61] Fargo Forum, 19 March 1941, p. 1.

[62] Grand Forks Herald, 20 March 1941, p. 7.

[63] Cavalier Chronicle, 21 March 1941, p. 1.

[64] Ibid.

[65] Ibid., pp. 1, 8.

[66] Grand Forks Herald.

[67] Grand Forks Herald, 25 March 1941, p. 2.

[68] Ibid., 18 March 1941, p. 2.

[69] Walsh County Record (Grafton, North Dakota), 20 March 1941, p. 1.

[70] Bennie Molde to Doug Ramsey, 18 March 1991.

[71] Grand Forks Herald, 20 March 1941, p. 7.

[72] Ibid., 28 March 1941, p. 16.

[73] Ibid., 25 March 1941, p. 2.

[74] Ibid., 15 March 1991, pp. 1A, 8A.

[75] Grand Forks Herald, 4 April 1941, p. 15.

[76] Ibid., March 1941.

[77] Ibid.

[78] Fargo Forum, 22 March 1941, p. 2.

[79] Crookston Daily Times, 17 March 1941, pp. 1, 5.

[80] Grand Forks Herald, 18 March 1941, p. 1.

[82] Grand Forks Herald, 18 March 1941, p. 1.

[83] Ibid., 19 March 1941, p. 5.

[85] Ibid., pp. 1, 3.

[86] Ibid.

[87] Ibid.

[88] Ibid.

[89] Grand Forks Herald, 18 March 1941, p. 2.

[90] Traill County Tribune, 20 March 1941, p. 1.

[91] Grand Forks Herald, 20 March 1941, p. 7.

[92] Fargo Forum, 15 March 1941, pp. 1, 9.

[93] Ibid., pp. 1, 5.

[94] Ibid., 19 March 1941, p. 1.

[95] Ibid., 18 March 1941, p. 8.

[96] Ibid., 19 March 1941, p. 8.

[97] Fargo Forum, March 1941.

[98] Interview with Georgia Maize by Doug Ramsey, February 1991.

[99] Fargo Forum, 18 March 1941, p. 6.

[100] Fargo Forum, March 1941.

[101] Ibid., 18 March 1941, p. 9.

[102] Richland County Farmer Globe (Wahpeton, North Dakota), 18 March 1941, pp. 1, 8.

[103] Fargo Forum, 18 March 1941, p. 11.

[104] Ibid.

[105] Fargo Forum, 20 March 1941, p. 8.

[1] Kittson County Enterprise, 19 March 1941, p. 1.

[2] Ibid.

[3] Robert Laude to Douglas Ramsey, 24 June 1991.

[4] Stephen Messenger, 20 March 1941, p. 1.

[5] Crookston Daily Times, 17 March 1941, p. 5.

[6] Stephen Messenger, 20 March 1941, p. 1.

[7] Kittson County Enterprise, 19 March 1941, p. 8.

[8] Warren Sheaf, 19 March 1941, p. 1.

[9] Ibid.

[10] Stephen Messenger, 20 March 1941, p. 4.

[11] Warren Sheaf, 19 March 1941, p. 6.

[12] Crookston Daily Times, 15-20 March 1941.

[13] Kittson County Enterprise, 19 March 1941, p. 1.

[14] Crookston Daily Times, 17 March 1941, p. 1.

[15] Norman County Herald, 19 March 1941, p. 1.

[16] Fargo Forum, 18 March 1941.

[17] Fergus Falls Daily Journal, 17 March 1941, p. 4.

[18] Ibid., 18 March 1941, p. 4.

[19] Wheaton Gazette, 20 March 1941, p 1.

[20] Morris Sun, 21 March 1941, p. 1.

[21] Swift County News, 18 March 1941, p. 1.

[22] Willmar Tribune, 19 March 1941, p. 1.

[23] Granite Falls Tribune, 20 March 1941, p. 1.

[24] Redwood Gazette, 18 March 1941, p. 1.

[25] Litchfield Independent Review, 20 March 1941, pp. 1, 4.

[26] Hutchinson Leader, 21 March 1941, p. 1.

[27] Pipestone Leader, 18 March 1941, p. 1.

[28] Worthington Daily Globe, 17 March 1941, p. 1.

[29] Fairmont Daily Sentinel, 17 March 1941, p. 1.

[30] Minneapolis Morning Tribune, 18 March 1941, p. 2.

[31] Mankato Free Press, 17 March 1941, p. 1.

[32] Ibid., pp. 1, 10.

[33] Fairbault Daily News, 17 March 1941, p. 1.

[34] Red Wing Daily Republican Eagle, 17 March 1941, p. 1.

[35] Albert Lea Evening Tribune, 17 March 1941, p. 3.

[36] Austin Daily Herald, 15 and 17 March 1941, p. 1.

[37] Rochester Post-Bulletin, 17 March 1941, pp. 1, 4.

[38] Winona Republican-Herald, 15, 17 March 1941, p. 1.

[40] Roseau Times-Region, 20 March 1941, p. 1.

[41] Warroad Pioneer, 20 March 1941, pp. 1, 2.

[42] Baudette Region, 21 March 1941, p. 1.

[43] Thief River Falls Times, 20 March 1941, p. 6.

[44] Crookston Daily Times, 17 March 1941, p. 1.

[45] Bemidji Daily Pioneer, 15 March 1941, p. 1.

[46] Ibid., 17 march 1941, p. 1.

[47] Itasca County Independent (Grand Rapids, MN), 21 March 1941, p. 1.

[48] Mahnomen Pioneer, 21 March 1941, p. 1.

[49] Congressional Record, 20 March 1941, p. 2400.

[50] Detroit Lakes Tribune, 20 March 1941, p. 1.

[51] Congressional Record, 20 March 1941, p. 2399.

[52] Congressional Record, 20 March 1941, p. 2401.

[53] Detroit Lakes Tribune, 20 March 1941, p. 1.

[54] Kittson County Enterprise, 19 March 1941, p. 5.

[55] Wadena Pioneer Journal, 20 March 1941, p.1.

[56] Brainerd Daily Dispatch, 17 March 1941, p. 1.

[57] Little Falls Daily Transcript, 17 March 1941, p. 1.

[58] Park Region Echo (Alexandria, MN), 20 March 1941, p. 3.

[59] St. Cloud Times, 17 March 1941, p. 2.

[60] Kanabec County Times, 20 March 1941, p. l.

[61] International Falls Daily Journal, 15 March 1941, p. 1.

[62] Ibid., 17 March 1941, p. 1.

[63] Itasca County Independent, 21 March 1941, p. 1.

[64] Aitkin Independent Age, 20 March 1941, p. 1.

[65] Hibbing Daily Tribune, 17 March 1941, p. 1.

[66] Ely Miner, 20 March 1941, pp. 1, 5.

[67] Cloquet Pine Knot, 21 March 1941, p. 1.

[68] Duluth News Tribune, 16 March 1941, p. 1.

[69] Ibid., 17 March 1941, p. l.

[70] Paul Douglas, Prairie Skies: The Minnesota Weather Book (Stillwater: Voyageur Press, Inc., 1990), p. 8.

Chapter IV: The Great Lakes Region and Northeastern United States: The Deadly Storm Subsides: Record Breaking Cold Temperatures

[1] <u>Minneapolis Morning Tribune</u>, 17 March 1941, p. 2.

[2] Ibid.

[3] Ibid.

[4] <u>New York Times</u>, 18 March 1941, p. 45.

[5] Ibid., p. 16.

[6] Ibid., p. 1.

[7] Ibid., p. 1.

[8] Ibid., 17 March 1941, p. 35.

[9] Ibid., p. 15.

[10] Ibid.

[11] <u>New York Times</u>, 19 March 1941, p 23.

[12] Ibid.

[13] Ibid., 18 March 1941, p. 1.

[14] Ibid., 19 March 1941, p. 1.

[15] Ibid., 19 March 1941, p. 23.

[16] Ibid., 24 March 1941, p. 33.

Chapter V: Aftermath and Conclusions

[1] <u>Fargo Forum</u>, 18 March 1941, p. 1.

[2] <u>Fargo Forum</u>, 19 March 1941, p. 8.

[3] <u>Grand Forks Herald</u>, 29 March 1941, p. 10.

[4] <u>Grand Forks Herald</u>, 18 March 1941, p. 7.

[5] <u>Chicago Daily Tribune</u>, 19 March 1941, p. 7.

[6] Ibid., March 20, 1941, p. 8.

[7] <u>Fargo Forum</u>, 18 March 1941, p. 5.

[8] <u>Grand Forks Herald</u>, 18 March 1941, p. 7.

[9] <u>Wheaton Gazette</u>, 21 March 1941, p. 4.

[10] <u>Fargo Forum</u>, 22 March 1941, p. 1.

[11] <u>Grand Forks Herald</u>, 8 April 1941, p. 2.

[12] <u>Fargo Forum</u>, 19 March 1941, p. 1.

[13] Ibid.

[14] Ibid.

[15] Fargo Forum, 18 March 1941, p. 1.

[16] Bemidji Daily Pioneer, 15 March 1941, p. 1.

[17] Fargo Forum, 19 March 1941, p. 1.

[18] Ibid., 18 March 1941, p. 1.

[19] Ibid.

[20] Fargo Forum, 18 March 1941, p. 7.

[21] Fargo Forum, 19 March 1941, p. 1.

[22] Ibid.

[23] Ibid.

[24] Ibid.

[25] Fargo Forum, 22 March 1941, p. 2.

[26] Ibid.

[27] Ibid.

[28] Ibid.

[29] Grand Forks Herald, 19 March 1941, p. 1.

[30] Ibid.

[31] Fargo Forum, 21 March 1941, p. 1.

[32] Grand Forks Herald, 21 March 1941, p. 1.

[33] Ibid.

[34] Fargo Forum, 19 March 1941, p. 1.

[35] Grand Forks Herald, 21 March 1941, pp. 1, 2.

[36] H.R. 2792, 77th Cong., 1st sess. (1941).

[37] H.R. 4156, 77th Cong., 1st sess. (1941).

[38] S.R. 1317, 77th Cong., 1st sess. (1941).

[39] Congressional Record, p. 3205.

[40] Fargo Forum, 20 March 1941, p. 1.

[41] Fargo Forum, Englevale Letter.

[42] Grand Forks Herald, 23 March 1941, p. 4.

[43] Walsh County Record, 20 March 1941, p. 1.

WORKS CITED

Newspapers provided the majority of information for this study. To offer a better understanding of the scope of this project, the authors are going to separate the Canadian and American newspapers in the following bibliography. The number of Canadian newspapers cited is not large enough to require further breakdown. The area most affected by the March 15, 1941, blizzard was North Dakota and Minnesota. The number of newspapers from North Dakota and Minnesota is quite large, so the authors are dividing those sources. The rest of the newspapers will be listed in one group. The authors looked at more newspapers than what is cited below.

Canadian Newspapers

The Boissevain Recorder. 20 March 1941.
Brandon Daily Sun. 17 March 1941.
Calgary Herald. 15, 17 March 1941.
The Carberry News Express. 19 March 1941.
The Daily Graphic. (Portage La Prairie, Manitoba) 17 March 1941.
The Dawson News. 15 March 1941.
Edmonton Bulletin. 15 March 1941.
The Leader-Post. (Regina, Saskatchewan) 17 March 1941.
The Lethbridge Herald. 14 March 1941.
Medicine Hat News. 15 March 1941.
The Morden Times. 20 March 1941.
Morris Herald. 20 March 1941.
Swift Current Sun. 15 March 1941.

Weyburn Review. 20 March 1941.
Winnipeg Tribune. 15, 17, 18 March 1941.

North Dakota Newspapers

Bismarck Tribune. 15, 17 March 1941.
Bottineau Courant. 19 March 1941.
Cavalier Chronicle. 21 March 1941.
Cavalier County Republican. 20 March 1941.
Devils Lake Daily Journal. 17 March 1941.
Dickey County Leader. 20 March 1941.
Dickinson Press and Dickinson Recorder Past, Richardton Times, and
Belfield   Review. 20 March 1941.
Edmore Herald News. 20 March 1941.
Fargo Forum. March 1941.
Grand Forks Herald. March and April 1941.
Griggs County Sentinel. 20 March 1941.
Jamestown Sun. 17 March 1941.
Lakota American. 20 March 1941.
Minot Daily News. 17 March 1941.
New Rockford Transcript. 21 March 1941.
Pierce County Tribune. 20 March 1941.
Richland County Farmer Globe. 20 March 1941.
Sargent County News. 20 March 1941.
Turtle Mountain Star. 20 March 1941.
Traill County Tribune. 20 March 1941.
Valley City Times Record. 18 March 1941.
Walhalla Mountaineer. 20 March 1941.
Walsh County Record. 20 March 1941.
Williston Daily Herald. 17 March 1941.

Minnesota Newspapers

Albert Lea Evening Tribune. 17 March 1941.
Aitkin Independent Age. 20 March 1941.
Austin Daily Herald. 15 and 17 March 1941.
Baudette Region. 21 March 1941.
Bemidji Daily Pioneer. 15 March 1941.
Brainerd Daily Dispatch. 17 March 1941.
Caledonia Argus. 21 March 1941.

Cloquet Pine Knot. 21 March 1941.
Crookston Daily times. 15-20 March 1941.
Detroit Lakes Tribune. 20 March 1941.
Duluth News Tribune. 16 March 1941.
Ely Miner. 20 March 1941.
Fairbault Daily News. 17 March 1941.
Fairmont Daily Sentinel. 17 March 1941.
Fergus Falls Daily Journal. 17 March 1941.
Granite Falls Tribune. 20 March 1941.
Hibbing Daily Tribune. 17 March 1941.
Hutchinson Leader. 21 March 1941.
International Falls Daily Journal. 15 March 1941.
Itasca County Independent. 21 March 1941.
Kanabec County Times. 20 March 1941.
Kittson County Enterprise. 19 March 1941.
Litchfield Independent Review. 20 March 1941.
Little Falls Daily Transcript. 17 March 1941.
Mahnomen Pioneer. 21 March 1941.
Mankato Free Press. 17 March 1941.
Minneapolis Morning Tribune. 18 March 1941.
Morris Sun. 21 March 1941.
Norman County Herald. 19 March 1941.
Park Region Echo. 20 March 1941.
Pipestone Leader. 18 March 1941.
Red Wing Daily Republican Eagle. 17 March 1941.
Redwood Gazette. 18 March 1941.
Rochester Post-Bulletin. 17 March 1941.
Roseau Times-Region. 20 March 1941.
St. Cloud Times. 17 March 1941.
Stephen Messenger. 20 March 1941.
Swift County News. 18 March 1941.
Thief River Falls Times. 20 March 1941.
Wadena Pioneer Journal. 20 March 1941.
Warren Sheaf. 19 March 1941.
Warroad Pioneer. 20 March 1941.
Wheaton Gazette. 20 March 1941.
Willmar Tribune. 19 March 1941.
Winona Republican-Herald. 15 and 17 March 1941.
Worthington Daily Globe. 17 March 1941.

Other Newspapers

Chicago Daily Tribune. 19 and 20 March 1941.
New York Times. 18, 19 and 24 March 1941.
Plentywood Herald. 20 March 1941.

Government Documents

U.S. Congress. House. 77th Cong., 1st sess., 1941, H.R. 2792.
U.S. Congress. House. 77th Cong., 1st sess., 1941, H.R. 4156.
U.S. Congress. Senate. 77th Cong., 1st sess., 1941, S.R. 1317.

Interviews and Letters

Bremseth, Odin, 22 March 1991.
Gronbeck, Mrs. H. J., 2 January 1991.
Larsen, D., 5 August 1990.
Maize, Georgia, February 1991.
Molde, Bennie, 18 March 1991.
Olson, Darrell, 1 March 1991.
Laude, Robert, 24 June 1991.

INDEX

Ada...201
Aitkin..247
Alberta...1, 15, 18, 20
Alberta Clipper, definition of...3
Albert Lea..220, 221
Alexandria..242, 243
Anderson, E.A...182
Anderson, Rosalie..84, 85
Argyle...182, 183
Austin...221
Austin Daily Herald...221
Bailey, Orland family...198, 199
Baitan, Arthur...31, 32
Ball, Senator..280
Bakke, Adolph et al..184
Baudette..178, 179, 227, 228
Baumgartner, Mrs William et al...66
Bearles, Harry et al...194, 195
Bellamy, Kathleen Shear...109-112
Bemidji...231, 232
Bemidji Daily Pioneer...231, 239
Benbo, Myron family..201, 202, 212
Benson...212
Berentson, Edwin..62
Bismarck...XI, 55-58
Bismarck Tribune..50, 55, 57
Bjerken, Jacob family...233
Bjork, Andrew..61, 62
Bjork, Burton..218
Blizzard, definition of..3
Boiger, T.J..142
Boissevain...35, 36
Boissevain Recorder...36
Bolles, Congressman..280
Bonaime, Sid family..199, 200
Bonzheimer, Mahlon..96, 97
Boostrom, Nelson farm..87

Bottineau County 60, 61
Brainerd 239, 240
Brainerd Daily Dispatch 239
Brandon 33, 35
Brandon, Martin A. 143
Bravendick, F.J., Meteorologist, Bismarck Bureau 56, 57, 274-276
Bremseth, Odin 73, 74
Bridgeford, Professor R.O. 211
Buckeye Limited Derailment 257, 258
Buckler, Congressman 279, 280
Buffalo Basketball Tournament 149, 150
Bunday, J.E. 100
Burdick, Clarice Bennett 134, 135
Calgary 23, 24
Carberry 36, 37
Carberry News Express 36
Carlson, August 182
Castle, Maynard family 238, 239
Cavalier 106
Cavalier Chronicle 106
Cavalier County 67-72
Charboneau, George 188, 189
Charon, Mrs. Nancy 115
Chicago 255, 256
Chicago Daily News 135
Chicago Daily Tribune 255
Chicago Weather Bureau 12, 49-51, 268, 269
Chisolm 248
Christiansen, Geraldine 220, 221
Christianson, Mrs. Maria 87
Clark, George 255
Cloquet 248, 249
Coger, Miss Harriet 64, 125, 126, 194
Condit, B.W. ....XIII, 131
Cooperstown 88-92
Crookston 185-192
Crookston Daily Times 172, 270
Crosby 52
Dauphin 32, 34, 38
Dawson 16, 18
Detroit Lakes 233, 235

Detroit Lakes Tribune 235
Dickinson 54, 55
Dickinson Press 54
Divide County 52
Donnel, C.A., Supervisor, Chicago Weather Bureau 269
Downs, H.A., Meteorologist, Chicago Weather Bureau 268, 269
Drayton snowplow operators 112, 113
Drift Prairie, North Dakota....................................46, 48
Duluth 249, 250
Duluth News Tribune 249
Ebel, Fred 31
Edmonton 20, 21, 22
Edmore Herald News 76
Ellendale 101, 102
Ellington, Elmer T. family..........................125, 126, 194
Ely 248
Engebretsen, Ervin 200, 201
Enger, Carl family..135
Erickson, Emil 58
Erickson, Steini 38
Fairbault 219, 220
Fairmont 216, 217
Fairmont Daily Sentinel 216
Fargo 136, 141, 144, 145
Fargo Forum ....III, 50,51, 148, 171, 263, 287
Fargo Weather Bureau 49-51, 267, 271
Fast, Issac I. 41
Fee, Roy 106
Fergus Falls 204, 209
Fergus Falls Daily Journal 205
Fingal 97, 98
Fingal Press 94
Foss, Ludwig family 203
Fosston 200
Fox, E.J., Meteorologist, Moorhead Bureau 51, 59, 269-274
Freis, C.V. 282
Frykman, Marian 192
Gedde, Peter family 238
Gentilly 190
Goodale, Jesse 38
Goodridge 230

Goodwin, George 195
Gordon, Gene et al 83, 84
Grace, Casmir...123
Grand Forks 118-125
Grand Forks Herald .VIII, XII, 80, 115, 117, 120, 122, 123, 171, 263, 284, 287
Grand Rapids 246
Granite Falls 213
Graves, A.N. "Bud" et al 88, 89
Great Lakes...253, 257
Green, Elmer family..193, 194
Griswold, E.W...74, 75
Gronbeck, Mrs. H.J. 100, 101
Grovum, family...231
Hagen, Representative..280, 281
Hallock...173, 175
Hanke, C.P...65
Hanson, Representative...280, 281
Harizim, A.W..115, 116
Hass, August et al 88
Hauser, Ernie...65, 66
Hector Airport 268, 269
Heldstab, Mrs. Harold 189
Hentjium, Andrew..86
Heuchert, Nicholaus family..109
Hibbing 247, 248
High Pressure, source of blizzard 1-5
Hill, Chester 216
Hiller, Ernotte..186, 187
Hillisland, Carl..87
Hoffman, Jacob family 71
Holt, Gene..187
Hope, basketball team 94
Horn, Albert..224, 225
Hoverson, Olger "Ole" et al...128, 129
Howry, Mike family 105, 106
H.R. 2792 280
H.R. 4156 280
Huidster, Nels et al 182
Hutchinson 214
Ingberg, Manie, Verle 230
International Falls..245, 246

International Falls Daily Journal 172, 173, 245, 270
Isobars, significance of 5
Jacobson, Albert family 99, 100
Jamestown 95, 96
Jenzen, Mrs. John 41, 42
Jet Stream, significance of 11, 12, 267
Johnson, Raymond 89-91
Johnson, Waldemar 184
Jones, Jesse, Secretary of Commerce 278, 279
Kallestad, Mrs. John 85
Kennedy 176, 177
KFJM Radio 49, 121, 122, 274
KFYF Radio 49, 275
Kitely, Mr. 18
Kittson County Enterprise 173
Kjos, Ted Farm 72
Knudson, C.N. 64
Knutson, T.E. and Lefsgren, Authur 188
Kroeker, C.K. family 42, 43
Lake Superior 253-255
Lake Superior Fishermen 253-255
Lakota 81-84
Lakota American 81, 82
Lankin 115
Langer, Senator, William 274, 277
LaRochelle, Mrs. Alphonse 190, 191
Larsen, R.D. 95
Larson, Bernice et al 148, 149
Laude, Robert family 176, 177
Lennox, John family 234, 235
Linser, Julius 243
Little Falls 240-242
Lichfield 214
Lockhart, Wilburt M. 14
Loken, Armand 188
Lokem, Martin et al 173, 175
Loney, Ed family 232
Looking For Candles In The Windows XIII
Lowe, William J. 266
Luzaich, Al 248
Lyytinen, Paul 249

Mack, Henry family 236
Mahnomen 232
Mahnomen Pioneer 232, 233
Maland, Elmer 203, 204
Maize, Georgia 145
Manitoba 32-38
Manitoba forecasts 32
Manitoba, the Red River Valley 39
Mankato 218, 219
Martz, Walter et al 68, 69
Mayville 131-133
McDonald, Agnus 263
McLeod, Louise 69, 70
Medicine Hat 23, 24
Medicine Hat News 23
Melland, Elmer et al 76, 77
Melland, Lawrence 77, 78
Meyers, Frank 125
Michael, Rudolph family 198
Michigan 255
Miller, Bob 89-91
Minneapolis-St. Paul 217, 218
Minneapolis Tribune ....VIII, 146, 171, 218, 285
Minnesota Weather Forecasts 171-173
Minot 58, 59
Military Activity, effects on 264, 265
Missouri Plateau, North Dakota 46, 48
Mitchell, Charles 277
Molde, Bennie 113, 114
Moorhead 141-145
Moorhead Weather Bureau 49-51, 269-271
Mora 244, 245
Moren, Berg 231
Morris 211, 212
Moses, Governor John Proclamation 266
Nahwaykeesick 42
National Weather Service 3, 11-15
Nelson County 81-87
Nelson, Ed 114
Nelson, Joseph et al 196
Nelson, Lincoln 148

Nelson, Newell..98
Nelson, G.N. et al...146, 147
Nelson "Peep"...214
New York...258-260
New York City...259
New England...260, 261
Nickel, Herbert...207-209
Nickerson, Kenneth..69, 70
Niversville...41
Nordberg, Paul family...61
Norden, L.S...243
Norman County...201-204
Norrie, Mrs. Eric..191, 192
North Dakota forecasts.......................................49-51
Northeastern United States.......................258-261
Northern Pacific Railroad.............................92, 93
Olson, Agnes..80
Olson, Darell..124
Ontario...256, 257
Ottertail County..204
Overmore, Alfred farm..135
Park Rapids...235, 236
Park River..114, 115
Patterson, John..14
Peewabic, Mrs. M...33
Pembina......................................103-105, 270, 271
Pembina County...103
Pennsylvania...257, 258
Peterson, Robert...184, 185
Peterson, Family...196, 197
Petruchek, Mrs. Anita...218
Pipestone...214, 215
Piquette, Ernest..61
Pisek...117
Polk County...185-201
Popowich, Nettie...32
Portage la Prairie...33, 37, 38
Potulny, Vic and Rose.....................................117, 118
Radio Stations...49, 283, 284
Ramsey, Laurence family..VI
Red Lake Falls...231

Red River Valley..39, 46
"Red River Valley Flash Storm" ....VIII, 39, 210, 218, 285
Red Wing 220
Redwood Falls 213
Reep, Melvin family 75, 76
Reep, Sever..85
Regina...28-30
Reichelderfer, F.W., head United States Weather Bureau....................271
Reinersten, S.G. 142
Reynolds, Ted family...246
Riopelle, Ivan...183
Rippy, Neumel...227
Rochester...221, 222
Rolla..62, 63
Rolette..63
Romine, Jessie..65
Roosevelt, Franklin..20, 22, 38, 59, 122, 138
Roseau...225, 226
Roseau basketball team et al 178-182
Ruch, Harold family..202
Rugby...63, 64
Runaway Boxcar 129, 130
Sanders, H.W. family...43
Sanderson, Ernest family 76, 77
Sandy, Oscar family..202
Sargent County 102
Sargent County News 102
Saskatchewan..24, 25
Saskatchewan Weather forecasts..24
Saskatoon 24, 26
Saskatoon Star Phoenix..26, 27
Sault Ste. Marie 256
Schroeder, Walter et al...143, 144
Schultz, Ralph W., Meteorologist, Hector Airport 267-274
Schlucter, Herbert family...106-108
Schulsan, Gilbert...57
Sear, Joe 204
Smaage, Bernice...84, 85
Smiley, Peter 85
Sollman, Captain Fred...253, 254
Solvedt, Erick family..182, 183

Spring flooding 266, 267
S.R. 89 277
S.R. 1317 280
Stamin, Joe et al 71
Stangler Sisters 98
Stassen, Governor Harold 265, 278, 279
St. Cloud 243, 244
St. Hilaire 230, 231
Stephen 178-181
Stephen Messenger 178, 179
Sterling, John family 108, 109
Sturger, Henry family 198
Swanson, Dr. L.O. 132, 133
Swift Current 27, 28
Swift Current Sun 28
Taylor, Warren family 96
Tenney, Arvid et al 237
Thief River Falls 228, 229
Thompson, Alvin family 79
Thompson, Edith 126, 127
Tracy, E. 91, 92
Trail County Tribune ....XIII, 131, 132
Treichel, Herman family 202, 203
Turner, Dave family 175, 176
Turtle Mountains 60
Tysdal, Lewis 209
Underdahl, Sig 185
United States Weather Bureau 11-14, 281, 282
Valley City 97
Vasicek, William J. 80
Vierkant, Oliver family 94
Virginia 247
Volland, Andy et al 195, 196
Wachal, Stanley W. et al 152-153
Wadena 236-238
Wadena Pioneer Journal 237
Walhalla Mountaineer 104
Walsh County Record 113
Wahpeton 150-152
Ward, Charles family 84
Warren 183-185

Warroad 226, 227
Waters, Frances 134, 135
WDAY Radio..49, 137, 138
Weather forecasting..12, 13
Weckwirth, Francis J. 229, 230
Weiner, Harold family 70, 71
Weir, Frank 219
Wermager, Tilman family..191
Weyburn 29-31
Wheaton..210
Williston 52, 53, 256
Willmar..212, 213
Windecker, Victor farm..31
Winnipeg..40, 41
Winnipeg Tribune 40
Winona..222-224
Winona Republican - Herald 223, 224
Worthington 215, 216
Yukon Territory..16, 17, 20
Young, Mrs. Willard..63
Younggren, Luke family 176